i'll try anything twice

i'll try anything twice

Misadventures of a Self-Medicated Life

CARLY SCHWARTZ

SWP

SHE WRITES PRESS

Published in 2026 by
She Writes Press, an imprint of The Stable Book Group

32 Court Street, Suite 2109
Brooklyn, NY 11201
https://shewritespress.com
The Library of Congress Control Number is available upon request.
ISBN: 979-8-89636-094-0
eISBN: 979-8-89636-095-7

Interior Designer: Tabitha Lahr

Printed in the United States

Names and identifying characteristics have been changed to protect the privacy of certain individuals.

For Cory and Kelsey, who knew I could do this.

And in memory of Kathy Trabue Weiss,
who lives on through some of my favorite people.

author's note

This memoir contains candid discussions of suicide, suicidal ideation, and related mental health struggles. These themes may be distressing or triggering for some readers.

The content shared reflects the author's personal experiences and is not intended to serve as medical or mental health advice. It should not be relied upon as a substitute for professional diagnosis, treatment, or support. Always consult a qualified health care provider regarding any mental health concerns.

If you or someone you know is struggling, please seek help. You are not alone. In the United States, you can contact the Suicide & Crisis Lifeline at 988 or visit 988lifeline.org for free and confidential support, 24/7.

To respect the privacy of those involved, the names and identifying details of certain individuals and organizations in this memoir have been changed. In some cases, characters are composites or representations of multiple people, and events may have been reordered or adapted for narrative clarity.

While this story is grounded in the author's personal experiences, it is not intended as a definitive account of any one person's life other than their own.

"What should young people do with their lives today? Many things, obviously. But the most daring thing is to create stable communities in which the terrible disease of loneliness can be cured."

—Kurt Vonnegut

"I decided I needed a complete makeover. Except this time, I'd make over my soul."

—Cher Horowitz, *Clueless*

prologue

I'm sitting cross-legged on the floor of a moldy tent somewhere in the jungle, approximately two hours east of the Panama City airport. In my shaking hands I hold a plastic bag I found billowing in the breeze by the outhouses.

I want to suffocate myself with this plastic bag.

A few yards away, keeping dry from the afternoon drizzle under a palm-leaf roof, my students are writing essays about sustainability while snacking on mass-produced peanut butter smeared on unsustainable bread. I've spent the past six weeks teaching them how to tell stories while they vacillate between wanting to make the world a better place and wanting to drink homemade rum and make out with each other.

But I don't care about my students. I don't care about anyone but myself and my own screwed-up brain, a soundtrack on a repeated loop telling me all the reasons I'm a failure, a symphony of self-loathing. Everything is heavy. My footsteps on the hiking trail. The monsoon-like rain. My fingertips, struggling to type out my weekly curriculums. My head on the balled-up sweatshirt inside my tent that I use as a pillow each night and, increasingly, each day.

I can only think of one way to stop these hateful thoughts—this heaviness.

I pick up the bag and gingerly place it over my head. Take a few breaths. The material expands and contracts with my inhales and exhales. Outside, the rain grows stronger, fat droplets plunking on the makeshift nylon walls. Inside my plastic cocoon, it gets hotter. My breath starts to speed up. Am I getting dizzy?

Before I can answer that question, my hands tear the bag off my face, animal instinct overtaking any will to want to die.

What the hell am I doing? How the hell did I get here?

I rip down the zippered door and stumble outside, gulping mouthfuls of fresh air. I can't tell if it's the rain streaking down my cheeks or my own tears. I sprint down the dirt path, my flip-flops sliding in the mud and leaving speckles on my calves, away from the tent platforms and through the banana trees. One of the reality-show producers approaches me with a camera balanced on his shoulder.

"Hiya, Carly!" he says in singsong. "Where are you off to in such a hurry?"

I push past him, hoping he isn't filming, knowing he is. Meltdowns make for great television.

"Gotta find Santiago," I mutter. The producer follows me a few paces and then gets distracted by a pair of giggling girls in bikinis doing a rain dance, open mouths poised toward the sky.

I spot Santiago in the teachers' hut sipping coffee from his thermos, hands gesticulating wildly, rapt attention focused on Max, the show's director. She came down to our eco-community a little over a month ago to film a TV series about our experimental school, a glorified study-abroad program where we're all convinced we can redesign humanity's societal paradigm together from our little speck in the wilderness. She's got a deal with a major network and everything.

From the way Max is grinning and gazing directly into Santiago's eyes, I know he's making her feel like the most interesting person in the jungle. He has a way of making whoever he's talking to feel like the most interesting person in wherever they might be.

As I approach them, Max giggles loudly and gives Santiago a playful little shove on the chest. "Santi, you think you're such a mind reader," she teases.

Normally, their flirting would have made me anxious, but I'm too numb to feel basic emotions. I stumble over to Santiago and manage to grab his hand.

"Hi, sweetie!" he says cheerfully, kissing me on the cheek. "Max was just telling me how she really likes the direction of our story arc. She wants to interview us together before dinner."

"You two are the romance of the season," Max adds.

I ignore her. These days, my relationship takes place more in front of the cameras than between two people in private. I can't remember the last time Santiago and I had a conversation about anything consequential. That's about to change.

"Can I talk to you?" My mouth manages to form words without me crying, but talking feels as gargantuan a task as everything else.

Max perks up. "Care if I join you two lovebirds?"

"Great idea!" Santiago agrees enthusiastically. "We can get a head start on today's storyline."

"No—I need to talk to you by myself," I say. This time it's easy not to cry because I'm starting to get pissed. I'm almost relieved Max's persistence and Santiago's camera-readiness provoke my capacity to feel anything but hollow.

I pull Santiago back toward our tent before anyone can object. By the time we reach our wooden platform, protected only by a flimsy tin roof, we're both soaked. The rain keeps hammering down. Now, out of earshot of anyone with access to a camera, the tears come freely.

"Oh, babe." Santiago pulls me into a hug and strokes my hair, finally paying genuine attention to me, which makes me cry harder. "What's going on? Are you having another bad day?"

"I've got to get out of here," I sob into his T-shirt.

"I know it's hard," he replies, kissing my ear. "I want to leave sometimes, too."

I yank myself away and look him in the eye, sniffling. For a minute it's like things were before, just him and me. Maybe I'm about to ruin it for good.

"Santi, I need to go *home*," I tell him. "I'm pretty sure I just tried to kill myself."

He inhales sharply, his sunscreen-protected face even paler than normal. "Sweetie?"

"I can't be here. It's too much. Everything hurts. It won't go away. It's not getting better. I want—I want to die."

As soon as I say it out loud, relief relaxes my whole body, and I start to cry again. Nothing frees you from wanting to end your own life more than admitting it aloud. Suicidal thoughts are fleeting, but the only thing that feels more permanent when they come is death itself.

Now, admitting my darkest, most shameful secret to Santiago, I'm jolted back into an existence that feels bearable. The memory of five minutes ago, poised to stop my own breathing with a bag over my head, is just a tale to tell. Part of a long and complex story that hasn't ended yet.

Santiago shifts into problem-solving mode, hero mode, his favorite mode. I can see his mind weighing scenarios and making calculations.

"Okay. Let's get you to the airport. We can figure out a plan from there."

Do I actually *want* to leave? The past few weeks have been some of the worst I've ever lived through. Every day, the voices in my head grow louder, reminding me why I shouldn't be in the jungle, that I'm nothing but a faker.

And yet the misery is peppered with moments of magic—euphoric sparks that light up my insides like fireflies, reminding me why I'm here, that I can do hard things. In those moments, any will to want to die feels as foreign as the local dialect spoken by the campesinos down in the valley.

But it's too late. Any chance I had of staying was shattered the minute I put that bag over my head. I need help, real help, and I'm not going to find it in Panama.

I wipe my eyes with the back of a dirt-smeared hand. I almost forgot I have actual responsibilities. That people are counting on me. "Will you deal with my students? I can't let them see me like this."

He pulls me back into a hug. I collapse onto his shoulder. "Of course, sweetie. We'll figure it out. Don't worry about them right now."

It's a strange feeling to love someone so deeply and envy them just as much. In many ways, I want to be Santiago. His unyielding charisma, his immunity to feeling dumb when he cracks a joke, his ability to make anyone he speaks to feel relaxed and comfortable enough to share their innermost thoughts and fears.

When we first got together, I thought that type of easy intimacy was reserved for me, that our fluid conversations were the result of two soulmates who had finally found one another. Now I know how shallow that intimacy actually is, how natural it is for him to peel back the layers of someone's truth with just a few sentences. Is it really intimacy if you dole it out to everyone who passes by?

Yet I still see myself next to Santiago and feel inferior. My own fears of one-on-one connections seem pathetic next to his interpersonal fluency. When he captures the focus of everyone around him, it stirs up my own inherent childhood desire to be the center of attention. Not that I'd do that by playing Taylor Swift songs on the ukulele, but in my fantasies, I'm equally enchanting. Equally worth spending time with. Instead, I don't even want to spend time with myself.

Twenty minutes later, we're in the front seat of our 4x4, my meager sweaty possessions shoved into my duffel bag. We begin the bumpy journey up the jagged, ironically nicknamed Suicide Hill toward civilization. The jungle swirls around me, a puree of technicolor dulled gray by my plagued mind. Through the storm obscuring our rearview mirror, I glimpse another truck.

"Shit. I think that's the TV crew."

PART ONE

one year earlier

chapter one

I arrived at Benito Juárez International Airport in time for dinner and pulled the crumpled, sweaty Post-it Note scrawled with Axel's address out of the pocket of my hoodie. He lived in a district called San Ángel. I wondered how far that was from the Condesa, which everyone seemed to think with great authority was the "cutest neighborhood in the world"—even people who had never been to Mexico City before. It was 2015, two months before Mexico's capital topped the *New York Times*' "52 Places to Visit" list, and this area had yet to become overrun with the explosion of expats who would swarm here in the impending years. In the weeks leading up to my arrival, I fielded unsolicited admonitions to "be careful" from almost everyone I told about my travel plans—most of whom knew nothing more about the country than what they read in clickbaity news headlines about cartel activity.

Everything I needed to survive for the next indeterminate stretch of time had been stuffed into a big blue backpack, the kind used for a multiday trek through the mountains or visiting a bunch of European cities by train. The rest of my worldly possessions were boxed up in my father's attic in Connecticut. I blinked away the airport fluorescence and scanned the row of luggage carousels, spotting my flight information from JFK. As I gazed at the conveyor belt for my backpack, I tried to recall the Spanish word for *suitcase*, but nothing came to mind. I'd taken classes steadily since the fifth grade, including a college minor and a semester abroad in Madrid. But now, at thirty years old, nearly a decade had lapsed without any meaningful opportunities to practice, and all my hard work had dissipated into inaccessible areas of my brain. My grasp of the language was minimal, at best.

I watched the colorful array of baggage from my flight make three full revolutions around the carousel before realizing my backpack was not among it. *There must be some mistake.* Maybe I forgot what the bag looked like, was too tired from the long journey and the all-nighter I'd pulled getting ready in nervous anticipation. I looked around at my fellow travelers retrieving their possessions until the conveyor belt dwindled to empty, anxiety rising from a gentle hum in my stomach to aggressive thumps in my chest. Fully panicked, my eyes darted around the arrivals hall until I located what must have been the baggage-services counter. *Maleta!* That was the word for suitcase.

I approached baggage services and looked helplessly at the uniformed man behind the counter. "¿Maleta?" I said, wincing at how American my accent sounded. "¿Dónde está mi maleta?"

He must have been used to this situation, because the airline worker remained unfazed by my combination of choppy nouns, incorrectly conjugated verbs, and hysterical hand gestures. He handed me a form with the phone number for Aeroméxico's "lost luggage" unit. Other than that, he explained slowly, there was nothing he could do. I looked down at my messenger bag, which didn't contain so much as a toothbrush or a change of underwear. Luckily, I'd been smart enough to stick my half-consumed bottle of antidepressants in one of the side pockets. A larger, three-month supply was stashed inside the big blue backpack. With all the changes afoot, I didn't dare screw with my meds.

A couple months earlier, I'd quit my job on the leadership team at what had recently been deemed the world's most visited online news empire. Through a combination of circumstance and a deep alumni network from my journalism undergrad, I'd wound up as one of the site's early editors, before its acquisition by a legacy media brand, domination of the SEO-based headline market, and considerable expansion into cities all over the country and, eventually, the world. I spent my twenties working my way up the masthead, first as founding editor of the site's San Francisco bureau and then on the management team at its headquarters in New York City.

Success at the media company meant being tethered to your laptop during all waking (and often sleeping) hours, churning out article after slideshow after article into cyberspace, fielding a steady stream of tweets and RSS feeds to ensure no piece of information hadn't been aggregated and repurposed with our own branding so we could rake in the page views. By the time I was twenty-nine, I'd amassed dozens of direct reports, led the newsroom's daily meeting, and was fumbling my way through management with the rest of my radically unsupervised and underqualified peers.

Every time I got praised or promoted, the brief sense of accomplishment and pride quickly gave way to impostor syndrome, insecurity, and hunger for my next achievement. My eyes burned from constantly seeing the world through a screen. Outside the office, I nursed a growing cocaine habit and a volatile off-and-on relationship with my boyfriend, Robbie. Inside the newsroom, I pushed through my hangovers and collapsed from exhaustion in our designated "nap room," where I sometimes spent the entire night if I needed to be on call to oversee coverage of international events like the Libyan uprising or the royal wedding.

I began to fantasize about what my life might look like if I blew it all up and did something completely unexpected. *Eat, Pray, Love* had been released a few years earlier, giving way to an influx of stories about wanderlusty women who traveled to exotic locales in service of "finding themselves." I grew increasingly attached to the idea of moving far, far away from New York City and the cutthroat journalism industry. As someone who had spent nearly her entire academic career studying Spanish but never quite mastering it, Latin America seemed like a natural destination to direct my daydreams. I escaped to conference rooms during the workday, feigning a "news emergency," so I could research fellowships and programs and travel opportunities in the southern hemisphere without getting caught.

Though my depression had been largely manageable since a catastrophic college experience first forced me to reckon with it, I still battled an inner monologue that nearly constantly reminded me why I wasn't good enough, smart enough, interesting enough, or successful enough. My only tangible skills for drowning out that voice included drugs, booze, work, and fights with Robbie that provided an avenue for me to divert my attention away from my own sense of self and toward whatever drama the two of us created. As the idea of a Latin American adventure took shape in my mind, I became convinced that walking away from life as I knew it would be my straight shot to self-love. "I yearn to see the world through my own eyes and not through a computer screen," I mused poetically as I laid my plans.

Somewhere along the way, I recalled an article I'd written about a microfinance fellowship program. The fellowship placed its recipients in regions all over the developing world, and though it was unpaid, it offered a supportive framework, a deep network of on-the-ground contacts in all the cities it operated in, and the opportunity to engage in meaningful work. I hadn't managed to save all that much money over the years, but I'd been prudent enough to stick my most recent Christmas bonus in a savings account without chipping away at it. Some quick math and a few Google searches led me to calculate that I could survive at least six months if I managed to be careful—the exact length of this fellowship. My acceptance into the Summer 2015 cohort, and subsequent placement in Mexico City, excited me more than any promotion at work ever had.

The stick-shift cab I hailed from the Secure Taxi Stand gasped and puttered its way through a maze of loud, bumpy blocks, passing taco stands, billboards emblazoned with unfamiliar series of numbers, and several groups of children playing dangerously close to the road. Talk radio blared from the speakers in Spanish so fast it sounded like one long tongue twister, and I tried to hang on to a few words, but all I managed to decipher was *hola*. By the time I'd become sufficiently carsick, the streets had grown wider and steadier, lined with large, ornate homes covered in vines and shaded by other manicured greenery. The driver pulled up to a yellow two-story villa with a Spanish colonial roof, partially hidden behind a grand iron gate.

For the first few weeks of my journey, I'd been offered a bedroom in the home of another graduate of the same fellowship I was about to start. All I knew about him was his name (Axel) and his country of origin (Germany). He seemed nice enough in our polite email exchanges, certainly generous to the point of allowing a stranger to move into his house. I handed the cab driver a tangle of pesos I'd pulled from the airport ATM and made my way up the stone path to the yellow house.

An extremely tall, bespectacled man with gelled curly hair answered the door, holding a basket of round, colorful fruits. "Ah, welcome!" he exclaimed in a strong German accent, ushering me inside. "Can I help you with your baggage? And where *is* your baggage?"

"I think the airline must have lost it," I replied, trying not to sound as anxious as I felt.

Axel sighed and chuckled. "Welcome to Mexico," he said. "Unfortunately this does not surprise me that much. But you will recover it, undoubtedly."

He led me inside an airy marble foyer with flower arrangements on seemingly every surface, and through a tiled hallway that led to a spacious kitchen. He placed the basket on the table and offered me something called a *mamay*, a traditional Mexican fruit he'd picked up at the outdoor market that afternoon. "They are so fresh, I eat them with a spoon," he said, slicing it down the middle. It looked like a neon-red mango. He extracted a large pit and handed me half.

I took a bite and tried not to make a face, swallowing the fruit down in one fleshy gulp. It tasted like a cross between a papaya and a rotten banana. "Mm," I said politely. "Thank you."

Axel clapped his hands together. "And we have so many wonderful local delights to show you," he said. "I trust you will fall in love with Mexico, just as I did. You also may never want to leave!"

A stout, round man with coffee-colored skin and buzzed black hair ambled into the kitchen. He smiled at me shyly. "Soy Felipe," he said, bowing slightly. Axel's roommate, I guessed. I managed to go back and forth with him for a few introductory sentences before scrambling my Spanish.

"Ah, hablas muy bien!" Axel said enthusiastically in a perfect Mexican accent. He continued talking at me in Spanish, too quickly for me to understand, and my confusion must have shown on my face because he switched back to English. "You've had a long trip," he offered gently. "Let's show you to your room, shall we?"

My "room" turned out to be an entire guest suite, a separate building accessed via a stone pathway through a lush garden behind the main house. The flowers were so bright they practically radiated from their stems, fat roses and frilly hydrangeas and spiky birds-of-paradise. Axel told me gardening was his favorite way to spend his days, second only to his flute practice, which took place every morning in the piano room and he hoped wouldn't disturb me. Felipe took French lessons a few blocks away each day before lunch, and in the afternoons they liked to go to the *tianguis* together, which is Mexico's equivalent of an outdoor farmers market. I couldn't help but wonder how he and Felipe garnered the resources to afford such a cinematic home, but since I got to reap the benefits for the next two weeks, I decided it would be rude to ask further questions.

They left me by myself to get settled, and I sat down on the guesthouse's single bed, testing it a few times, alarmed by its stiffness. I looked around the space, stark and pristine compared to the colorful main building, and wondered what happened next. All my stuff was still in transit somewhere. I was suddenly alone, my adrenaline drained from navigating transit, meeting strangers, and picking my way through dusty Spanish phrases. With nothing left to do, thoughts of Robbie washed over me. I missed him so much. I wished so badly for him to be here with me, to speculate on the source of Axel and Felipe's independent wealth, to see if he thought mamays tasted as gross as I did. We would undoubtedly have already come up with a catalog of inside jokes about my first forty-five minutes here.

Though the past two years had been tumultuous, Robbie had been my best buddy. Sure, we had a knack for bringing out the worst in one another: When we weren't passionately fighting or passionately reconciling, we were egging each other on to take the tequila shot, text the drug dealer, traipse to the after-after-after-party to keep imbibing long past sunrise. On our first date, we met up at a jazz bar in the West Village—we'd loosely known each other through mutual friends in San Francisco, and he'd moved to New York City a few months after I did—and he convinced me to snort a line of cocaine right off the table, in the middle of the crowded venue. As mercurial as our relationship was, I also found our connection exhilarating, a welcome distraction from the intensity of both my job and my low self-esteem. The unwelcome realization that I'd be navigating through Mexico by myself, and not inside our fiery two-person universe, crushed me. I couldn't remember the last time I'd felt so lonely, so far from anything familiar.

I took off my only clothing, a long-sleeved T-shirt and yoga pants, and folded it carefully on the uncomfortable bed. I'd have to turn my underwear inside-out or wash it in the sink until my luggage arrived. I turned the shower knob to the hottest setting, and freezing water came out of the nozzle. I missed my bathtub in Williamsburg, grimy as it was. I held my fingers under the stream, waiting for the cold water to turn warm. Ten minutes passed and nothing changed. I sighed and climbed underneath the showerhead, letting the frigid sensations jab at my pores like tiny needles. I shivered as the water trickled over my body. Alone in that austere guesthouse, enclosed inside the intricately tiled shower, a grain of sand on the map of one of the world's most populated cities, nobody could hear me cry.

chapter two

After a labyrinth of phone calls, Mexican hold music, and broken Spanish, my big blue backpack arrived at Axel and Felipe's villa a few days after my flight. I pulled out my clothing items one by one, unrolling each T-shirt and dress individually and hanging them in the guesthouse closet. These would be my only possessions for an indeterminate amount of time. I'd never been one to guard my items with any particular care—my dirty clothing at my apartment in Brooklyn had grown into a mountain on my desk chair each month until I hauled it to the laundromat down the block, orphaning socks and pairs of underwear along the way—but this backpack filled with belongings was the closest thing I had to any sense of home. It felt grounding to be a little precious about it.

With the contents of my luggage emptied into nooks and crannies of the guesthouse, I felt less like a trespasser in the space. I slipped the backpack shell under the bed.

Yet something didn't feel quite right. I'd unpacked piles of wrinkly clothes, an extra computer charger, a binder full of background information for my fellowship, and a tangerine-scented candle I'd purchased impulsively during my final drugstore run. But my antidepressants. *My antidepressants!* The final thing I'd slipped into my bag before checking it at the airport had been a ninety-day supply of nortriptyline, ordered with my father's discount code at Costco. Now, that comically large pill bottle was nowhere to be found. I pulled the empty pack back out from under the bed and checked inside every crevice to make sure I wasn't going crazy. I turned it upside down and shook it. Nothing came out except for a couple crumbs and a safety pin. Panicked, I patted down every item of clothing in the closet and dresser. Still nothing but fabric.

I still had a seven-day supply of pills left in my messenger bag, which gave me a week to secure a local source for the medication that sustained my life. Luckily, there was a *farmacia* on seemingly every corner of this city. I left the guesthouse in search of the nearest one, rehearsing the Spanish phrases I'd need in order to successfully complete this transaction as I wandered around the cobblestone alleys and wide avenues of San Ángel. My friends back home joked about how easy it was to supposedly buy narcotics like ketamine and OxyContin over the counter at Mexican drugstores. How difficult could it be to find what I needed?

I entered the first drugstore I saw, which featured a cartoon caricature of a bald man writing on a prescription pad on its awning, and greeted the on-site pharmacist with a big smile. "Hola," I said brightly, still cringing inside by how foreign my accent sounded. "¿Tienes una droga que se llama nortriptyline aquí?"

The pharmacist, a bored-looking woman with an eyebrow piercing and pink streaks in her hair, typed something onto a keyboard with her glittery acrylic nails. She shook her head and clucked her tongue.

"No," she said crisply. "No los tenemos aquí." *We don't have this here.*

I willed myself not to become frantic. I tried spelling the medication once more. The woman shook her head again.

"Okay," I replied, my breath quickening. "¿Dónde podría recogerlo?"

She shook her head again. "We don't have this in Mexico," she responded in perfect, impatient-sounding English. "They don't manufacture it in this country."

With that, she moved on to the customer behind me. I backed away, trying to absorb what she'd said. They didn't have my brand of antidepressants in the entire *country*? What was I supposed to do? I couldn't stop taking these pills now, of all times in my life.

I blanketed the entire neighborhood, visiting every farmacia I passed, most of which bore the same cartoonish doctor on their signage. Each person I spoke to gave me the same response: "No los tenemos aquí." After several hours of this unsuccessful scavenger hunt, I made my way back to Axel and Felipe's yellow house.

Axel brought me a cut-up mamay—my fourth in as many days, and I was actually starting to like them—as I did my best to recount my dilemma without crying.

"You'll just have to sneak your medicine down here," he replied breezily. "People do it all the time."

I hadn't gone a day without antidepressants for ten years.

Growing up in a competitive academic environment, I developed at an early age an exhausting habit of pathologically comparing myself to others and never measuring up in my own mind. I excelled at finding reasons to dwell on my inferiorities rather than celebrate my accomplishments. It didn't matter that I won awards for my writing or earned a spot in the all-state choir; my shortcomings were oh-so-much easier to focus on. I was a terrible athlete, I was only chosen for supporting roles in the school plays, I didn't have the discipline to learn more than a handful of guitar chords. Each of my successes felt like a minor detail compared to all the things I sucked at, and anytime I so much as interacted with one of my peers, I became distracted by a ruminating voice in my head reminding me of all the reasons that person was better than me.

As I journeyed deeper into my teenage vortex of self-loathing, my father became mired in his own bout of severe depression. The details in my memory are hard to conjure—I was either too caught up in my own adolescent solipsism to pay attention to what was going on at home or triggered enough by his behavior that I learned to cope by blurring it out. But I do recall evenings he spent in bed or in front of our family's boxy desktop computer, clicking aimlessly around on fantasy baseball websites, too numb to join us at the dinner table.

At some point, he began sleeping in the guest room, separate from my mother, and one of the only vivid images I can picture in my mind from that time features my father trudging out of the master bedroom and down the hallway, clutching his favorite pillow. Eventually, his depression lifted, and as my understanding of my own mental illness began to take shape as a young adult, my dad became one of my closest confidantes. Nobody else could empathize with my darkness in quite the same way.

I graduated in the top ten of my high school class, an achievement I quickly brushed off, and headed to college in the Midwest, a short flight from my childhood home in Connecticut. Determined to manufacture a sense of belonging, I wriggled my way into a tight-knit crew of guys and girls, and I even joined a sorority. But the hateful voice in my head only grew louder, and with unrestricted access to cheap alcohol for the first time, I learned that I could temporarily drown it out by partying. Not without severe consequences, though: My drinking usually resulted in blacked-out temper tantrums in which I sobbed and flailed and said horrible things to my friends. I almost always woke up the next day with a throbbing head and an overwhelming sense of dread that I'd have to profusely apologize for some sort of mysterious havoc I'd wrought the night before.

A couple years into college, my parents told me they were getting a divorce. I hid from the sad reality of my newly fractured family by partying harder. My binge drinking became so routine that I pretty much exclusively vacillated between being wasted or recovering from being wasted, and I rarely attended lectures or opened my books, save for the journalism classes that I still managed to legitimately enjoy. I had never considered suicide an option before, but eventually, thoughts of taking control over my internal bully began to flicker through my mind. Every time that notion appeared, a reminder that if I really wanted to, I did, indeed, have the power to end my own life, I felt relieved enough to let the thought pass. *I'm not the kind of person who would ever actually do that,* I'd tell myself.

Then, sitting in the back row of my international relations seminar one afternoon, I had that familiar realization that it was within my own authority to put an end to my misery. This time, the thought lingered—simply hearing it in my head wasn't enough relief to make it go away. The teacher's assistant was explaining the theory of anarchy, drawing complex diagrams on the whiteboard, and all I could think about was the anarchy in my own mind. If anarchy meant there were no rules, then why did I have to keep following the rules? Look at how far the rules had gotten me. I was two decades old, and I wanted to die. And there was no reason I couldn't. I could find a way to go peacefully, to free my friends and family of the burden of being around me, to turn off my sorry thoughts for good. I left class feeling better than I had in months: empowered and resolved, with an end to my suffering in sight.

My sorority was having a recruitment event that night, so I knew my roommates wouldn't be at our apartment, a dimly lit three-bedroom we'd rented above a popular breakfast diner in town. I texted them that I had a migraine and had to miss the event, and they wrote back telling me they hoped I felt better. I stopped by the drugstore on the way home and bought a bottle of Tylenol PM. I practically skipped down the frigid sidewalk to my front door. I was really going to do this. Relief was mere moments away.

Back in my bedroom, I turned my iPod to my favorite album, Wilco's *Yankee Hotel Foxtrot*, and plugged it into my speakers. I put on the most comfortable outfit I could find, one of those imitation Juicy Couture velour two-pieces that had been so popular in the aughts. I brought the pills and a bottle of vanilla-flavored Smirnoff into bed and sat on the mattress, pulling my down comforter around me. Opened the bottle and took a few pills, washing them down with the syrupy, fiery liquid. It was so easy. So painless. I took another handful of pills, another swig of vodka. No consequences. By the time the pills were gone and the bottle of Smirnoff was half empty, I felt warm and far away from my thoughts, my mind humming only with cozy white noise. I curled up into the fetal position and closed my eyes. The last thing I remember is leaning over the side of the bed to throw up all over the floor.

I woke up in a dark, sterile hospital room that smelled like bleach, on a stiff bed. My legs had fallen asleep, and there was a catheter shoved up inside my crotch. It took me several minutes to figure out where I was, to make sense of everything that had transpired leading up to this point. When I remembered, I panicked. I was trapped inside my body. I was still breathing. I was alive. I was relieved, terrified, disappointed, and exhausted all at once.

Over the next several days, as a lineup of doctors and nurses poked and prodded me, as I transferred to a youth psych ward in the suburbs, as my parents flew out separately from Connecticut, I pieced together what happened. My roommates had returned early from the sorority event. They popped into my room to see how my headache was and smelled the vomit on the floor. Discovered my unconscious body. Traumatized, they called 911. Paramedics took me in a blaring ambulance to the emergency room. Doctors saved my life by pumping my stomach full of charcoal. If my friends hadn't decided to come home when they did, things could have turned out a lot differently.

During those early weeks recovering from my suicide attempt, I didn't really grasp the gravity of what I'd done. It was almost as if I had known all along that this would be the outcome, that my second chance was an already-written story and not a lucky last-minute decision my roommates made to end their night early. I spent a week in the youth psych ward making drawings, writing long journal entries, and doling out advice to the younger patients. A parade of friends came to visit, still shaken. School administrators mandated that I return home for the rest of the academic year, address my issues in earnest, and check in with them when summer rolled around to see how my mental health was doing. I dutifully followed my parents, who were still only living a short drive away from one another, back to my hometown in Connecticut. I snuggled up with my childhood dogs on the futon in my mother's new apartment and set out to get well.

Conquering my depression became a project, a purpose. My destructive inner monologue was replaced by a determination to rebuild my life—a common phenomenon that doctors often refer to as a "flight into health." I got a new psychiatrist, started on a regimen of antidepressants, enrolled in an intensive outpatient program at a mental health facility in Hartford, and doubled down on making sense of my darkness. I listened to Thich Nhat Hanh audiobooks and read Pema Chödrön essays, learning about how to live in the present and reframe negative thoughts into neutral ones.

Meeting other seemingly normal people who struggled in the same ways I did, learning that my problems were not unique, was nothing short of revolutionary for my twenty-year-old self. Under the care and supervision of others, in community with people like me, I felt seen and heard in a way I hadn't before. Releasing the thoughts that had tormented me for years, from inside the walls of my mind out into the open air of group therapy sessions, was a newfound freedom, a welcomed lightness. Hearing others—young and old, male and female, awkward and self-possessed, professional and artistic, shy and outgoing—express similar fears and longings made me feel both unique and part of a tribe. I had never been able to diagnose my issues before with clinical terms. *Severe depression. Generalized anxiety disorder*. Other people had also been bestowed these labels by seemingly authoritative figures, and there were documented courses of treatment available to all of us.

In the years that followed, my daily dose of antidepressants became a solemn ritual: I brought them with me when my doctors deemed me healthy enough to return to college, and I found a new psychiatrist to write the same prescription when I moved out to San Francisco upon graduating. Along the way, I developed an equally religious marijuana practice, and the combination of SSRIs, an increasingly demanding career, the steady haze of pot smoke, and a distracting social life served as a sizable buffer between my depression and my ability to move through the world. It was never gone, exactly, but it never consumed me again. I felt like I had power over my disease and not the other way around.

Now, alone in a foreign city with no career, social life, or weed dealer, I wasn't about to give up the only other item on that list that might keep me from spiraling back into the depths of my deeply familiar pain. I needed to get my hands on my brand of antidepressants, and fast.

If anyone would know how to help me solve this predicament, it was my best friend Devon. Dev could come up with a creative solution for almost anything in a pinch: a wine bottle opened with the sole of a shoe when nobody remembered to bring a corkscrew, a side hustle helping startup founders fill in their LinkedIn profiles when you needed cash quickly. Before she moved to San Francisco in her early twenties, she spent a couple years living in Buenos Aires, where she ran a thriving small business selling electronics on the black market: She knew her way around shipping almost-but-not-entirely-legal goods south of the border. And not least importantly, Devon was the most loyal friend I'd ever had. One time, she spent an entire day at the Oakland DMV helping me retrieve the car of a guy I was casually dating before he could return home to find out I'd accidentally gotten it towed.

I first met Devon at a bar above the Stockton Tunnel, where we'd both been dragged to a mutual acquaintance's "Happy Independence Day" party, a celebration in which the host wanted to prove to her guests that she was absolutely fine and thrilled to be marking another year without a boyfriend. Devon and I bumped into each other while we were both hiding out in the corner trying not to get roped into drinking watermelon mojitos and taking selfies and belting out "All the Single Ladies" with the rest of the giggling young women in attendance. She told me she had just arrived in San Francisco for a job at a pal's solar energy startup after spending three months trimming weed in Humboldt County. Her long, uncombed hair and flowy floor-length dress suggested the kind of effortless hippie chic my insecure New England–bred self would never embody.

I had been in San Francisco for a couple years at that point, having moved there for an unpaid internship in the fact-checking department at a now-defunct magazine, later transitioning to a boring job at an ad agency that made commercials for a gasoline brand. (I'd yet to weasel my way into online news—that would happen the following summer, after they syndicated a series of blog posts I wrote on behalf of a local political candidate.) Devon epitomized the sort of confident, carefree spirit I fantasized about one day becoming as I played online Scrabble at my desk and counted down the minutes until my workday ended.

"Want some of these nugs?" she asked me before even introducing herself, pulling a jelly jar full of her recently harvested marijuana out of a shabby oversize purse. "I don't smoke pot, but I always seem to find myself with a bunch to give away." We were fast friends.

Using the ancient Nokia that Axel had loaned me until I was able to procure a Mexican SIM card, I dialed Devon from my San Ángel guesthouse. I knew her number by heart even though she'd changed it no fewer than three times since I'd known her—she lost her phone with the same frequency other people went grocery shopping. Hearing her voice on the other end warmed my insides and relaxed my entire body; I sank onto the bed with a comfort I had yet to experience since arriving in a foreign country earlier that week.

"I knew it was you," she said by way of greeting. "Who the fuck else would be calling me from a random number that starts with a plus sign?"

"Devon. Oh my god. I miss you so much." We hadn't lived in the same city since I'd moved to New York two years prior, but we still conversed all day long on a variety of mediums: text message, Gchat, popping silly links onto each other's Facebook walls. Her presence was a constant thrum that formed the foundation of my existence. I didn't realize how much I relied on our constant contact until I'd gone without it these past few days for the first time in at least half a decade.

In the background, I heard what sounded like elaborate harp music clashing with emphatic spoken-word poetry. "Are you guys having some sort of event or something?" I asked.

"Unfortunately, yes." I could practically hear Devon rolling her eyes through the phone. "Hang on, let me go up to my room to spare you from this nonsense. Thea decided to take *harp lessons*, of all things. She thought it would be fun if eighty of her closest friends came over so she could show them what she's learned."

Devon lived in the Avalon, a fifteen-person communal home in SF's Mission District named by its inhabitants after a defunct 1960s music venue. It was part of a wider trend of "modern communes" that had been popping up all over the city in recent years, in part to address rising rent prices, in part as a nod to San Francisco's history as the birthplace of the hippie movement, and in part because everyone we knew flocked to Burning Man each August and didn't want to stop living that way during the other eleven months of the year. These communal houses took many forms, from gritty art warehouses in the burgeoning South of Market district to cozy single-family homes in Twin Peaks, but each of them boasted a colorful roster of ever-changing residents and an equally colorful moniker.

Devon and two of her friends, a successful startup founder and the founder's twin sister, had established the Avalon a couple years earlier when trolling Craigslist for a place to live and stumbling upon a historic Victorian mansion from the late 1800s. I loved hanging out there, and I stayed with Devon in her king-sized, four-poster bed almost every time I visited San Francisco in the years since I'd left.

But I always felt a little intimidated, too. Devon's housemates were confident, creative, visionary types who sprawled across the ornate living room furniture having casual conversations about particle physics on a Tuesday afternoon. They shared groceries, toilet paper, hopes, and dreams: a chosen family that provided the kind of omnipresent support I'd never experienced outside nuclear relatives. And while Devon remained fully aware that the activities inside her home were often ridiculous enough to merit a *Saturday Night Live* sketch parodying San Francisco at its most annoying, I knew how much she cared about the community she helped create.

Her healthy skepticism kept the whole thing honest instead of earnest, and I loved that about her.

From my perch on Axel's guest bed, I explained my conundrum with the antidepressants. As expected, Devon had a quick fix.

"You know Simon? He just moved out? He's doing his residency at one of the big hospitals here," she said. "He can write a prescription for almost anything. And he's rad—he always gets us whatever we ask for. For some reason, a bunch of people wanted animal dewormers for some party last weekend, and he delivered. I don't ask questions." I knew she was rolling her eyes again.

I didn't remember who Simon was, but Devon insisted that wouldn't be an issue. She'd have him call in a ninety-day supply of whatever meds I needed as soon as we hung up the phone. Then, she explained, she would sew the pill bottle inside a teddy bear and mail it to Axel's address with no return address.

"And you're sure this will work?" I asked, starting to feel better already.

"Well, no," Devon admitted. "But it's worth a shot. And worst case, we can split the cost of a round-trip ticket for you to come back to the States and pick up some more. You're in *Mexico,* for fuck's sake, not Madagascar."

I couldn't help but laugh. Devon had a way of making even the most dire problems sound like minor inconveniences.

Sure enough, the following week, a DHL shipment with my name on it arrived on the doorstep of the yellow house. The stuffed elephant inside—Devon's favorite animal—was so cute that I almost felt guilty slicing it open. And there, inside its belly, was a humongous plastic bottle containing everything I needed to keep my depression under control until my next trip home. My first international travel crisis had been successfully averted.

During my earliest weeks in Mexico, my surroundings felt like a giant blurry mass, my rusty collegiate Spanish returning to my vernacular at a frustratingly slow pace. My hunger to understand and absorb my new home propelled me forward, my senses activated at all times. I'd never felt so new, so alone, so out of place—and so invigorated, especially as everything I saw and spoke and tasted gradually sharpened into focus. Around every street corner, across each intersection, was a new universe to explore.

The fusion of old-world and modern metropolis was striking: the corn maze of crowded stalls at the traditional outdoor market, whole chickens butchered with giant scissors as shoe-repair guys pounded on boots with hammers and older gentlemen played wind-up accordions for just a few pesos. Then, across the street, a sleek artisanal "marketplace" that may as well have been San Francisco's Ferry Building, all clean lines and wooden floors and fancy wares like chili-pepper-flavored ice cream and freshly shaved serrano ham. In traditional and contemporary settings alike, everyone I met approached me with the same generosity and warmth, eager to share their country and culture with me as soon as they realized I was a gringa from the United States.

My new roommates, Felipe and Axel, were obviously a couple, even though they slept in identical beds in identical separate rooms. ("We are old-fashioned," Axel would later explain.) They met when Axel was on the same microfinance fellowship I'd soon be starting; Felipe was the recipient of one of their grants, and Axel had been dispatched to his dry cleaning business in the state of Veracruz to make sure everything was up to par. Eventually, they moved in together in the yellow house, though how or with what resources they'd acquired it remained unclear. The pair loved to go to the tianguis together on Thursdays, Mexico's answer to a farmers market, only a few blocks away. I joined them a couple times, enchanted by the bounty of mangoes and papayas and cheap avocados, charmed by the elderly women hand-pounding tortillas onto griddles to make tacos out of exotic ingredients like corn fungus and squash blossoms.

My fellowship assignment was to take place at the local branch of an international microfinance NGO a couple blocks off Mexico City's main boulevard, the Paseo de la Reforma. I'd work at the office for several days a week, sifting through the profiles of individuals who borrowed money from the organization in order to start their own small businesses: convenience stores and hair salons and chicken farms, located out in the countryside several hours' drive from the city. I'd be visiting ten of those borrowers in person to learn more about their businesses and ensure the loans were going to good use, journeys that would take place over the course of several road trips organized by employees of the NGO, in partnership with the American organization administering my fellowship.

On my first day at the office, a young woman with caramel-colored bangs wearing a fuchsia blazer met me at the entrance and introduced herself as Rosario. She was to be my main point of contact during the fellowship, she explained, and would be accompanying me on all the borrower visits in the countryside. She showed me to a windowless room with cream-colored walls and a worn carpet and said that's where I'd work when I was on-site.

"You're a special guest," she told me in Spanish with a wink. "That's why we're giving you your own room." I managed to understand every word. Since arriving a few weeks earlier, my childhood grasp of the language was slowly re-revealing itself in the corners of my brain. Though I still couldn't decipher everything that was said to me, especially in the speedy local dialect, words and phrases were starting to solidify, and I no longer felt stranded on an open sea without anything familiar to buoy me. I had a long way to go, but I wasn't completely lost. Every legible sentence I formed felt like a small victory.

Rosario and some of her coworkers offered to take me to lunch at a taco stand nearby. "We never go out to lunch, so this is exciting for us," Rosario explained, again in Spanish, again to my understanding.

"Rosario habla muy bien el inglés," another woman interjected with a knowing smile. Rosario's forehead reddened beneath her bangs and she shook her head shyly.

"It's okay," I told her in her native language. "We're in Mexico, so we'll speak Spanish if you want." Rosario smiled and nodded. Eureka! More full sentences that made sense.

Lunch was awkward in the way that plucking dusty vocabulary words from the bowels of your memory can only be. After exchanging pleasantries about the weather (rainy season would soon be upon us) and how lucky I was to be spending my first couple weeks in San Ángel (Frida's and Diego's original art studios were there, had I walked past them yet?), the women started chit-chatting to one another too quickly for me to understand. My head ping-ponged back and forth; I thought I heard something about a sister's wedding, and something else about pyramids, maybe a party this weekend.

I strained to look interested, but my mind wandered to Robbie. I wondered what he was doing at that exact moment as I picked at a plate of *el pastor* two thousand miles away. Did he miss me? Was he already seeing other women?

Before I left New York, Robbie and I had considered every possible scenario for how our union would evolve, from breaking up entirely to him moving to Mexico with me. We eventually landed on "open relationship." It was more his preference than mine—to my great annoyance and frequent anxiety, Robbie maintained flirtatious relationships with many women and was always spouting irritating polyamory rhetoric, like suggesting that finding new sex partners might bring the two of us closer together. I didn't much care for the idea of my boyfriend sleeping with other people, but I wasn't ready to lose him. Not when I was leaping into a brand-new world without anything else connecting me to my former life. Not after we'd been through so much and still, miraculously, kept showing up for each other. For all his faults and all our dysfunction, Robbie was such a familiar force. And, quite inconveniently, I was in love with him: a hard spell to break.

An open relationship made perfectly logical sense to me. I was off on a grand adventure, meeting throngs of new people. The comfort of a long-term boyfriend paired with the freedom to explore other connections would be the best of both worlds. But I'd never been great at letting logic dictate my emotions, and the thought of Robbie going on dates—or worse, being intimate—with other women made me feel physically ill. I knew the only way I'd survive this arrangement would be to pretend it didn't exist. So I told Robbie our open relationship was to take the form of "don't ask, don't tell": Whatever he did when I wasn't around didn't concern me.

Except it *did*, of course, concern me. During my first month in Mexico, I couldn't shake the consuming, sickening thought of my boyfriend having sex with people who weren't me. Instead of letting myself explore my own romantic connections, I became obsessed with the idea of finding out who Robbie might be pursuing. I had a hunch. He'd returned to San Francisco a couple days after I moved to Mexico: He was living off online poker savings, which meant he could be based anywhere, and he didn't have a whole lot of friends in New York aside from our party crew. According to photos that had recently surfaced on his Facebook feed, he'd been spending a lot of time at Devon's commune, the Avalon, lately. That meant there was a not-small possibility that he'd picked things back up with Ari again.

I didn't know Ari well; she'd moved into the Avalon after I had already left for New York. She and Robbie had a brief fling during one of our "off" phases; they'd hooked up at Burning Man the previous summer and he flew out to San Francisco to visit her a couple times. Even then, I detested the idea of Robbie spending his nights with someone who shared four walls with my best friend. Devon, who was never a big fan of his and certainly never a big fan of our relationship, refused to say much on the matter aside from "I can't figure out what so many amazing women see in that guy." And Ari *did* seem amazing; her bountiful energy and musical laugh were infectious. I had no choice but to hate her.

Rosario gently tapped me on the shoulder, and my uncomfortable thoughts momentarily dissolved. I was back in the cafeteria, more than two thousand miles away from my messy relationship. I forced myself to tune back into my coworkers' fast-paced conversation; it seemed like they were still discussing their weekend plans.

"We're doing karaoke for my sister's birthday," the woman to Rosario's left told me in Spanish. "You should join us if you don't have plans."

"¡De acuerdo!" I replied, a little too enthusiastically. A local activity with local friends? I was starting to feel like I belonged here. And for the rest of our lunch break, brief as it was, the question of my boyfriend's love life was no longer relevant.

chapter three

The grand, leafy boulevards of the Condesa were just as resplendent as every travel writer suggested. I plopped down on a wrought iron bench on the corner of a wide cobblestone sidewalk—the kind that ran right through the center of the street, as was common in this area of the city—and watched the passersby, joggers and dog walkers and couples traipsing arm in arm. My feet were starting to hurt, the soles of my shabby combat boots wearing thin.

On days I didn't have to work, I chose a different area of the city to explore, always making the long trek from San Ángel to other neighborhoods on foot. I passed red double-decker buses, discount shoe stores, squat pastel apartments with cracked facades, and white-haired women wearing aprons, selling tacos from shiny silver carts. Today I'd chosen to head north, a mission that ended up taking several hours.

Though it had been sunny all afternoon, the skies had quickly darkened, and a droplet of rain plunked onto my forehead. As soon as I registered its wetness, a chorus of raindrops followed. No, a chorus would be describing it too politely. This was more like a heavy metal mosh pit of rain, a cracked-open sky releasing a cacophony of liquid. I'd heard about surprise afternoon storms during Mexico City's summer months, but I didn't expect them to be this aggressive, or to happen so suddenly. I raced to a pizza shop on the corner for respite, but by the time I reached the doorway, I was completely drenched. My clothes stuck to my skin like Saran Wrap.

I glanced around the restaurant, shaking off my limbs, noticing how my surroundings perfectly embodied everything I'd come to love about this city's fusion of the old world with the modern. The venue itself could have been a tavern from the Middle Ages, sturdy high-top wooden tables and matching stools, concrete walls with no decorations, patrons sipping on glass mugs of beer, a stone pizza oven carved right into the wall itself. But the menu, a nondescript faded piece of paper tacked by the door, boasted all the offerings of the fanciest pizza spots in Brooklyn, exotic ingredients like figs and goat cheese and jalapeño honey and hand-cured Spanish prosciutto, vocabulary words I'd never learned in school and needed my phone to translate into English. The beer, too, appeared to be locally brewed and artisanal. Outside, rain still gushed from the clouds, forming sinister, murky puddles, so I grabbed a seat by the oven and attempted to warm myself.

At the table next to me, a man with a graying ponytail and a jolly potbelly spoke to his dining companion loudly, vacillating between Spanish and English. He wore a tie-dyed shirt that said PEACE, LOVE, AND KARATE CHOPS, featuring the silhouette of someone giving a high kick. The guy across from him, clad in a tight polo shirt buttoned all the way to the neck and narrow, oval-shaped glasses, appeared to be hanging on to his every word. I instantly wanted to be sitting with them. *Well, what the hell,* I thought, and motioned to the loud one's T-shirt.

"Perdón," I said in my best local accent as I approached them. And then, continuing in Spanish: "Where did you get your shirt?" I never would have so brazenly approached a stranger in America, but something about traveling drains your shyness from you.

"Ah, a gringa?" The ponytailed man bellowed in perfect, accent-free English. "I just got back from the States myself!"

I grimaced and switched to my native tongue. "Was I that obvious?"

Ponytail chuckled, and Polo Shirt slunk his face into his beer mug and averted my gaze. I stood there for a beat longer than felt comfortable, then Ponytail pulled out the stool next to him. "Join us for a slice, gringa? It's looking soggy out there!"

I gratefully climbed onto the stool, and Ponytail flagged the server down and ordered me a beer. It tasted just like the thick, hoppy stuff I drank at all the sleekest breweries back home. As Ponytail and I chatted, and Polo Shirt eyed us silently from behind his mug, I learned the two men were enjoying a happy hour after the class they co-taught at the continuing education center in the nearby Roma Sur district.

"What do you guys teach?" I asked.

"Creativity," Ponytail replied.

I tried to look enthusiastic instead of confused. "Is creativity something you can teach?"

Ponytail laughed, a rumbling guffaw that shook his entire body. "Of course it is, gringa! Maybe not where you come from, but everything is possible here in Mexico. As you will soon learn, if you stay here long enough."

I couldn't help but be enraptured by his magnetism. We chatted effusively over several more pints of beer, Polo Shirt chiming in with a grunt or an affirmation here and there. I told them about my past as a journalist, my skepticism about digital news, my first impressions of their city, my own philosophies about creativity. Ponytail radiated with tales of his most recent trip to America, where he attended a design-thinking workshop in Austin and went kayaking with the bats on the river at sunset. "Cool city, but their tacos—no bueno," he laughed. "You Americans think you know Mexican food, but let me tell you, there's no such thing as a burrito down here. You made that shit up."

"Excuse me, but I believe Tex-Mex is a whole type of cuisine in itself," I retorted, matching his laugh.

"I like Tex-Mex," Polo Shirt piped up.

Ponytail snorted. "You two: loco! What am I even doing here?" He took a large gulp of beer. I felt buzzed and happy, infused with a traveler's confidence. I wanted more: more new experiences, more new people, more of my new city.

Polo Shirt glanced at his watch. "I need to head home," he said, looking me in the eye for the first time. His eyes, I noticed, were a beautiful shade of crystal blue, an unexpected match for his tan skin and black hair.

Ponytail laughed his hearty laugh. "Oh yes, Vicente here has a new baby. And how could we have forgotten? Can't leave your wife alone for too long with that screaming thing!" He clapped his friend on the back and rose from his stool. "And how about you, gringa?"

I shrugged. "I should get home, but it's all the way on the other side of town. San Ángel."

Ponytail clapped his hands together. "Then we walk! It's a beautiful evening for a walk."

I glanced out the window. The sun was peeking through the trees again, and water dripped sporadically and non-menacingly from the pizza restaurant's overhang. I shrugged again. "I don't even know your name," I mock-protested.

Ponytail grinned. "Well, let's fix that. I'm Alfredo. And it would be my pleasure to take you on a long walk." Alfredo extended his meaty hand, and I took it.

The two of us meandered across the city for hours. We stopped inside a department store to try on funny hats and at his favorite *birria* stand to sip savory broth out of little plastic bowls. Alfredo told me the names of different agave plants and that Mexico came from an Aztec word for "bellybutton of the moon." Along the way I heard his life story; he moved to Mexico's capital for university after growing up on the outskirts of Guadalajara, and he worked in the tequila-exporting industry for a while in his twenties, which brought him to border cities in Texas and California. He was twice divorced and currently entangled in a messy custody battle with his second wife for his son, and the details sounded obscure and ugly. To make himself feel better, he engaged in torrid encounters with one of his creativity students, whom he described as "the true love of my life."

"How do you know if someone is the true love of your life?" I asked. My mind flashed to Robbie gallivanting with other women, but I quickly shook away the image, like a child erasing a drawing on an Etch A Sketch.

Alfredo paused and considered my question. "You know, I'm not sure," he replied. "But I do know I like you."

I felt my ears grow hot, until I realized Alfredo wasn't hitting on me. He was merely regarding me as a fellow individual, someone whose company he'd enjoyed for the past several hours.

"You're not like the other gringos," he continued. "They come down here, they eat our food, they visit our museums, they drink our mezcal. They refuse to learn our language. They think they have all the answers. But they never stop and listen to us Mexicans to find out if their answers are the right ones."

I knew what Alfredo meant. In my less than a month in Mexico City, I'd already encountered a certain "social-impact warrior" archetype at expat networking events and during my search for more permanent housing. Well-intentioned white people wearing flowy local fabrics and long beaded necklaces, loudly pitching their ideas for "making the world a better place" between sips of Dos Equis, bitching about capitalism and colonialism while bragging about "how far the dollar goes here" in the same sentence. I knew it didn't sit quite right with me, but I was too green in my travel journey to understand why.

"You, you ask questions," Alfredo continued. "Good questions. And you hear what I have to say in response."

I smiled sheepishly and averted my eyes to the ground. I'd never been good at taking a compliment. We'd reached the yellow house, and I extracted my old-fashioned brass key from my purse, shrugging away this kind man's kind words.

Robbie surprised me with a plane ticket to fly back to the US and meet him at Burning Man. When he told me via Skype, my immediate reaction disarmed me: I didn't want to leave Mexico so soon, to pull myself out of the new life I'd been steadily building. I missed him, though, and often to the point of discomfort. So I batted away those feelings and smiled into the grainy computer camera, telling him that I couldn't wait to see him and all our friends.

"I know, babe, it'll be so great," he said, shoving his unruly dark hair out of his eyes. I had an urge to reach through the screen and brush a lock of hair behind his ears, a move I often made while we were together that he described as "grooming."

It took me years to admit that Burning Man sounded like fun, and even longer to finally get my act together and go. Burning Man was a way of life for a huge chunk of San Francisco residents: Entire stores on Haight Street exclusively sold costumes and supplies year-round for the event, which still takes place for a week around Labor Day, and everyone from my boss at the ad agency I worked at after college to the musicians who played pop-up shows on Valencia Street had a designated "camp" they went with.

When I lived in San Francisco in my mid-twenties, I thought I was making a brave political statement by refusing to attend and poking fun at my friends for taking the event so seriously. After all, the city felt great when it cleared out: In late August, you could snag last-minute reservations at even the most popular restaurants, and it was so much easier to find parking! (Not that I owned a car or anything.) It wasn't until I moved to New York and missed my friends on the West Coast that I decided to join a camp to see what all the fuss was about.

Burning Man draws tens of thousands of people who proudly identify as "Burners" to Nevada's remote Black Rock Desert annually and forms the basis of a vibrant international subculture that involves costumes, bass music, drugs, openheartedness, and undeniably extraordinary large-scale art. Burners spend several months, sometimes the full year, planning elaborate theme-camps ranging from roller rinks and beauty salons to breakfast restaurants and burlesque theaters. Then they load up their U-Hauls and head out to the desert—known in Burner lingo as "the playa"—and build it all from scratch, knowing that in just seven days, they'll have to remove everything just as carefully as they constructed it.

Creating a temporary city for eighty thousand weirdos in harsh, dusty weather conditions is a unique kind of forced hardship that brings people closer together, and the bonds formed during Burning Man remain strong enough to last throughout the rest of the year. In recent years, it's grown into more of a tasteless billionaire bacchanalia—a laughable symbol of tech excess and reckless consumption—than a remote destination for free spirits to explore their outer limits of self-expression. But at the time Robbie extended his invite, I loved the event as much as everyone else in my social circle. Even if it meant taking a break from all the progress I'd made in Mexico, I couldn't help but relish my giddy excitement.

Seeing Robbie for the first time since we'd parted ways, though, was anticlimactic at best. I arrived in the desert at 2:00 a.m. on the "Burner Express," Burning Man's shuttle bus from San Francisco, toting a garbage bag filled with costumes I'd collected from Mexican flea markets. It took me another couple hours to find his camp, its only signifier a giant rainbow-colored geodesic dome that was impossible to spot in the dark. I hailed a ride on a golf cart decked out as an LED-lit armadillo and scouted as best I could.

When I finally made it to Robbie's tent, I found him curled up in a heap on top of a deflating air mattress in the corner, one leg extending from the side of a pilly blanket. I crawled over beside him and attached myself to his torso like a koala bear. He grunted and turned over.

"It's you," was all he said, his breath sour. His body felt like a stranger's. I nuzzled my face in the crook of his elbow anyway.

It didn't take me long to realize I'd left my meds on my bedside table in Mexico City. As I pulled costumes out of the garbage bag one by one to show Robbie, my toiletry bag was conspicuously absent from the pile. "Oh, fuck," I groaned. Not again.

Robbie seemed deeply inconvenienced when I dragged him to the medical tent with me to ask one of the volunteers how I might be able to obtain my antidepressants. Her psychiatric qualifications were dubious at best. "Let me see if the on-call doctor knows," she said, twirling her braided hair, which was woven with fuzzy purple ribbon.

When she reappeared a few minutes later, she told me that, no, Burning Man didn't have anything that remotely resembled a Walgreens. I'd either have to drive several hours to Reno and back or do without them for the week.

"What happens if she does without them?" Robbie asked impatiently.

The volunteer shrugged. "I'll ask." She turned on her heel and Robbie sighed.

I remembered something about a psychiatrist in the past telling me that this type of medication has a strong half-life, and that I could go up to several days without it before feeling withdrawal symptoms like aches and dizziness. I'd never tested that theory myself, but as long as I could get more on the drive back to San Francisco before I caught my flight, I reasoned, the effects probably wouldn't be that bad.

The volunteer confirmed my hypothesis when she returned. "Yeah, you'll be fine," she said. "I mean, you might feel a little sad. But it's Burning Man, so even if you get sad, you won't stay that way for too long."

That was a good-enough answer for Robbie. "Babe, let's *go,*" he said, pulling me toward the rack where we'd parked our bikes. "I want to make it to the foam party before the line gets too long."

We bumped into Ari, Devon's roommate and the woman I suspected to be my boyfriend's other lover, at the foam party. She hugged me just as magnanimously as she greeted Robbie. Her wavy chestnut-colored hair was streaked with desert dust, giving it a luminescent quality that matched the shimmering kimono she wore over a flattering one-piece bathing suit. "Your Mexican adventure sounds so special!" she said, as if we were old friends who knew everything about each other's lives.

A group of naked people dressed as a caterpillar doing the conga line danced past us. Bubbles from a machine in the corner circled over our heads, and Robbie popped one with his finger and grinned. He pulled a small baggie full of white powder out of his cargo shorts.

I spotted someone I knew from my New York party scene behind the DJ decks and made my way over to say hello, leaving Robbie and Ari alone with his bag of drugs. I admittedly loved going to Burning Man with all my friends each summer, pushing the limits of both my self-expression and my physical strength. But all the pomp and circumstance felt a little bit ridiculous compared to the work I'd been doing in Mexico, spending time with farmers and fruit sellers in the country's farthest-flung pueblos, learning the local slang with Rosario and our colleagues. I didn't want to be just another bleeding-heart, white-savior type who flew back to party in the United States at her every whim. Then again, I was a well-resourced American woman doing social-impact work in a developing nation. If it looked like a duck and quacked like a duck, then maybe I should lose the sanctimonious attitude and accept the fact that I was just as cringeworthy as everyone else.

I exchanged a dusty hug with my DJ acquaintance and scanned the gyrating, foamy bodies for Ari and Robbie. I finally spotted them on a faded couch in the corner. They sat so close together she was practically in his lap, their eyes fixed on one another's as they spoke, their mouths inches apart. My boyfriend looked to be hanging on her every word as if she were the second coming of Socrates. I ignored the somersaults in my stomach and made my way over.

At the end of the week, Robbie and I decided to go on a "date night." This basically consisted of biking around Burning Man's horseshoe-shaped streets, scoping out camps giving away free alcohol. When we were both good and drunk, sipping warm gin and flat tonic from our steel camping mugs, Robbie's mouth curled into a grin. He had that familiar look on his face, the one where I knew he was going to suggest we do something naughty.

"Wanna go to the Orgy Palace?" He winked and took another slug of gin.

The Orgy Palace was one of Burning Man's oldest camps, a tried-and-true desert tradition. A massive, opaque dome, it was one of the only air-conditioned structures on the playa and hosted piles of sweaty bodies, twenty-four hours a day, consummating their existing relationships or fleeting connections or everything in between. I had never been inside, but almost all my friends who'd experienced it had a good story. I just knew there was only one rule: You couldn't enter alone. And with Robbie, as I'd reminded myself so many times that week, I wasn't alone.

"Let's do it," I said, and swallowed down the rest of my drink in one gulp. I felt unsteady on my feet, maybe even a little bit dizzy. To be expected after a week of indulgence under the hot sun, I reasoned.

A squat bouncer stood in front of the Orgy Palace wearing a dog collar and tiny leather chaps. He looked like a cartoon toad getting ready to visit a dominatrix. He had us pull a number from an apparatus that looked a lot like what you'd use to order roast beef from a deli counter.

"Wait over there," he instructed, pointing to a canopied area packed with people milling around outside the enormous dome. A neon-pink sign hung above the entrance, asking all of us, "What's your pleasure?"

Robbie and I herded ourselves into the waiting area. A DJ covered head to toe in glitter with a pair of rhinestone antlers on his head was spinning a down-tempo set. All around us, scantily clad bodies were smushed against each other on the dance floor, flung across couches, making out on top of beanbags, and sprawled over a giant oriental rug. Another deli-counter device, a digital number counter, announced that the dome was "now serving 357." Our number was 462. This was going to be a long night.

We settled onto the rug next to a couple in matching Patagonia fleece tops—not the expected attire for a group sex party, but maybe that's what made them feel approachable. Robbie instantly struck up a conversation with the woman, who had a zigzag shaved into the side of her otherwise-limp brown hair, and I was left to fend for myself with the guy. His salt-and-pepper buzz cut matched his salt-and-pepper stubble. He offered me a stick of Doublemint gum.

"I'm Ben," he said, close enough to my face that I could smell his minty breath. "First time here?" His hand casually grazed my inner thigh and he let it linger. I didn't stop him: I was already so far outside my comfort zone that stating my needs felt like a moot point, and I'd never been one to find questions of overt consent an aphrodisiac. Once, at a sexually charged "conscious connection" party at the Avalon, someone asked me if he could please put his arm around me, and when I said yes, he asked if he could please kiss me on the cheek, and the whole process felt so rehearsed and mechanical that I ended up making an excuse to leave.

"Yup, never been here before," I answered Ben, unwrapping the gum, savoring the familiar mass-produced flavor on my tongue. "Robbie and I are on a date." I motioned toward my boyfriend, who was engaged in such an animated conversation with Ben's female counterpart that he'd ceased to notice me.

"Muffy and I haven't either," Ben told me. "We got married last month up in Portland. Burning Man's our honeymoon. We've never done anything like this before."

This statement prompted a lot of questions, none of which I could ever ask aloud. *Why are you spending your honeymoon having sex with a bunch of strangers? What inspired you to wear Patagonia to an orgy? Is Muffy actually a real name?*

Instead, I just smiled at him and tried to lean in a little closer so I'd seem as intimately connected to my new acquaintance as Robbie was to my new acquaintance's wife. We sat there awkwardly, as our partners flirted with each other beside us, listening to the DJ set and vaguely bopping our heads along to the music. "Good tunes," I commented dumbly. Ben nodded in agreement. We continued to sit, chewing our Doublemint in silence, and I pretended not to notice Robbie whisper something in Muffy's ear.

The number counter flipped to 374. Muffy's eyes lit up. "Benny, that's us!" she squealed. She hugged Robbie goodbye. "Hopefully we'll see you two in there."

Ben glanced at me nervously. "Guess that's our cue, then. Nice to meet you, uh . . ." He gestured in my direction, but before I could tell him my name, they were gone.

Watching the newlyweds traipse away together, I felt smacked by the realization that I wanted to be, quite literally, anywhere other than where I was in that moment. My disgust with Robbie after witnessing his little display with Muffy was so palpable that I could feel it sizzling on my skin.

"Hey, Robbie?"

He was gazing at a pair of women wearing only nipple pasties swaying in unison beside the DJ booth. "Yeah, babe?"

"I think I'm gonna head home. I'm not feeling well."

He reluctantly turned to look at me. "What are you talking about? This is supposed to be fun."

I hugged my knees into my chest and looked down at my feet. "Well . . . I'm not having that much fun."

Robbie sighed as if he were conversing with a petulant three-year-old. "Then let's get the fuck out of here." He rose to his feet and stormed toward the exit.

"Robbie—wait," I protested, following him out. "Can you just *wait?*" *Can you stop to think of anyone but yourself for just one minuscule second?* I wanted to shout.

He mounted his bike. I jogged after him and got on my own saddle, pedaling hard to keep up as dust billowed around our tires and disintegrated into the frigid desert night.

"Robbie!" I screamed. "So you're just going to ride away from me? Just like that?"

"I'm so sick of this!" he hollered back. "You've been in your head this entire goddamn week. Acting like you're better than all of us because you decided to go live somewhere else. Well, guess what? You're not!"

Now we were riding side by side, weaving through the uneven

dusty ground, dodging costumed revelers, shouting at each other. "Maybe I am!" I shrieked. "But I'm not canoodling with *your* best friend's roommate right in front of your ugly fucking face!"

Yelling into the open air felt visceral, a release of years of pain and anger our relationship had caused me, pain and anger I suppressed every time the two of us got back together again. We reached our camp and I threw my bike on the ground, livid, oblivious to anyone around me who might hear us fighting.

"Are you being serious?" Robbie roared back at me. "Are you in third fucking grade?" He gestured toward our sleeping space. "At least your quote-unquote best friend's roommate appreciates me. Or it sure seemed like she did the night before you showed up here."

When I was a kid, I used to have all-consuming temper tantrums. My entire body would be overtaken by a crackling, full-throttle rage. It was like my ego didn't exist and my id had pulled a release valve. I would scream until my throat hurt, cry until my body convulsed, throw my toys and clothes around, and collapse onto the floor. As a young adult, I only experienced this kind of hysteria when I was blackout drunk in college—my frustrated friends had to force me into bed flailing and howling on more than one occasion. Eventually, I grew out of it, even though my drinking habits didn't wane much. But sometimes, I still threw tantrums in my dreams, and I would wake up sweaty and breathing heavily, stung by the return of my unrestrained childhood. I had not, until now, engaged in this behavior in the real world as an adult.

Robbie's admission changed that. As soon as he told me about Ari, I lost control. I wailed as loud as I could: an ugly, full-throated cry, an inverted mating call that woke up whoever was sleeping at our camp. I lunged at Robbie and hit him in the chest and he grabbed my forearms to stop me. I wriggled free of him and sprinted toward his tent. I tried to yank down the tarp, tear down the whole structure, and when it wouldn't budge, I ripped open the door and grabbed his bin of costumes. I dumped them all on the ground, spread them around, smeared the fabric in dust, kicked them with my combat boots. My insides felt like they were on fire, my outsides cold and reptilian, my head floating like a helium balloon above my neck. I was so dizzy I thought I might pass out, but my rage kept me focused on the present moment.

Robbie caught up with me and grabbed me by the waist, picking me up and heaving me up over his shoulder. I was shaking, clawing at him, pulling on his hair and his flesh, but his strength overpowered me. He carried me inside the tent and gently placed me on top of the air mattress, stroking my hair, telling me to breathe. "Look at me," he said quietly. I wiped my runny nose with the back of my hand and sniffled, meeting his eyes through my tears.

"You are out of control," Robbie continued in a measured, patronizing, terrifyingly calm tone. "If you keep this up, I'm going to bring you back to the medical tent."

I spat in his face.

chapter four

I pedaled hard into the open desert, tires skidding on an unkempt lump of sand, dust particles smashing into my eyes and nose and mouth, channeling all my feelings into the velocity of my feet as I rode faster and faster. I whizzed past the massive steel replica of the word *Love* (ha!), screeched around a 1970s VW van dressed up like an LED-lit caterpillar. A big dust storm was stirring; already miniature tornadoes of particles were spinning up from the cracked earth, the landscape in front of me clouding over with cream-colored puffs. Pedaling through all that dust without toppling over became my only objective, a welcome distraction from my mood.

I must have been a full mile away from the city when the storm finally hit. I pulled my goggles and mask over my face. Everything around me was dense with dust. I put my hand in front of my face and couldn't see it. Full whiteout, as they called it. Only thin layers of fabric and plastic between me and the forces of nature. Although my natural instinct was to curl into a ball and protect my orifices until the storm passed, some primal proclivity took over, a longing to be part of the planet's fiercest elements. I lay down on the ground next to my bike and spread my arms and legs wide, the same angel pose I made when I first set foot on this land. Surrendered my body to the majesty of the desert. With the blurring of my senses came the blurring of my feelings, and the image of Robbie and our doomed relationship dissolved, temporarily, from my mind.

The sun was setting as the storm softened and passed. I gathered my things and walked my bike back toward civilization. After Robbie's and my blowout the night before, I'd slept on a couch in our camp's communal area and spent most of the next day skulking around like a zombie. Clearly our fight had not taken place in private, as everyone who passed me stopped to see if I was okay. *Was* I okay? I was drained of all resources, my body limp, my eyes puffy. But I also felt a relief I hadn't experienced since Robbie and I first got together in that jazz bar all those years ago. By late afternoon, I was able to shove down a couple energy bars and chug a Pedialyte, which gave me just enough motivation to take off on my bike into the open desert.

As I approached the cluster of camps that made up Black Rock City's core, I decided to veer away from mine and Robbie's and go visit my friend Pixie. Pixie had a knack for shimmying her way into thrilling, absurd scenarios, which made her the perfect person to pal around Burning Man with. Surely, she'd be able to keep my mind off my shattered relationship.

I leaned my bike outside the shipping container that doubled as her camp's ostentatious costume closet and dressing room. Sure enough, she stood in front of the full-length mirror, pulling a glittery tutu over her tie-dyed tights. Her new husband, Mister Jones ("just call me Mister," he'd told me earlier that week), sprawled beside her atop a beanbag chair, puffing on a nineteenth-century tobacco pipe and nodding at his wife's outfit approvingly.

Pixie and Mister met six days ago, on the first night of Burning Man. He'd been driving a golf cart maniacally, zigzagging around the playa in uneven circles, when he screeched up next to her. "Get in," he'd said simply, patting the furry magenta passenger seat. Pixie giggled coquettishly and climbed aboard. I'd bumped into the two of them a few days later wearing matching ring pops at a pancake-breakfast disco. She and Mister were soulmates, she explained, and they'd gotten married in a small ceremony atop a fire-breathing car decked out like a pirate ship. A guy dressed as a lizard had officiated, as someone down below played the bagpipes.

"Carly!" she squealed now as I stepped up into the shipping container. "You're beautiful, you're beautiful, you're beautiful!" She rushed over and wrapped me in a giggly hug.

Mister nodded at me from the beanbag chair and took another puff of his pipe, then wordlessly passed it to me. I took a small inhale, sputtering as I coughed out the harsh smoke. "What are you guys up to tonight?" I asked hoarsely.

Pixie clapped her hands together. "Mister's friends are throwing a party at the Oval Office, and you're coming with us!"

The Oval Office was the most notorious "plug-and-play" camp at Burning Man. While many longtime Burners embraced the event's participatory culture, building their own living quarters and bringing their own food, a faction of wealthy attendees spent their week in camps where they didn't have to exert themselves. Some had twenty-four-hour chefs, others had assistants on hand to erect hexayurts and shift pods, and almost all had fancy RVs plugged into an easily accessible electric grid.

I'd heard rumors about parties at the Oval Office, which allegedly featured top-shelf champagne, oysters, and go-go dancers. I couldn't begin to imagine how to keep oysters fresh for a week in the hot desert sun, but their power source was probably a lot more advanced than my camp's handful of solar panels. Though it didn't exactly jive with the way I preferred to spend Burning Man, I was deeply curious to see if the rumors were true. I followed Pixie and Mister onto that same storied golf cart he'd been driving the night he wooed her, and we careened out into the incandescent, swirling night.

The Oval Office was lavish in the way one can only create overindulgence in a wind-whipped, dark desert. Fire burned everywhere: from artfully scattered lanterns, from the tops of light poles, from the ends of dancers' batons in a velvet-curtained performance area. Servers decked out in corsets and miniskirts handed out champagne flutes to partygoers wrapped up in warm fur coats. House music throttled from a state-of-the-art speaker system. But the dust didn't discriminate; that familiar white sheen coated every surface.

Mister's golf cart puttered to the entrance and he helped Pixie down from the passenger side. I clambered out of the back seat, a third wheel eager to make new friends, and headed toward the fire dancers. A skimpy woman wearing goggles, a stovepipe hat, and black fairy wings handed me a glass of champagne from a waitress's tray, and I tossed my head back, downing it in one sip. She refilled it within seconds. Pixie and Mister joined us with another guy, and they each plucked their own champagne flute off the tray.

I made eye contact with the new guy as we sipped our drinks in unison. He had floppy hair, crescent-moon eyes, and a grin that took up his entire face. A blip of attraction flickered through my chest when I remembered I was newly single.

"I'm Carly." My voice was still raspy from puffing on Mister's pipe.

"Ooooooh, Carly, this is Coco!" Pixie trilled. "He and Mister met at a leadership summit in the Maldives last winter. And Coco, this is Carly. She's one of my more impressive friends." She giggled as my face reddened—though I secretly liked when my professional credentials came up in conversation, I still had no idea how to handle it graciously.

I wasn't quite sure what a leadership summit consisted of, but I had a feeling many of tonight's guests at the Oval Office attended them regularly. Coco grinned even wider. "Pleasure," he said, cocking his glass in my direction. His foreign drawl disarmed me; I couldn't tell if he was British or Australian or just one of those mysterious international people whose parents whisked them from Hong Kong to Paris to Dubai as a kid. "Want to go for a stroll? I'm feeling antsy." His eyes met mine conspiratorially.

I nodded; he took my hand and guided me toward the camp's entrance. "What brings you to the Oval Office tonight?" I asked.

Coco shrugged, still grinning. "I'm crashing here for the week. It's my first Burn, so I wanted to land somewhere comfortable."

He twirled me around in one effortless motion as we passed the fire dancers. It felt natural and not contrived. We bounced our bodies to the beat of the music, warmed by the fire, and he grabbed my hand and twirled me again, dipping me at the finish like we were ballroom dancing in an ornate banquet hall.

"So what do you do, Impressive Carly?"

"I'm a journalist," I replied. Even though I wasn't sure if that was true anymore, it had been my boilerplate response to this question for years. I told him about my former role at the online news outlet.

"No shit!" Coco gave me a high five. "Their preview of this year's Burning Man art was the reason I decided to come."

I had written that piece—one of the last things I'd posted before I left. It gleaned more than a million page views, and my boss had praised me for it in front of the entire staff.

"That was my story," I told Coco. "None of the other editors are all that interested in Burning Man."

That grin again, as he wrapped his arms around me and pulled me in closer. "Pixie was right," he said in my ear. "You *are* impressive."

And then I was kissing him. I couldn't tell who leaned in first, but all of a sudden we were making out as the fire dancers whirled around us. I could feel music vibrating in my head, my fingertips, my boots.

As our faces parted, Coco grabbed my hand and pulled me toward the bustling activity beyond the Oval Office's perimeter. "Come on," he said, winking. "Let's get out of this dump."

In his own words, Conrad Cunningham Jr.—known to his friends, business partners, and everyone else as simply "Coco"—ran a town in Panama, in the middle of the jungle. Naturally, I had a lot of questions.

"Are you, like . . . the mayor?" I asked him.

"Kind of," he replied. "I'm building. I'm a builder. I want to build the world's most sustainable modern town."

"Do jungles have towns?"

He chuckled. "They will now."

It all sounded very vague and grandiose and romantic. Coco explained that his father was a real estate developer originally from Sydney. Though he mainly dealt in strip malls, along the way, he'd acquired a vast piece of undeveloped land in Central America, in a thicket of jungle about two hours outside Panama City. Coco, who'd earned an MBA from Oxford, was looking to get into the family business but was bored by the idea of Australian big-box retail. So his dad partitioned off a few acres of the Panama land, a former cattle pasture in a deep valley surrounded by wild rainforest, and gave it to Coco.

"You mean he just handed it to you?"

Coco shrugged. "Not literally with his hands."

In addition to real estate, Coco was captivated by urban design and systems thinking, well-versed in Jane Jacobs and Donella Meadows alike. He believed in a human-centric approach: Communities were nothing without people, and people were nothing without education. He'd decided to prototype his town by starting with a school.

"It's like a research institute," he explained. "We're studying the early versions of everything we want to build together. Agriculture, biology, outdoor recreation, small business . . . we're envisioning how that will all look together in a thriving community one day."

He was using a lot of buzzwords, like "market innovation" and "systemic sustainability" and "circular economy," but I was fixated on the idea that this could be someone's regular life. I pictured Coco lounging in a hammock under a palm tree, writing lesson plans in a leather-bound notebook and sipping a strawberry daiquiri. Naturally, he loved the idea of what I was doing in Mexico on my fellowship, and he gushed about his own microfinance program that he was in the process of launching for local Panamanian entrepreneurs. Was there anything this guy *didn't* do?

Coco continued to pontificate about the future of cities and ecological development as we glided from party to party in the frigid, sparkling night. A pulsating energy typical of Burning Man's final evening permeated the air. We stopped in front of a monster truck decked out as a cruise ship. A DJ in a captain's hat stood on its hood spinning a lively set, and we started dancing again. Robbie's unkempt face felt like a distant memory; here in front of me was a magnetic, worldly man who thought I was as brilliant and interesting as he was.

I was still giddy, drunk on our breathless banter, by the time the sun peeked over the jagged ridgeline. My camp was a speck across the playa, miles away, and Coco put his hand on my lower back and offered to walk me home.

The pastel traces of early morning stirred as we arrived. A couple of my campmates hung around the makeshift kitchen, boiling water for a French press, as other wrung-out partiers, costumes awry, parked their bikes and splattered themselves like bird poop onto various pieces of dusty furniture. I searched the area for Robbie, but he was nowhere in sight. Coco kissed me on the cheek and slid something into the pocket of my fake-fur coat.

"In case you ever find yourself in Panama," he murmured. "A media mogul like yourself might be amused by our humble little town."

Watching the outline of Coco's body fade into a smudge as he sauntered away, I reached into my pocket and pulled out his business card. *Ico-Inna,* it said in yellow embossed letters across the top. Below it: *Coco Cunningham, Chief Executive Dude.*

Devon drove me from the playa to SFO, the closest airport with a direct flight to Mexico City. Dev was the kind of Burner who had no problem criticizing some of its more intolerable aspects—she wouldn't be caught dead at the Oval Office, for example—but as a devotee of magnificent art and a student of subcultures, she almost always took part in creating one of the more astonishing large-scale pieces on display. She rolled with the kind of Burning Man crew that was more likely to wear work boots than glittery headdresses and usually arrived in the desert several weeks in advance to help construct whatever spectacular thing she was working on that year.

To me, the process of building big Burning Man art seemed more daunting and complicated than even building a house, but nobody knew their way around a power drill like Devon. Though she was my closest friend, we rarely saw each other during Burn week.

In the passenger seat of Devon's Westfalia, I recounted my breakup with Robbie. The whole chain of events—the Orgy Palace, the middle-of-the-night temper tantrum—sounded so melodramatic and ridiculous in retrospect that I couldn't help but laugh.

"Do you think it's for real this time, though?" she asked. Devon had been privy to all our prior splits, which never lasted that long.

"I think so," I said. It certainly *felt* more real: I wasn't pining for Robbie or convincing myself we had unfinished business. I couldn't wait to get back to Mexico and continue what I'd started down there.

"Well, I hope so," she said. We watched the long two-lane road bend between the mountains in silence.

"You know," Devon added after a few minutes. "Ari is not the boogeyman here. I think you'd actually like her if you gave her a chance."

The memory of Robbie and Ari snuggled up on the couch at the foam party hit me with a chest pang. "She slept with my boyfriend," I snapped.

Devon looked over at me and gently put her hand on my shoulder. "With your full permission."

I sighed. She was right.

"I just hate how the other woman always gets blamed in these situations," Devon continued. "I'm friends with both of you for a reason. I like to think I have decent taste in people."

We stopped at a Walgreens in Reno so I could pick up a fresh supply of antidepressants. Devon's doctor friend had managed to call some in for me that morning. I'd been fending off feelings of lightheadedness for a few days, and I couldn't tell if it was from medication withdrawal or something more benign, like desert exhaustion or excessive partying or post-breakup languor. But I didn't want to find out. I opened the prescription bottle and swallowed one of the pills dry as Devon eased her van back onto the freeway.

She put her hand back on my shoulder. "I'm glad to see you taking care of yourself with these," she said. Devon was the only person from my post-collegiate life who knew anything about my suicide attempt. "Maybe you don't want to fuck with taking a break from them again."

I rested my cheek on the window as we passed signs directing us toward Truckee. "No," I agreed. "I'm definitely not gonna fuck with that again."

I'd later come to refer to the months following my breakup with Robbie as "*la edad dorada*"—the golden age. I returned to Mexico confident and single, ready to meet people and finish out my fellowship with a triumphant flourish. I went on dates with handsome locals and took salsa dancing lessons. I traveled to the jungles of Chiapas, the mountains of Oaxaca, the vineyards of Querétaro, and the beaches of the Yucatán. I moved into a one-bedroom apartment in the trendy Roma Sur district for a month by myself, my first time living alone, and stayed up late on the roof deck under the stars, writing and sipping mezcal.

At work, I drove several hours into the countryside to learn about biodigesters—the process of turning animal waste into fuel for your stove—and met the farmers using small loans to pay for the equipment that made that happen. These were individuals who'd previously used harmful wood-burning stoves to heat their food, many who suffered early onset lung complications as a result, now able to not only recycle the cow manure on their property but turn it into a renewable form of energy. I allowed the biodigester's inventor, a handsome American entrepreneur with an environmental science degree from UC Santa Cruz, to take me on a date the week after our tour. Over tequila and hunks of bread and cheese in a dark cantina tucked off a vibrant corridor, he told me about his company's growth, the biodigesters he'd built in Kenya and Cambodia, his solo surf trips to the dangerous state of Guerrero. I pitched a story about his invention to a well-known business publication, and after interviewing him at his kitchen table, he led me upstairs to his bedroom.

With only a few weeks left until I finished my fellowship, I realized that, for the first time in my life, I didn't know what was coming next. Ever since enrolling in my competitive high school, I'd been in a pipeline of sorts, exiting one era only when it was explicitly time to enter a new one: education, more education, job, another job. Even leaving my journalism job to come to Mexico was highly premeditated—an adventurous plan, but a plan nonetheless. Now, I found myself staring into an abyss, only white space stretched out before me. It felt thrilling and maybe a bit unsettling. I only knew one thing for sure: I wasn't ready to return to the United States. I liked living out of my big blue backpack, lighting my tangerine-scented candle every time I landed in a new bedroom, keeping tabs on my meager possessions, each subsequent day a novelty. With the uncertainty came a confidence I'd never embodied before, one that said, "I'm in charge of my life, and I get to actively choose what happens tomorrow."

So I fished Coco Cunningham's card out of my wallet and sent him an email to see about heading farther south to Panama to check out his "town." If I wasn't going home, I reasoned, I may as well go learn firsthand about the most outrageous thing I'd ever heard. A few days passed before I heard from him, and then there he was, in my inbox.

Hey Media Mogul! Was wondering if we'd ever cross paths again. Things are electric down here in the jungle. We are building something the world doesn't even know how badly it needs. I could use someone with a storyteller's mind. Come check it out? All you have to do is board the plane, and I'll take care of the rest. Hugs, CC

This seemed as worthwhile an opportunity as anything else. I booked a one-way ticket to Panama and waited to see what would happen next.

During the final week of the fellowship, my coordinator Rosario and I took the bus to Ixtlahuaca de Rayón, a small municipality several hours to the east of the capital city, in the state of Mexico. We were on a trip to visit the last borrower on my list, a woman named Dominika who had set up a composting operation with her microloan. Her son, Jorge, met us at the bus station in a boxy Honda Civic that looked like it was from the 1980s. He wore glasses and a pink button-down shirt, oddly formal for farming attire, and smiled shyly at Rosario, just as formal in her stiff blazer. Rosario climbed into the front seat of the Honda and the two of them chattered away, too quickly for me to understand. My Spanish had gotten a lot better over the past six months—so good, in fact, that I'd been able to compile an entire report about my borrower visits without visiting Google Translate once—but I still had a hard time whenever I was the only native English speaker in a group of Mexican people. The local slang was often too nuanced to grasp.

Ixtlahuaca's modest urban center soon gave way to its outskirts. Jorge drove us past shacks and concrete convenience stores with hand-painted signs, and eventually, we found ourselves on a narrow road climbing up and down the rolling hills. We whizzed past groves of avocado trees, cow pastures bracketed from the street by fences made from wooden sticks, and the occasional church. Every so often, we crossed a perpendicular dirt road but didn't make any turnoffs. I started to feel carsick as the Honda made a series of switchbacks, and I gripped the door handle and swallowed hard. Rosario turned around to face me. "Dominika is a very special woman," she told me in Spanish. "You are going to like her a lot." I caught Jorge's eye in the rearview mirror and he smiled, his cheeks flushed with modesty and a son's pride.

Finally, we did turn off onto one of those dirt roads, and the car barrelled and bumped its way into a forest. Several houses dotted the landscape, concrete like the convenience stores in the main part of town, many with thin tin roofs and the same wooden fencing from the drive. We parked next to a pickup truck at the end of the road. A stone path led down into a tiny valley encompassing a three-room main house and two greenhouses. I followed Rosario and Jorge down the pathway, which was lined with lush potted plants: agave and tomatoes and spiky cacti.

A plump, beaming woman wearing a plaid apron greeted us at the door. "Chicos!" she exclaimed, giving Rosario a big hug and a kiss on each cheek.

"Doña Dominika," Rosario replied, returning her embrace. "Le presento a Carly, nuestra compañera de los Estados Unidos."

"Hello, sweetheart," Dominika said in Spanish, giving me the same hug and cheek kisses. She smelled like freshly baked bread and flowers. "Welcome to my home, my business, my everything."

"Dominika's the queen of her kingdom," Rosario said proudly. "One of our best borrowers. You won't believe all the things she does."

Dominika swatted at Rosario and shook her head with the same modesty as her son. "Please, come inside."

She ushered us into a garage-like room filled with some of the most beautiful flower arrangements I had ever seen: bouquets bursting from baskets, collages of petals and colors arranged in a way that looked both deliberate and of nature's intricate hand itself. "Dominika grows all these flowers herself," Rosario said. "She uses our loans to buy seeds and supplies."

"And I've paid them all on time!" Dominika chimed in with a laugh. "This way, this way to the kitchen. I hope you're hungry!"

Come to think of it, I *was* hungry. My lunch had consisted of a bag of lime-flavored potato chips on the bus and a sliced mango dusted with chili powder I'd purchased from a street vendor when we arrived in Ixtlahuaca. Dominika led us into a small kitchen attached to the flower room, where a table was set with a bright-blue tablecloth and four folding chairs. Something that smelled meaty and salty simmered on the stove, and Dominika ladled what looked to be a hearty soup into gray ceramic bowls. "Sit, sit," she instructed us, placing the steaming bowls on the table. "My sister made these bowls herself with black clay from Oaxaca."

Jorge, who had been so quiet since we'd arrived that I forgot he was there, raised his spoon and dug into his soup with such vigor it could have been his first meal in weeks. I took a bite myself—it was absolutely delicious. That's the thing about Mexico: Whether you're at the nicest restaurant in the city, a taco stand by the bus station, or a kind woman's house deep in the countryside, the food is guaranteed to be an eruption of the best flavor combinations you've ever tasted. Though the soup was simple, chunks of meat in a savory broth with cooked carrots and potatoes, it tasted like Dorothy opening her eyes and seeing color for the first time in Oz. As if she could read my mind, Dominika smiled. "The cow meat comes from my neighbor down the road," she said. "She also receives your loans to keep her farm running."

Over the course of the meal, I asked Dominika a series of questions, learning that she was more than a gifted florist and five-star chef. She also grew tomatoes and mangoes, which she sold at the local market, and built a lucrative composting business after attending a workshop led by a traveling "sustainability coach" in Ixtlahuaca. It's a closed loop, she explained: The worms in her greenhouse munched on her food scraps, which in turn transformed them into rich soil that she repurposed for her tomato plants and flower beds. She sold liters of the byproducts at the local market. Dominika was so taken by the magic of composting, she said, that she taught all her neighbors in her village and even led her own composting classes at the local church. Now, she told us brightly, almost everyone who grows crops within a ten-mile radius also fully recycles their food waste.

"We'll throw nothing away today," she said, showing us the bucket by the sink that contained onion skins and carrot peels from the stew. "Here, let's take it to the greenhouse together."

I had never seen such contentment and pride, such an immersed and dedicated work ethic, for such simple pursuits. I was enraptured by Dominika and her story, her gregarious and generous disposition, her lovely farm, her quiet existence. Worlds away from the illuminated switchboard of my hyperconnected, metropolitan life. I could have spent all day with Dominika, pulling weeds from her tomato plants, feeding scraps to the worms, without checking my phone or wondering what my friends were up to. Here was someone so in touch with the rhythms of the earth that her life hummed alongside their ebbs and flows. She had dirt under her fingernails, her hands strong and callused from decades shaping her own natural surroundings. Though my own life back home was rife with seemingly unlimited material resources, I suddenly deeply envied hers.

Floored by this realization, I followed Dominika into her greenhouse and watched as she spread our leftovers onto tall beds of soil and earthworms. What would it be like for me to feel such a calm satisfaction with my everyday pursuits? To stop striving for my next bout of success and appreciate the present moment?

Perhaps finally breaking free from Robbie had been the first step toward finding the answer to that question. Perhaps my upcoming venture into the Panamanian jungle would bring me even closer. I pictured teaching Coco Cunningham how to compost in the same way Dominika was now showing me, methodically collecting the scraps of whatever food he and his crew harvested in the wild, the tropical breeze cooling my cheeks. Contented and in flow—deeply unfamiliar states for me. Just like prior fantasies about my future, this one could be as flawless as I designed it to be.

For now, I watched Dominika navigate her own enchanted world, eyes and smile brightening her already-friendly face, as she concluded her tour. On my way out, I hugged her tightly and thanked her for opening my eyes to a new way of life, for sharing a slice of herself with me.

"It's only because you wanted to learn," she replied. "Your curiosity is your light inside you. Use that light to guide yourself forward."

chapter five

Panama City's skyline surprised me. I'm not sure what, exactly, I'd pictured: a remote tarmac in the middle of a field, stray chickens waddling around in the grass, just like in a documentary I once watched about the Jonestown massacre? A village, similar to Dominika's, slanted tin roofs stacked on top of each other, farmers peddling citrus fruits from their wide pockets? When my plane descended toward a sleek, modern city skyline not unlike Miami or another built-up beachside metropolis, I was shocked.

"¿Estamos en Panamá?" I asked the guy sitting next to me, a businessman with slicked back hair scrolling through spreadsheets on his iPad. A painfully obvious question, given the flight attendant had just announced our impending descent.

"Yes, Panama City," the businessman replied in accent-free English, as if my inquiry had been perfectly reasonable. "I come every month to meet with clients. Your first time here?"

At least I wasn't the only one who asked obvious questions. I nodded.

"You'll love it," he said. "Don't forget to visit the Hard Rock Cafe. And you can go shopping in the beautiful new mall by the Trump hotel."

Hard Rock Cafe? Trump hotel? Clearly I wouldn't be finding chickens in any pastures.

The plane landed with a gentle thud and the businessman slipped his iPad into his leather briefcase. I had no idea what I was doing or where I was going; the only thing Coco had told me was to meet him by the baggage claim. I spotted him almost immediately, that same floppy hair and mischievous grin, cleaner than the time we'd met in the dust-soaked desert, sporting a handsome tropical tan. "Well, if it isn't the media mogul herself," he greeted me.

I looked down at my outfit—embroidered pajama pants from the Ciudadela market, a baggy T-shirt. I certainly didn't feel like a media mogul. But before I could protest, Coco leaned in for a hug. "Mexico looks good on you."

"Panama looks good on you, too."

"Then we must be doing well for ourselves," he said, grabbing my big blue backpack with mock difficulty. "My god, woman, what did you bring with you?"

"Oh, you know . . . just everything I own," I said.

"How romantic," Coco replied. "The wayward traveler. And where will she go next?"

"You tell me." I followed him into the parking lot and he unlocked a giant white SUV. He threw my backpack in the trunk and opened the passenger door. I pointed toward the glistening city skyline. "I'm guessing your jungle-whatever isn't that way."

"She's as smart as she is beautiful." Coco winked at me. "Panama City is the Dubai of Central America. I don't care much for Dubai. I am building something a little bit different. You'll see."

He eased the SUV onto a long, flat two-lane highway and drove toward the horizon. With the city behind us, all I could see in the distance were hills and trees and a sky as blue as my own eyes. As we drove, Coco expounded enthusiastically about the future of education, informing me that the school he was building in his jungle community would "blow up the pedagogy paradigm as we know it." This winter, they'd be hosting the designer in residence at one of the world's biggest tech companies to build a custom design-thinking curriculum for his students.

"Design-thinking isn't a thing," I replied.

Coco chuckled. "Well, of course it isn't," he said. "But it's one of the hottest buzzwords out there and we have our finger on the zeitgeist."

"Coco Cunningham, you are the most talented bullshitter I've ever met."

He winked again. "At your service."

The highway passed under an orange pedestrian bridge with peeling paint packed to the brim with people, as if they formed a human archway that opened into a new civilization. The other side looked like one of those suburbs you'd find off the exit of any major United States highway: strip malls on either side of the road, big-box retailers with local names. I could only tell we were in another country from the throngs of people milling about on the side of the road, some huddled under bus shelters, others selling knickknacks, reggaeton music blaring from multiple directions. A white school bus decked out with a custom graffiti paint job and flashing LED lights pulled up at one of the shelters, spilling dozens of people out into the town and collecting several more.

"That's called a Diablo Rojo," Coco said, pointing at the bus. "The Red Devils. They rival even the most elaborate art cars at Burning Man."

The suburb gave way to the countryside, acres upon acres of lush green land, dotted with the occasional shack or abandoned basketball court. As we drove, Coco talked excitedly about his project, barely taking a breath, a whirling dervish of ideas. He spoke of turning his jungle property into the first fully functional, thriving town in such a remote area. He was using his education program, whose tuition bore a hefty price tag, to both fund his vision and prototype his plans. The agricultural students were building out a permaculture farm; the outdoor-recreation kids were going out with machetes to hack trails through the dense forest surrounding his land. Biology researchers studied the local flora and fauna. Business students tested out different enterprises that could be viable, such as a general store and a restaurant. A hospitality team was designing an epic-sounding vacation package. I had a hard time getting a word in—each time Coco paused for more than thirty seconds on a subject, it reminded him of something else, and that tangent would derail us onto a new topic.

"Ico-Inna," I finally managed to interrupt. "You call yourselves Ico-Inna, but what does it mean?"

Coco chuckled and shrugged. "It comes from the native dialect of the folks who once populated this area," he said. "I honestly can't remember what it stands for. But doesn't it sound perfect? Ico could be a nod to all our efforts in the sustainability space."

"Like an eco-village?"

"Precisely."

"So you're appropriating an Indigenous vocabulary word without even knowing its definition?"

Coco shrugged again. "I'm sure they won't mind."

I was partially turned off by his cavalier, entitled attitude—he was the walking embodiment of all the "social-impact warriors" I detested. But something about him felt different. His ideas sounded new and special, things I'd never heard at an expat happy hour before. I found myself enjoying our banter, his sassy answers to all my confident challenges. So I lobbed the ball back over to him. "What you're saying is, you're basically a colonialist."

"Miss Carly, I prefer the term *eco-colonialist*," he said. "We're doing genuine good out here. You'll see. I'm a firm believer in owning your privilege. Making something meaningful with your resources, if you're lucky enough to have them. I am humble enough to admit that."

I didn't see anything humble about Coco Cunningham, but this was undeniably fun. We entered a village that reminded me of Dominika's rural neighborhood in Mexico. Coco steered the SUV onto a dirt path. Children played by the side of the road, and a young woman wearing an apron flipped what looked to be small yellow pancakes on an outdoor griddle. A river gushed alongside the village, behind it only a dense tangle of forest. We pulled into the driveway of a red house.

"¡Hola, Mónica!" Coco shouted to the pancake-flipping woman across the street. And then, in Spanish: "Meet my friend Carly." His Aussie twang made his use of the local language sound forced and naive, almost like he was making fun of himself by exaggerating his mispronunciations. But Coco seemed dead serious as he approached the woman with a big hug.

"Mucho gusto," Mónica said to me with a warm smile.

"You've got to let Carly try one of your famous *patacones*," Coco said in his silly-sounding Spanish, grabbing one of the tiny pancakes straight off the griddle. Then, to me, in English: "Patacones are a local staple. We live off these things. Smashed plantain, a little oil. Simple pleasures." He kissed his fingers. "A gift from the Panamanian gods."

I took a bite. It tasted like salt sprinkled on top of nothing, if nothing had a potato-like texture. "Yum," I said with my mouth still full, swallowing it down in one starchy lump. I recalled the first time I tried a mamay on the day I arrived in Mexico, how they ended up becoming one of my favorite local treats. If I stayed here long enough, I'd undoubtedly learn to love patacones, too.

A willowy woman with long, unkempt hair and even longer legs strode toward us. She wore tiny denim shorts and a top that looked like it was made out of a handkerchief. She kissed Coco on the mouth for a noteworthy amount of time. "Oh, hey, babe!" he said after their faces parted. "This is Carly, the famous media mogul I've been telling you about. She's here to see what we're up to. Carly, this is my girlfriend, Olivia."

"Nice to meet you, I'm Liv," Olivia said—another posh international accent. She extended a bony hand. Her fingernails were perfectly manicured. Did she live in the jungle, too? Was a nail salon part of Coco's business plan? Nothing made sense yet. I took Olivia's hand and introduced myself. Coco hadn't mentioned a girlfriend in any of our prior exchanges, least of all during our night together at Burning Man.

I sifted through the Rolodex of questions flipping through my head and settled on one. "Is the red house yours, too?"

"All mine," Coco said proudly, hugging Olivia from behind and lifting her slightly in the air. "We're in the village of San Miguel. Getting to the jungle can be a challenge—"

"To say the least," Olivia interrupted.

"We stop here at Casa Roja on our way in and out," Coco continued. He pronounced it *CASS-uh ROE-hah*. "It's also where my education and public health students post up for the semester. We teach in the local school and help out in the medical clinic."

So Coco's empire extended beyond the borders of his mysterious jungle property. He'd infiltrated the local community, too. Was there anything this guy *didn't* do?

". . . plenty of beds inside; you can crash here whenever you want," Coco was saying. "Hot water, the works. But you'll get a good night's sleep in one of our ranchos, too."

Before I could ask what a rancho was, we were back in the SUV, Olivia riding shotgun, me now relegated to the back seat. "This is where the real fun starts," Coco said, waving goodbye to Mónica and her patacones through the glass of his window.

He drove over a rickety bridge to the other side of the river, toward the opaque forest. I half wondered if we were just going to smash into the trees, pulverize them into jungle stew. I didn't know Coco *that* well. Had he kidnapped me? Was I about to be sacrificed as some sort of weird cult ritual? A pang of anxiety rippled through my body. Before my mind could spin out any further, Coco guided the vehicle onto an unmarked, muddy trail.

"There's only one path that leads to Ico-Inna," he said. "It's a bumpy one. Buckle up."

The sky was an inky blue when I woke up, a few stars still scattered, the first traces of sunlight forming an outline around the plantain trees. I rolled over on my air mattress and looked at the ceiling of my hut, its crosshatch pattern of woven banana leaves. There were no walls; I felt the early morning air directly on my skin. I stretched, wiggled out of my sleeping bag, and climbed the ladder that led me down to the bare ground. I heard the murmur of talking nearby, and I wandered over in its direction.

Isa stood in front of a giant pot on a long wooden table, ladling something liquid into a mug. "Good morning, Carly," she greeted me warmly. Traces of a local Panamanian accent melted into her voice, a detail that made everything she said sound remarkably soothing. "I hope you slept okay in the rancho."

I smiled at the kind, tiny young woman in front of me. The pot was bigger than her entire frame. She grabbed another mug from a hook on the wall and filled it, passing it over to me. "This is called cowboy coffee," she explained. "We make it every morning and drink it black. The beans come fresh from Boquete, the coffee country."

I took a sip. It tasted watery, a few grounds floating in the cup, but it warmed me in the early morning chill. Birds chirped; everything smelled green. I was really in the jungle.

Coco, Olivia, and I received a hero's welcome when we arrived the evening before, a king returning to his loyal subjects. The rough, ragged road had concluded with the SUV negotiating its way down a nearly vertical decline—"Suicide Hill," Coco informed me with a casual grin—and I gripped the door handle, terrified the entire vehicle would topple over. He navigated the rocks and crags with an expert's precision, though. A shallow river flowed by at the bottom, marking the end of the path, but I still didn't see anything that resembled civilization. Coco hit the accelerator and charged right through the water, which sloshed around the tires. On the other side, through a clearing in the trees, I spotted a few two-story wooden structures, their rooftops crafted from sticks and leaves. Someone in a bikini was pulling weeds at the base of one of them.

"Welcome to Ico-Inna," Coco said proudly, draping his arm around Olivia. "The jungle called, and we answered." He parked the SUV next to one of the wooden structures.

The bikini-clad woman sauntered over with a basket full of weeds. "Isa!" Olivia exclaimed, and the two of them hugged. Isa turned to me.

"You must be Carly—Coco has been talking about you all week," she said, opening her petite arms toward me. I tried not to stare at her bronze corn-cob abs. "Chef Lola is cooking a special meal for you tonight."

"You have a chef here?" I blurted, returning Isa's embrace.

"What, you think we live like animals?" Coco interjected. "Come on, I'll show you around."

He strode around the property arm in arm with Olivia, greeting everyone he passed with a high five, a wink, or an offhanded personal comment. Each individual we encountered was as tanned, toned, and beautiful as Isa and Olivia, wearing just as little clothing. They all looked to be in their early to mid-twenties, a bit younger than me, but not so much that I felt awkward or out of place. In fact, every single one of them said the same thing, that Coco had told them all about me, that they couldn't wait to hear about my work, that they were so excited someone with a career like mine would come all the way down to the Panamanian jungle to see what they were up to. A gaggle of folks convened under one hut set back by a stone path from the rest.

"This is the staff rancho," Coco said. "No students allowed. Prime hangout space. You'll usually find something fun going on here."

"Except when Coco comes by!" a guy with Hawaiian shorts and a man bun said, clapping him on the back.

"Bullshit; fun follows me everywhere," Coco teased. "Hand me that bottle."

Man Bun grabbed a dusty liter from a makeshift wooden shelf and gave it to Coco, who took a gulp directly from the spout. "Shots all around?" Coco asked mischievously. We passed the bottle back and forth, each taking a big swig. The liquor was hot, syrupy, and disgusting. It burned my throat and I tried not to gag. It must have shown on my face because Man Bun grinned and rubbed my lower back.

"You'll get used to it," he said. "This is called Seco. They make it here in Panama. Doesn't go down super easy, but makes you feel so good. I'm DeLong, by the way. Everyone here calls me by my last name."

"I don't even know what your first name is," Coco said, and DeLong gave him a playful shove. "Let's continue our tour."

Coco led me to a colorful thicket of trees and plants, magenta vines curling around smooth trunks, spiky leaves sprouting from various heights, more stone pathways snaking through. "This is our crown jewel," he said. "The permaculture farm. We're building an entire food forest so we can feed ourselves for generations. The whole thing was designed by a sustainable-farming pioneer who came down from Costa Rica. Do you know about permaculture?"

I'd heard the word a few times but always assumed it was a fancy way to describe gardening. Coco informed me that permaculture was, in fact, the practice of living fully in tune with your natural surroundings, amplifying and caring for the plants already native to your location, enriching the soils with the compost from their own fruits. "Living in harmony with the food you grow, rather than degrading the soil with years of monoculture that strips it of its nutrients," he explained. "We're the opposite of mass-produced soybeans. Each plant is meant to be here." I pictured Dominika, at home in her greenhouse, struck by the notion that these people designed their lives according to the same set of values.

At the edge of one of the stone paths, another tanned body was digging up the earth with a garden hoe. He smeared his dirt-covered hands on his khaki shorts as we approached and held out his palm for Coco to shake. His long, wavy hair was shoved under a trucker hat. I caught his eyes. Here before me was the handsomest man I had ever seen.

"I'm Jesse," he said shyly, with a half smile.

"Farmer Jesse makes everything happen," Coco said.

Jesse blushed. "Not really. I'm just planting a coffee tree. Want to help?"

Yes, yes. Yes, I wanted to help. Coming to Panama was the right decision indeed.

Dinner was absolutely delicious—something peanutty and pineappley, the richest tropical flavor combinations I'd ever tasted. Sprinkled on top of the stew were green shards that looked a lot like shredded arugula. Chef Lola, another tan and attractive creature with a lip ring and a pink pixie cut, explained that the green leaves were called katuk, a plant species native to this area. "It's a natural source of energy," she said. "Go ahead, try it—kind of tastes sweet, like sugar snap peas."

I spent the next few days hiking, bathing in a swimming hole at the edge of a waterfall, eating psychedelic mushrooms that DeLong had plucked directly from cow manure on the neighbor's farm, gathering eggs from the chickens so Chef Lola could make us breakfast, and learning how to hack banana leaves off trees with a machete. To call it paradise would be to cheapen the experience. I felt comfortable and peaceful among Coco's team, brave young people who dared to live differently. Here I was, jumping off rocks into a refreshing river while my former colleagues back in New York endured long meetings and stared at their laptops in a newsroom.

On my fourth day living this serene, luscious jungle life, Coco told me to pack my things. He had a surprise for me; was I ready to take a little trip? He hadn't steered me wrong yet, so I zipped up my big blue backpack and tossed it in the back seat of his SUV. DeLong, Farmer Jesse, and Chef Lola piled into another 4x4 on the property and followed us out. Olivia and Isa hung back by a rancho with linked arms and matching bathing suits, waving goodbye.

"Where are we going?"

Coco flashed his signature grin, a look I was starting to get used to. "Oh, you know," he said as we began the treacherous journey up Suicide Hill. "Just a private island for the weekend. No big deal."

"Excuse me?" A thrill zipped up through my torso and out my appendages. A private island! I had never come close to anything like this before.

"Yeah, some washed-up tech bazillionaire bought a piece of land off the coast and has his sights set on a sustainable farm. I met him at a gala in Panama City. One thing led to another, and I offered to bring some of my crew by for a couple days to see if we might be able to do some consulting." Coco spoke so casually of his sumptuous lifestyle that I tried not to look too bedazzled.

We drove back the way we came, through San Miguel and past Casa Roja, under the crowded pedestrian overpass between the strip malls, past the airport exit, and straight through the city's main highway. Eventually, the skyline disappeared behind us again, and we found ourselves on another long, flat two-lane country road. I stared out the window, taking it all in, feeling that familiar peace and steadiness I'd experienced in the jungle this past week.

"You know, Media Mogul," Coco said eventually. "I didn't just bring you out here to show off my little world. I mean, there's no reason we can't have a good time. But just in case you were wondering, I'm not that generous of a person. Everyone always has an ulterior motive."

So there was a catch. There had to be a catch. My stomach churned. "What's your ulterior motive?" I asked, trying not to sound nervous. "You're not going to, like, sacrifice me in some sort of weird appropriated ritual?"

Coco patted my thigh. "You don't have enough meat on your bones to feed any of us," he replied. "But no. I want you to work for me. I want you to move down here to Panama, join our mission, and become a permanent part of Ico-Inna. I've been looking for someone like you for a long time."

I took in his offer, my mind a merry-go-round of visions for what my life could be. I saw myself sautéing katuk in a cast-iron pan with Chef Lola, cracking jokes with DeLong, rising with the sun. I saw myself splashing around in the river and learning how to identify different bird species. I saw myself just as tan, just as beautiful, as everyone I had met. But why *me*? What could I possibly offer Coco that he didn't already have?

He answered that question before I could ask it aloud. "I want to build a media empire," he said. "People need to know what Ico-Inna is all about."

Coco proceeded to outline his vision for me in a monologue so polished that I wondered if he'd practiced it in front of the mirror before I arrived. The next program he wanted to create at his school would be focused on storytelling. He needed people to document all the exciting, cutting-edge things happening at Ico-Inna to attract investors and permanent residents. Social media, newsletters, a video series, the works. A quarterly glossy, polished magazine. All produced through a program I'd design myself, by aspiring journalists who'd move to Ico-Inna to learn from *me*.

"And I'll pay you the big bucks," he added. "Three thousand dollars a month. Cash. No taxes or social security or any of that bullshit. That'll get you far in Latin America. You'd be my highest-paid employee. But you're worth it, Miss Mogul."

My mind raced for the rest of the car ride—more of a series of sprints than a long, steady marathon. I pictured myself typing curriculums late at night under the moon, bringing a group of wide-eyed college students all over Panama, trekking through the mountains with video cameras perched on their shoulders or scribbling in their notebooks on the beach. I had never considered education as a career path before, but back in the newsroom, I'd designed a series of workshops that taught new employees how to write viral stories in our voice, how to craft headlines that would click, how to aggregate from other outlets without stealing their work. I was a leader there—I could be a leader here, too. I could create something that had never been done before. I could revolutionize journalism education! And then, when my program became a success, when there was nothing else out there like it, students all over the world would clamor for an acceptance letter. I would change my own life *and* the lives of other people for the better.

By the time Coco parked the car beside a rickety-looking dock that led to a pristine body of water, my hands were trembling and my heart was pounding. Ripples expanded in every direction as I waded in up to my ankles, shattering the lake's glassy surface with my jittery feet. This was a new feeling for me: I had never felt so high on my own ideas, soaring on sheer potential.

"Think it over," Coco said as if he could read my thoughts. He handed me a life jacket and took my hand, guiding me into a motorboat tied to the dock. "Spend a few more days here with me, see if you find inspiration, and let me know if you want to be part of this crazy thing."

The other Ico-Inna truck pulled up and came to a stop next to Coco's SUV, and out piled Farmer Jesse, Chef Lola, and DeLong. They all had somehow also managed to procure life jackets, and they traipsed down to the dock, laughing and chatting. The boat jostled as each one of them climbed in.

"Conrad Cunningham, since when do you know how to drive a boat?" DeLong teased.

"Who said I know how?" Coco winked. "Let's see what happens, shall we?"

He started up the motor and we buzzed away from the dock, toward whatever adventure was coming next.

It stormed most of the weekend on the private island, so the five of us passed the time playing cards and drinking Seco straight out of the bottle. The tropical rain gushed down in lush, plentiful sheets, and the flora seemed to become even greener before our eyes with each droplet that touched it. Unlike the formidable summer thunderstorms I'd grown up with on the East Coast, this rain felt welcoming and cozy, at home with its surroundings. DeLong and I even went snorkeling by the shore during one of the lighter drizzles, and while we didn't see any fish, we did laugh and splash each other with the familiarity of old friends.

Why, exactly, we were on the island remained unclear: Its proprietor was nowhere to be found, the home he'd built for himself echoing with emptiness. Coco said we had free rein of the place to explore the grounds and see where we might establish a permaculture farm. But I got the feeling the rich guy who owned it was some sort of business acquaintance of his, and Coco had merely brought us all to this private blob of land in an effort to impress us. I didn't know him well, but I did know by that point that impressing people was one of his favorite activities. I didn't mind, as long as I got to reap the benefits.

On our final night in the estate, we sat on the banana-leaf-shaded deck, smelling the rain and telling stories. I was sprawled out on a beach chair wearing a bathing suit and a soft, fuzzy robe Coco had procured from the master bedroom closet. We passed the bottle of Seco around, getting collectively drunker as the sky dimmed to navy blue. I felt warm and a little bit giddy. Unless I was imagining it, I'd been exchanging flirtatious glances with Farmer Jesse all night. His glorious face could have been carved into marble by a sculptor, his eyes innocent and curious as they flashed at mine. Our gazes locked again as Coco bellowed the punchline to a belabored joke, and I smiled. Farmer Jesse smiled right back beneath his dirt-smeared trucker hat.

"Alright, kids," Coco said to nobody in particular. "Ask and you shall receive."

I was pretty sure none of us had asked for anything. Nevertheless, he pulled a small baggie filled with white powder out of his cargo shorts pocket and shook it like a maraca. "Our media mogul hasn't yet sampled some of Panama's finest."

"Ooooh, the island provides!" DeLong said, grabbing the bag from Coco's fingertips. He dumped a little pile on one of the deck's bamboo side tables. "Anyone have a dollar?" I'd recently learned that Panama used the American dollar as its currency, a relic of the majority of the twentieth century, when the United States governed the comings and goings of canal activity.

Because everything we had done that weekend had been lavish to the point of parody, Coco extracted a $100 bill from his wallet and handed it to DeLong, who was busy cutting the cocaine into fat lines. "You see, we're right along the Colombian trade route," Coco explained. "The shit that passes through Panama is unlike anything you've tried back home. It's too early in its journey to be cut with any of that nasty crap they add to it along the way. Baking soda or deworming meds or whatever. This is the purest powder you'll ever have."

DeLong snorted a line and passed me the bill. I leaned over and shrugged. "I'll try anything twice," I quipped, and everyone else chuckled approvingly.

I breathed in the drugs, feeling the familiar nasal sting I'd endured during so many late nights and early mornings with Robbie in New York. When the line was gone, I swallowed and took a deep breath and let the first tingles of euphoria overtake me. Coco was right. The high felt clean, almost healthy, in a perverse way.

In no time we'd finished the bag. Our conversation grew louder and faster and more urgent, each thing we had to say more important than the next. The high that had carried me through the weekend was so augmented I could feel it in my fingernails. I took another shot of Seco and got up to go to the bathroom. As I was washing my hands, I heard a light tap at the door.

Farmer Jesse stood on the other side, glancing at me shyly. Wordlessly, I took his hand and pulled him into the bathroom with me. Pulled his hat off and set it by the sink. He stroked my cheek with his palm.

"This is fun," Farmer Jesse said, his voice barely louder than a whisper. "You're fun."

I threw my arms around his neck and kissed his angelic face. It was the only thing left to do. I pushed him up against the door as we kept kissing, ravenous, my hands in his long hair, his fingertips running up and down my back. He flipped me around and I hoisted myself up on his waist, wedged between his chiseled body and the wooden door.

The house was eerily quiet when we finally tiptoed out of the bathroom; everyone seemed to have gone to bed. But I was wide-awake, the residual cocaine high making my pores sparkle and my heart pound, the Seco morphing my surroundings into a satisfying swirl. I padded down the hallway and knocked on the door of the bedroom where Coco was staying.

He greeted me wearing a plush robe identical to the one I'd had on earlier, his grin so wide it sliced his face in half. "Well, well, well," he said, pulling me inside.

I sat down next to him on the bed. He touched my knee. "You know," he said, his fingers massaging my thigh, "Liv and I have an open thing going on. She wouldn't care if—"

I took his hand off my leg and placed it back onto his lap, brushing him off. "No. Coco. That's not why I'm here. I'm not trying to seduce you."

He shrugged, unfazed by my casual rejection. "Then what brings you into my bedroom in the middle of the night?"

I took a breath. Sometimes the moments that change your life forever feel as insignificant and inevitable as breathing. "I wanted to tell you—I accept," I said. "I accept your offer. Count me in. Let's build a media empire together."

Coco's grin reappeared, his eyes little half-moons of delight. He gave me a loud, fat high five and pulled me in for a tight hug. "Let's do it," he said. "Let's build a media empire."

chapter six

The customs line at Tocumen International Airport wound its way through not one but two rooms, moving at the pace of the tide. Fresh off a bumpy flight from San Francisco, my nerves were high, my body tense, and I was desperate to clear the government officials and get to the jungle as quickly as possible. Several bodies ahead of me, a group of people around my age wearing ostentatious fur coats and the kinds of hats you see on beautiful women's Instagram posts from Joshua Tree shuffled toward passport control. They were undeniably headed to the same destination as me: Ico-Inna's epic annual New Year's Eve extravaganza.

After accepting Coco's offer, I'd stayed in Panama for another week, touring his offices in Panama City and meeting some more of his well-connected local friends. Ico-Inna's Panama City locale astounded me—metal bunk beds crammed into rooms with cracked ceilings, the mattresses wrapped in faded and pilly sheets. Coco explained that anyone from Ico-Inna who was passing through the city on the way to catch a flight or take care of any sort of business stayed in one of the bunk beds. Sometimes, the staff took long weekends there and enjoyed the modern amenities of an urban lifestyle (Sushi! Manicures!) before returning to their banana-leaf huts. I held my breath as I examined a fridge full of moldy food in the kitchen and used a stained toilet in a dirty half bathroom. But Coco had a *lot* of properties to manage—it made sense that the city outpost was the least meticulously cared for.

He and Olivia shared an apartment one floor below that was significantly better maintained. "I head back and forth a few times a week," Coco explained. That he spent so much time in Panama City surprised me: When I'd pictured his life before seeing it in person, I'd imagined him passing most of his days holed up in a hammock tied to a palm tree, scrolling through his phone while his staff fed chickens. His walls were lined with bookshelves containing tomes on urban philosophy and sustainability, everything from *Blessed Unrest* to *Operating Manual for Spaceship Earth*, and he frequently quoted obscure authors or exclaimed "I have a book for you to read!" before pulling something off his shelf and handing it to whoever he was talking to. This, too, surprised me; Coco's swaggery demeanor didn't suggest he was much of a bookworm. I was, in turn, impressed.

It soon became clear that the drugs he offered us on the private island weren't just for a special occasion. When he was in Panama City, Coco fielded many visits from his dealer Joaquin, the great-grandson of a communist spy who had escaped from Russia and reinvented his life in Latin America before his gruesome assassination in the mid-sixties. Joaquin was trying to restore his family's legacy with a fledgling DJing career, but so far, he was only able to secure a gig as the resident Thursday-night background music at a boutique hotel's adjoining restaurant. He supplemented his income in other ways, and Coco was one of his top customers.

Joaquin spoke freely, almost proudly, about his ancestral past, recounting his great-grandfather's murder-by-letter-opener in chilling detail to anyone he shared his white powders with. For the rest of my inaugural week in Panama, I, too, became a regular customer. My cocaine binges fueled multiple nights of scrawling in my notebook, my thoughts spilling out faster than my pen could document them, dreaming up plans for Coco's and my media project.

Before the New Year's party, I returned home to the United States to prove to my parents that I hadn't been kidnapped and brag to my friends about the upcoming phase of my life. I spent Thanksgiving in Connecticut with my father, who told me he was proud of the opportunities I manifested for myself and pleased that my depression had subsided for so long, and Christmas in San Francisco with my mother, who told me she didn't trust this "Ico-Inna experiment" one iota.

"It sounds like a scam to me," she offered, unsolicited. "There's no such thing as a town in the middle of the jungle. It's too good to be true, and life doesn't work like that. Who is this guy, anyway? Just some rich kid whose daddy bought him some land?"

I didn't tell her that she wasn't incorrect about the means by which Coco acquired his jungle parcel. There was nothing shady about Ico-Inna, I promised her and reassured myself. I had seen it firsthand, after all. There were banana trees for shade and fresh katuk leaves for dinner! How could that possibly be a scam?

And thus, after swapping out a few items in my big blue backpack, buying a pair of Muck boots for the rainy season, and hugging my parents goodbye, I was back on a plane to Central America. "You don't want to miss our epic New Year's," Coco advised. Tickets were $1,000 a pop, and he'd convinced 250 of his closest friends to buy them at face value. As Ico-Inna's newest employee, I got to go for free.

I trudged along in the customs line, anxious to make it through to the other side and start the party. I tried to eavesdrop on my co-revelers up ahead, but I couldn't make out what they were saying. I took the Octavio Paz novel I'd bought at a used bookstore in Mexico City out of my backpack and tried to parse through his literary use of Spanish. I got bored after a few pages and put the book back inside my backpack. I put on the most recent *This American Life* podcast episode, something about the politics of propaganda, and forced myself to concentrate on Ira Glass. His soothing voice calmed my jitters a bit. Finally, after what felt like several hours but was only forty-five minutes according to my watch, I handed my passport to the customs agent.

"What brings you to Panama?" she asked me in Spanish.

"I live here now!" I declared proudly. Then I realized I didn't have anything that even slightly resembled a visa. "I mean . . . I'm living here for the next few weeks. With a friend," I backtracked.

On the other side of customs, by the baggage claim, I spotted a lanky guy in a trucker hat and mesh shorts holding a clipboard. His backpack was fastened across his chest as if he were about to embark on an arduous hike. He rushed over in my direction, looking like he had something very important to tell me.

"Carly Schwartz?" he said hurriedly. "You're Carly Schwartz, right?"

"How do you know my name?" I was taken aback by his unabashed enthusiasm.

He blushed. "Coco told me to look for you," he said. "So I googled you to see what you looked like. You've had . . . quite the career."

I brushed off the compliment. "Do you work for him, too?" I asked.

"For this weekend I do," the skinny guy replied. "I live in Minneapolis, but I came down for the party. I was a student here a couple years ago. The education track. I wrote my thesis about teaching methods in rural Latin America. Got my master's program to pay for it and everything." He blushed again. "And I'm sure you were burning with curiosity to hear my life story. Sorry. I'm Santiago, by the way."

He smiled and I noticed a small speck of black food nestled in his front teeth. I had the sudden instinct to reach into his mouth and pluck it away. But I kept my hands to myself.

"Nice to meet you, Santiago. I'm Carly. But you seem to already know that."

"Heck yeah I do," he said with exaggerated cheerfulness, side-hugging me with his clipboard-free arm. "Sounds like we're about to spend a lot of quality time together."

I was eager to get in a cab and head to San Miguel, where a 4x4 was supposedly waiting to deposit me in the jungle. "Why's that?" I asked. "Do you know where the taxi stand is? I want to make it down to Ico-Inna before dinner."

Santiago's face fell. "Coco didn't tell you?" he said.

"Tell me what?"

"You're on airport duty with me. Until tomorrow morning. Tons of flights are coming in with party guests. We have to check them in and show them how to get to Casa Roja."

Coco hadn't told me anything about "airport duty," or any other tasks, for that matter. I was under the impression I'd be able to enjoy the party like everyone else. After my turbulent seven-hour flight, the last place I wanted to hang out was the airport. I wanted to dip my feet in the river with a bottle of Seco in my hand. I wanted to find Farmer Jesse.

"I think there must be a mix-up," I told Santiago. "Coco told me to meet him in the jungle tonight."

"Are you sure? Because he said very clearly to look for Carly Schwartz."

I checked my phone. Sure enough, there was a WhatsApp message from Coco that I hadn't yet seen.

Media Mogul, welcome back! Hey listen, I need you to do me a solid. We're short-staffed at the airport so it would be great if you could help greet my guests tonight. Okay, thanks! Look for a strapping young lad named Santiago. He'll tell you what to do. See you tomorrow. Hugs, CC

I sighed, trying to hide my disappointment from the eager guy in front of me. "Well . . . guess we're about to get to know each other pretty well!" I forced a smile.

Santiago gave me a side-hug again. "Yeah! Let's have our own New Year's Eve party right here at scenic PTY. I hear it's the hottest new club in Panama."

I couldn't help but laugh. "Does this club have a bar?" I played along. "Because I could really use a drink."

At the airport restaurant on the second floor, I poured two shots of whiskey into my cappuccino as Santiago sipped his chamomile tea. Our conversation flowed easily.

He told me all about his career as an aspiring comedian and showed me videos of himself singing silly songs on YouTube, including one making fun of my former media employer. We lamented the state of digital media and hungrily discussed a recent podcast that deconstructed journalism's flawed ad models. His pitch-perfect impression of its host had me exploding with giggles. I shared my vision for the media program I was planning to build at Ico-Inna and he listened with rapt attention, his brown eyes as big and round as dinner plates, nodding and hanging on my every word.

"I think you're really onto something," he said when I was finished. "Education as a form of content creation. And a living laboratory in the jungle! This is going to create a new paradigm for how journalism is taught." I swelled with excitement and pride. His unbridled enthusiasm made me feel invincible.

We greeted party guests into the wee hours of the morning, until the airport was almost empty. Each person who arrived was more cartoonish than the last, and Santiago and I stifled laughter and tried hard not to make eye contact as we directed them toward their shuttles to San Miguel. There was Urth Collective, a three-piece acoustic band Coco hired to perform. "We've got some heart-opening tunes to share," their lead singer, Bartholomew, assured me as he hoisted his guitar up from the baggage claim. His sideburns were so long they traveled down to the sides of his chin, which was, in turn, hairless.

Then there was Aliki, an energy healer from Venice Beach who wore a long lace caftan and perfectly applied makeup. She insisted on snapping a selfie with me and Santiago for her followers. "I like to show them real moments, you know, when I'm shabby and traveling," she explained. "Realness is the only way you can ever really connect, you know?" And then there was Cass, the assistant to a big-tech mega-billionaire ("chief of staff," she corrected me), who was helping him get into the vertical-gardening business and wanted to see what Ico-Inna's farm was all about. She barely looked up from her phone to acknowledge us, and she had Santiago carry her bags all the way to the shuttle like a bellhop. "I can't *believe* she didn't tip you," I whispered under my breath, and he coughed loudly to cover his snicker.

By the time we sent the last group of revelers to San Miguel, it was nearly 2:00 a.m. The next guests weren't slated to arrive for at least five more hours. "Should we just camp out here?" Santiago said, slumping onto the ground. "My hat makes a great pillow."

I had a better idea. "Let's get a room at the airport hotel," I suggested. "Make Coco pay for it."

Those dinner-plate eyes again. "Coco would *never* agree to that!"

I shrugged. "I bet he would. Let me text him."

Coco's response came within minutes—clearly, for him, the party was just starting. Also clear was his good mood, because he replied simply, *Go for it! Get your beauty rest and make sure you look sharp for the next batch tomorrow.*

"And that's how it's done," I said to Santiago smugly, showing him Coco's text.

Santiago shook his head in disbelief. "Never in the four years I've known Coco Cunningham has he ever paid for something like this."

"Well, maybe you've just been hanging around with the wrong people," I teased, grabbing his arm and heading toward the exit.

The hotel room had matching queen beds, and we each climbed into one. It felt comfortable and easy to share a room with this person, as if we were old friends on vacation together. It was hard to believe we'd only met a few hours earlier.

Santiago fell asleep right away, snoring softly. But I couldn't turn my mind off. Thoughts blazed through my head: I imagined the program I was about to build, going back to my alma mater to recruit students and share my success story. I thought about my mother's skepticism and how I couldn't wait to prove her wrong. I fantasized about finding Farmer Jesse as soon as I arrived in the jungle tomorrow and pulling him behind the greenhouse with me.

Then I started to feel anxious because I knew I only had a couple more hours to bank some rest before a whirlwind ensued. The more I tried to sleep, the more awake I felt. I turned over on my side and watched Santiago's peaceful breathing. I tried to match my own breaths to the rhythm of his.

Was it love at first sight? Definitely not. Santiago was so animated and flamboyant our first twenty-four hours together that I assumed he might be gay. My suspicions were overturned when he told me he was going through a divorce, and her name was Sarah.

Santiago's parents were from Ecuador, but his dad was an entomologist whose research took him all over the world. Santiago himself had been born in French Polynesia and raised in Arkansas. His parents were currently living in Botswana, where his father was studying ant colonies. I thought of my dad and stepmom in suburban Connecticut and my mom and brother in the Bay Area and felt instantly less interesting, even though Santiago treated me like the most fascinating person in the world.

"You seem a little young to be a divorcé," I said. "How old are you, anyway?"

I expected him to tell me we were around the same age, so I was surprised to find out his twenty-fifth birthday would be in April. He and Sarah had been college sweethearts at the University of Missouri, where Santiago stayed on an extra year for an accelerated master's while she made ceramics. They both came from quasi-traditional families and felt pressure to get engaged when they moved in together, and a wedding happened quickly after. It only took a year for their marital bliss to give way to the flagrant realization that they were poorly matched. "We never even fought," Santiago said. "It was just so obvious we weren't meant to be together that we just kindly and compassionately agreed to go our separate ways."

For a twenty-four-year-old to freely use such nonviolent communication as *kindly and compassionately* was striking. Though six years younger than me, Santiago seemed wiser and more grounded in so many ways. By the time we'd finished up our airport shift and took a 4x4 into the jungle together for Ico-Inna's multiday celebration, I felt like I'd made a new best friend.

The New Year's party buzzed with a similar energy as that Oval Office camp at Burning Man where Coco and I first met. Cosmopolitan influencer types packed into the jungle, participating in sunrise raves on the riverbank, jewelry-making workshops, nature hikes, and guided meditation sessions. At night, Ico-Inna's large wooden yoga platform transformed into an elaborate stage, where startup founders gave talks and musical acts performed.

Ico-Inna's residents hustled to produce the smoothest event possible: Chef Lola led a team of interns in the kitchen who cooked from first thing in the morning until deep into the evening, former students kept Seco and boxed wine flowing at a twenty-four-hour open bar, and staffers flitted around picking up refuse and keeping the venue looking pristine. As media director, I chatted with attendees, filming interviews and sound bites about their Panamanian adventure. Sentiments were similar ("This is breathtaking! I'm invoking my inner child! The critters are so cute!"), but I figured I'd be able to knit them into some sort of story after the fact.

Behind the scenes, though, was a bit of a shit show. Coco spent the entire weekend hobnobbing with attendees and guzzling Seco, barely acknowledging the robust operation of indentured servitude keeping things running. Every once in a while, he'd discover a tablecloth out of place or a long wait at the bar, and he'd bellow, "*Who* the *fuck*?!" But other than that, Ico-Inna's proletariat went largely ignored. In hushed corners, I heard staffers complaining about the privileged elite who were making a mess of their land, of the hours they were forced to work in the sun, of the assholes Coco surrounded himself with.

For the most part, I stayed out of these conversations, though I tried to make sympathetic small talk with Isa and DeLong, who seemed too busy to even crack a smile. Santiago took on the role of peacemaker, making quips about how "Coco will be Coco" and reminding people of all the good networking opportunities up for grabs right on their own land. Ico-Innans seemed to really listen to him, and oftentimes, grumpy attitudes flipped into laughter after one of his simple interactions. I watched closely, struck by his charisma, his gentle ease with people of all personality types.

By the third night, my admiration of Santiago had morphed into a little crush. I liked watching his gangly body make its way through the throngs of revelers, lighting everyone's faces up with chitchat along the way. When he picked up a guitar and led the guests in a silly improv sing-along, I stood by his side, belting out lyrics louder than the others and hoping he'd find me as amusing as I found him. At a happy hour dance party by the river, I let my body brush against his in a way that felt natural, not awkward. Finally, the two of us settled down together on the grass to watch that evening's series of talks and performances. The first person onstage was a singer-songwriter from Coco's hometown in Australia, who sang a moving piece he'd written about his struggles with depression.

"I have depression," I whispered to Santiago, too comfortable with him to worry whether or not he'd judge me. "Sometimes it's really bad."

He squeezed my hand while the guitarist finished his song. We kept holding hands through the second act, a woman's carefully crafted humblebrag about work she'd done with orphans in Southeast Asia. By the third performance, a Polish experimental electronica duo that Coco's girlfriend, Olivia, had met at an after-hours party in Berlin, my body was warm and sparkly all over. Santiago's fingers felt like they had been interlocked with mine since the day we were born. I asked him if he wanted to go for a walk, and we snuck away.

We strolled over to the river, neither of us acknowledging that our hands were still interlocked. Stars freckled the clear night sky, a tropical breeze blowing wisps of hair around my face.

"What does depression look like for you?" Santiago asked. He sounded genuinely curious, and before I knew what I was saying, the truth tumbled out.

"It was really bad for a while," I told him. "I hated myself so much that living my life became impossible. I overdosed in college—I almost died. I just wanted to turn it all off."

I'd never recounted those facts aloud to anyone besides Devon. Hearing my own voice form the words felt like I was simultaneously unearthing my most shameful secret and describing someone else. Tears formed at the corners of my eyes, and yet I somehow didn't feel embarrassed. I wanted this man to know everything about me.

Santiago brushed his fingers across my forehead and pushed a wayward strand of hair behind my ear. He looked at me very intently. "I am so, so glad you're alive," he said, almost a whisper. "What a gift to be alive together, in this moment, right now."

Then he leaned over and kissed me. It felt different from other people I had kissed—his lips were deeply familiar and also brand-new. A confluence of lust and comfort, two feelings that had never coexisted for me before. We stayed like that, kissing by the river, until the performances ended and the faraway crowd erupted into a hearty cheer. I couldn't help but feel like they were applauding the two of us.

Santiago and I remained glued together after our night by the river. We picked up a bartending shift together and played off each other's personalities, a performative duo for all the thirsty party guests. We coordinated transportation out of the jungle and to Panama City for the last night of the event, a yacht party on the Pacific Ocean organized by Coco's drug dealer. We kissed under a dome of fireworks. Coco had slipped me a bag of cocaine en route to the city, and I kept sneaking away to the bathroom to re-up my fix. Santiago didn't want any, though—he said he didn't have that much experience with drugs and didn't like purposely feeling out of control. I couldn't think of anyone else in my life who readily admitted they were capable of having fun without some sort of substance involved.

Coco had organized a four-day retreat to a black-sand surf beach after the party ended for Ico-Inna staff to "decompress" before the semester started. Santiago wasn't due to fly back to Minneapolis until the following week, so he joined us. The beach was as idyllic as a computer's desktop background, cerulean waves foaming against the shore, neon sunsets slashing the sky at twilight. Santiago and I had our own private hotel room, and we spent most of the trip intertwined together under the covers, two matching puzzle pieces that had finally found one another, talking about our visions for our lives and our plans to make them a reality.

Santiago dreamed of owning an experimental comedy theater one day, of spending his twenties building a community of performers who would convene around his performance space, often with his own name headlining the marquee. But it was about more than just making people laugh, he explained. He wanted to take the world's most pressing issues, climate change and child poverty and identity politics, and distill them into hilarious bits for his audience to learn from while they enjoyed themselves. "Like a Social Impact Second City," he said, a fluid mantra that suggested it wasn't the first time he'd rattled off that tagline. "I want my performances to have a positive impact on humanity."

For my part, I talked more about disrupting media education by building the journalism school of the future in the jungle and using it as a prototype that could be replicated all over the world. Santiago stroked my cheek. "You're so smart," he murmured. "Your brilliance is so sexy."

In the evenings, when we finally managed to peel ourselves off each other, we plopped around a bonfire with the other Ico-Innans, Santiago strumming a guitar and encouraging everyone to make up funny improv songs. DeLong, a burgeoning freestyler, rapped over the beat of the guitar, his diatribes reducing all of us to hysterics, and we bounced along with the beat, our faces illuminated orange by the flames. "You and Santiago are *so* cute together," Olivia whispered, hooking her arm into mine as we swayed our bodies by the fire. "What a catch. He's really special."

"*Really* special," I agreed, my body bathed in lust as I watched his fingers brushing the guitar strings, his wide mouth open toward the sky with carefree confidence.

When the luxurious absurdity of our vacation finally came to an end, I rode with Santiago in a taxi to the Panama City airport. We snapped a photo of ourselves together outside Departures. "I'm never going to forget this week," he said. "Like . . . whoa."

"Was it even real?" I replied, gripping his body toward mine in a hug so tight I could have cracked his rib cage.

"Who cares if it was real," he whispered into my ear. "If it wasn't, it was the best dream I ever had."

"I don't know if I'll ever see you again," I said, suddenly choking up at the thought of our week together reduced to a memory.

"We'll find a way," he said. "I know we will."

He rolled his suitcase through the automatic doors. I watched the back of his body disappear into a smudge before I headed back to the taxi stand and hailed a ride to Coco's apartment.

chapter seven

My dreamlike romp through the stratosphere continued during my first few months in Panama, my mind a twirling disco ball of ideas, my elevated mood carrying me from the jungle to the city and back again. Students arrived for the winter semester, attractive, wide-eyed wanderlust types in their late teens and early twenties, and I watched on the sidelines as the Ico-Inna staff pulled off an elaborate orientation and began grinding on their separate education tracks. Coco had recruited the students via an aggressive Facebook marketing campaign that involved photos of beautiful women in bikinis on a riverbank and headlines like "This Could Be Your Life."

I laid the groundwork for my own media curriculum, thumbing through the news-philosophy book Santiago had given me, clicking around on my favorite websites to create an archive of the best examples of storytelling I could find. Even though many of the staffers seemed wary of my close relationship with Coco, solid friendships started to form; I grew more comfortable cracking jokes with DeLong and trying on items from Olivia's impressive collection of vintage clothing. On nights in the Panama City outpost, I slept on a bottom bunk and barely noticed the squalor: the dusty linoleum floors and the mildewed shower with the torn curtain. None of it mattered because I was happier than I'd ever been.

I didn't think of our constant cocaine use as a problem; it merely felt like a detail, part of our unconventional way of life. I often spotted Coco's dealer popping in and out of his Range Rover in front of our building in the city. A couple times, he even came out to the jungle for a visit. We drank boxed wine under the stars and did key bumps and he told me about his childhood attending a boarding school not unlike my own, a continent away from the country that led to the violent demise of his ancestor.

It didn't concern me when we started doing coke before breakfast, a line and an espresso to start the day, nor did I feel weird when Olivia and DeLong and I finished a baggie before greeting the students in San Miguel the day they arrived. In fact, I relished the surge of energy it gave me as I led them on the hike to the jungle, navigating Suicide Hill, adrenaline overpowering any of the drug's residual jitters. Our shared debauchery gave me a sense of belonging, even after the effects of the cocaine wore off.

Everything I looked at, every conversation I had, sparked a new idea for my burgeoning media empire. The possibilities of what I could create felt limitless, be it a media conference in the jungle to which I'd invite all my old journalism colleagues, or my soon-to-be hit podcast about the future of towns (not that I'd recorded anything yet, but I told myself I would, soon). Coco fed my insatiable imagination for success; we spent long nights at his apartment in the city pontificating about the impact we'd make as we rubbed white powder on our gums, grinding our teeth and interrupting each other until sunrise. Olivia usually joined us for these marathon ego sessions, keeping quiet but also keeping up, making sure our wine glasses were full and the music matched our mood.

Whenever I was in Panama City with good internet service, I called Santiago via Skype before bed. We texted so often, via so many different messaging platforms, that I could barely keep up with all the musings we exchanged. We spoke breathlessly about our schedules and what we were reading that day and how much we missed each other, typing our responses too quickly to keep the conversation flowing in any rational way.

"I somehow never run out of things to say to you," I told my computer screen one night from the bottom bunk. "The email I wrote you the other day . . . I reread it; it must have been five thousand words."

He laughed. "Send me ten thousand more tomorrow, and I'll still think they're the most interesting words I've ever read."

"Well, good, because I made a list of things to say to you in case I forgot some of them." I pulled my Moleskine cashier's notebook out of my messenger bag, which I'd begun to carry around with me everywhere, scribbling ideas whenever I felt a moment of inspiration. And it was true—I added many of those thoughts to a running list of things to talk to Santiago about, because I never wanted to feel like he was too far away from my brain.

When my mother called to check up on me, I was delighted to let her know that her instincts about Ico-Inna had been all wrong. We really *were* building something incredible, I told her, and right now we were in stealth startup mode, all hands on deck, one project after another.

"You sound hyper," she observed. "Are you sure you're okay down there?"

I almost hung up the phone like a petulant teenager. But I was an adult now, I reminded myself, several thousand miles away from my parents and capable of making my own decisions.

So I took a deep breath instead. "No, I'm not hyper, Mom. I'm just inspired. I've never been so inspired by anything in my entire life."

Here's what I didn't tell her about: Coco's explosive temper. Since an incident with one of the New Year's performers demanding payment in cash rather than a wire transfer, I'd seen Coco blow up a handful of times. Was it scary? No, but it also wasn't fun. Something shifted and his charismatic personality clouded over with an unbridled rage, his crescent-moon eyes bloodshot, spittle flying from his mouth as he shouted. I'd seen him direct this fury toward his Ico-Inna staff on occasion, yelling at DeLong for trying to organize a companywide request for raises, degrading Farmer Jesse for killing the coffee tree he'd planted a few months earlier, and even screaming at Olivia when he thought nobody else was listening. But he had yet to say anything unpleasant to me;

our relationship remained amicable and playful, full of banter and sarcasm and inside jokes. I decided that as long as he respected me, I, in turn, would continue to respect him.

In February, Santiago came back down to Panama for a hobnobby gathering of "thought leaders" Coco was hosting on Ico-Inna's property. Santiago had been trying his hand at being a professional comedian back home in Minneapolis, picking up gigs on Taskrabbit here and there to fund his modest lifestyle, so, needless to say, he had some free time. ("The Easter Bunny would be a better Taskrabbit than me," he often joked. It's true that I couldn't picture him holding a screwdriver or hauling boxes, but I admired his dedication to his dream.)

By then, I lived nearly full-time in one of Coco's friends' guest rooms in Panama City's trendy Casco Viejo neighborhood, visiting the jungle most weekends to check in on things. I found I didn't love being stuck out in the wilderness for long periods of time: There was no Wi-Fi to text Santiago with, and the relatively compact area teemed with kids at least ten years my junior. I preferred building a life as the city dweller I'd always been, with a lush, exotic locale to decamp to for a couple days at a time. Coco and Olivia seemed to gravitate toward a similar arrangement, so I usually had people to hang out with when I wasn't in the jungle.

Santiago had officially declared himself my boyfriend recently, even going so far as to tell me he loved me. I eagerly volleyed the sentiment right back, though the conversation took place over the not-particularly-romantic Facebook Messenger. We were thrilled at the chance to be together in person again and told Coco we'd handle all the transportation logistics for the conference. Just like how we first met!

"You two are so nauseatingly adorable that I might need help cleaning the vomit from my shoes," Coco chided when I offered up the airport gig as a testament to our love story.

I was nervous to see Santiago in person again, even though we communicated so often in the digital realm. What if those same crazy feelings didn't return? What if it was all just something I'd built up in my head? The night before he boarded his flight to PTY, I acted guarded and snippy, finding fault in everything he said to me, his wide-eyed optimism grating at my nerves.

"Sweetie, is something wrong?" Santi asked gently, his face taking up my phone screen, his fat lips pursed in concern. The fact that he didn't immediately escalate my behavior into a fight disarmed me.

"Of course not," I managed, finding a reason to end the conversation soon after.

But all those feelings felt like somebody else's life story when I saw him at the airport the next day, striding through customs wearing his trucker hat and a radiant smile. I practically sprinted in his direction, attacking him with my embrace, kissing his neck all over. Oh, he smelled so good.

Back in the jungle, Ico-Inna's staff and students had been scurrying around like the mice from *Cinderella* to get the property ready for the networking event. It had been, to put it mildly, a hot mess. The students recently discovered that the staff didn't mind if they drank Seco and partied with them. DeLong was now dating one of the outdoor-recreation kids, a nineteen-year-old from Kansas with overgrown blond dreadlocks whom he proudly introduced to me as the love of his life. Projects fell by the wayside—more plants in the farm had shriveled up in recent weeks, igniting Coco's fearsome temper, and people spent more time swimming in the river than they did studying.

Not to mention the physical state of the place: It was a wreck. Chef Lola's kitchen was in constant disarray, beer cans and empty wine boxes littered the bottom of the ranchos, and a pile of discarded air mattresses sat squashed by the yoga platform, water from a recent rainstorm pooling in their crevices. The bathrooms were grimy and the showers smelled like mold. I surveyed the scene and felt instantly grateful for my cozy queen-sized bed in Casco Viejo.

There was no *way* this jungle disaster would be cleaned up in time for Coco's VIP guests. I felt embarrassed for him and made a mental note to ask if my media program could be mainly based in the city.

But the Ico-Innans worked tirelessly to make a miracle happen, and by the time the event began, the jungle looked just as pristine as its Facebook ads. The thought leadership summit, which took place annually in a different exotic locale each time, was an invite-only, exclusive event that Coco had attended in Morocco one year. Once you landed a spot on the guest list, you had to pay two grand to the organizer, a Viking-like man named Hendrick who spent most of his time on a ranch in Idaho planning future conferences. He had a way of making people with decent jobs sound like extraordinary A-listers: This year's attendees included the UN's social media coordinator and a soap opera actor, and he introduced them as a "top diplomatic communications leader" and a "household television star."

The idea was for all these enthusiastic, motivated people to get together and exchange ideas and drink wine in order to "unlock the world's potential." I couldn't help but wonder why none of these burgeoning world leaders felt guilty booking a carbon-spewing jet for a weekend at the "world's most sustainable town," but given that I myself had traveled to Ico-Inna by plane, I kept that thought to myself. I also wondered where Coco and his team were disposing of all the garbage they'd collected during their cleaning rampage—another thought I didn't say aloud. As far as I'd seen, Panama didn't have much recycling infrastructure.

As Ico-Inna's media director, I was instructed by Coco to spend most of the conference with his documentary-filmmaker friend, Max. Max was a two-time Cannes festival short-film finalist who never went anywhere without a camera balanced on her shoulder, poking around for stories. Coco told me that she'd floated the idea of making a film about Ico-Inna more than once. "The thought of my project getting that much publicity gives me a boner," he said brazenly, and I rolled my eyes but agreed to try my darndest to charm her.

The event itself involved, from what I could deduce, a series of self-aggrandizing workshops in which each guest shared their "superpower" and explored how they could use it to make the world a better place. In other words: social-impact warriors on steroids. I had always despised the phrase "make the world a better place," finding it hollow and moderately arrogant (who was I to decide what made the world better?), but Hendrick looked so earnest and excited about gathering these groups together that I decided to humor him by participating. His burly Viking arms held up sheets of paper with indecipherable diagrams connecting each attendee to one another, formulating ideas that sounded pretty unrealistic to execute. When it was my turn, I said my superpower was telling stories, and at least a dozen people approached me afterward to pitch articles about themselves that they wanted me to write. I was in the middle of telling the soap opera actor, who was peddling a gluten-free children's cereal he and his wife invented, that I had my hands full running Ico-Inna's media program when Max buzzed by with her camera. That was my cue.

"Hey, Max!" I waved, turning away from the soap star. "Want me to show you around?"

"This place is fascinating," she said, not missing a beat, positioning her camera lens on my face. "Why don't you give me the insider's tour."

I'd been a journalist long enough to know that any conversations I had with her would be better off the record. "I'll give you more of the dirt if you put that camera down," I said with mock sass, and, to my surprise, she obliged, snapping on the lens cap and meeting my eye with a warm smile.

"You got it. Let's go for a little walk."

I was even more surprised by how easy it was to talk to Max as I gave her a tour of the grounds, pointing out the ranchos, the plantain trees, the showers Coco hired a local team to build using water from a nearby stream. Her questions were direct without being probing, her demeanor fast-moving without feeling rushed. She asked all the standard inquiries: where Coco's money came from, why people chose to live here, what our best practices were for cohabitating together harmoniously. I had spent enough time with Coco by that point to rattle off the full PR pitch, to enthusiastically tell her how Ico-Inna could serve as a microcosm for sustainable communities all over the world. But something about Max's demeanor felt casual, like I was chatting with a friend, and by the time we made it to the riverbank I found myself recounting how Santiago and I met at the airport and fell for each other within a few days.

"How romantic!" she purred. "You can't make up a love story like that."

"I know, I pinch myself over it every day," I said, gazing at my boyfriend across the river, where he was perched on a rock engaged in an animated conversation with the girl who ran the UN's Facebook page.

Max studied me studying Santi. "I like your story, Carly," she said. "It's interesting. Why you came down here. To give up such a big career in search of something different."

I felt genuinely touched by her compliment. "I'm exploring different versions of what success might mean to me," I replied. It sounded so good as I said it that I actually believed myself.

"This is all just so fascinating," Max added. "Really, really fascinating. So many layers of the onion to peel back. Coco seems like such a complex guy, and with characters like you and Santiago, well . . . I think I could really have something here."

I almost burst out laughing at our good fortune. To have this entire project documented on camera, for the world to see? Is this what it felt like to be truly, deliciously, unequivocally happy?

That night, as our guests bopped around under the stars in an MDMA-induced dance party (Coco's drug dealer had come out to the jungle to spin a techno set and get everyone high), I realized I'd forgotten to take my antidepressants with dinner. I snuck away from the festivities and headed toward the staff rancho. I passed the meadow dotted with cheap tents where the guests were staying: Coco had a mass delivery of camping supplies shipped down from

Walmart the week before when he realized nobody would have anywhere to sleep.

The MDMA was just starting to kick in, and I felt tingly and euphoric. Hendrick had explained earlier that he very much condoned the use of substances at his events. "Anything that opens our hearts and connects our souls," he said when Coco offered up his dealer's supply. There was no question my heart was open, wider than it had ever been. Even though the summit's stated purpose was undeniably ridiculous, even though Ico-Inna wasn't 100 percent sustainable just yet, none of that mattered, because I was content inside my own mind. And after a lifetime of all my joy coming with some sort of caveat, that felt like enough.

I reached the director's rancho and unzipped my big blue backpack. My bottle of antidepressants was dwindling. I'd managed to secure a ninety-day supply in the US over the holidays, but I'd been living in Panama for almost three months now. I counted the pills: five left. There was no way I'd be able to smuggle more medication down here in less than a week.

Did I *really* need these anymore? I felt better than I ever had in my life. I couldn't imagine anything impacting my mood for the worse. I was in love, in a relationship that was so much healthier than my last. I had abundant sources of support, an interesting passion project to work on, a source of income, adventures on the horizon. A prime setup, really. And these pills were nothing more than an inconvenient detail—a chore tethering me to the United States, shackling me to my former life.

I recalled Devon reminding me not to mess with my dosage after Burning Man last summer. But Devon hadn't seen me in more than six months. She didn't know how confident I'd become, how capable of living in the moment without second-guessing myself. She'd be so proud of the person I'd grown into since arriving in Panama.

I put the bottle in my pocket and headed back to the dance party. Along the way, I stopped by the kitchen. I tossed the remaining pills into the trash bin on top of the dinner scraps and went to find Santiago.

chapter eight

Depression doesn't return overnight, in full force. It seeps in slowly, a steady drip, drip, drip of unpleasant moments until there's enough discomfort to fill up an entire bathtub, until you're so heavy you sink beneath the surface. Your sandal breaks on a cobblestone street and the idea of buying a new one feels too hard and stressful. *Drip.* Your boyfriend has a flirty conversation with someone else in front of you, and you're convinced he's going to leave you for that person. *Drip.* You meet a successful friend of your roommate, the creator of Panama's answer to Groupon, and instead of admiring his work, you become fixated on the fact that someone younger than you has clearly made more money. *Drip.* Your curriculum isn't ready in time for the semester to start, and you can't conjure the motivation to finish it, so you wallow in your ineptitude instead. *Drip, drip, drip.*

It was around the time when Santiago permanently moved down to Panama that my bathtub started to collect water. Coco had hired him to run the entire study-abroad program, with the prestigious title of president of the Ico-Inna Research Institute, which was too big an offer for a twenty-four-year-old to pass up, even one who had his heart set on a comedy career. When Coco offered him the gig, I was ecstatic. My good-luck streak just kept continuing. And my roommate didn't mind if he stayed with me in our apartment, either.

Moving in with a long-distance boyfriend you've only been dating for a few months? And who was on the cusp of becoming your boss, even though he was more than half a decade younger and less professionally experienced? What could go wrong?

Though I was already starting to feel a little bit off when Santiago arrived, the excitement of having him close overpowered any pinpricking feelings of gloom. We quickly adopted traditional domestic roles: I unpacked his suitcase in my closet and made him smoothies in the morning; he worked on his laptop from our bed and told me I was beautiful and how much he appreciated me. Our first week together felt like all our other times, developing our individual projects side by side, cheering each other on. The summer semester would start in one month, and I was deep in the throes of designing the media program, making connections all over the city, photographers who would give guest lectures and reporters who would take us on a field trip to the offices of the local newspaper, *La Prensa*.

Santiago devoured books on leadership and management, spending long hours at Coco's apartment mapping out strategic plans while Olivia and I did lines of cocaine and flipped through old design magazines. Though he had a master's degree in education and was deeply passionate about the field, Santiago had never held a formal leadership position at any sort of organization before, and he was determined to succeed at Ico-Inna. It wasn't necessarily his long-term goal, but he figured that it would boost his credibility in some way or another.

After our domestic bliss started to wear off—and my depressive drips had begun to collect into a shallow puddle—it became clear that despite our shared ambition to do something meaningful during our time in Panama, Santiago and I had very different philosophies on how to make that happen. To put it plainly: He was a workaholic. Every person he met became someone he might benefit from professionally; he couldn't have a conversation without selling himself in some form or another.

He spent mornings and nights and weekends hunched over his computer, spewing networking emails into cyberspace, furiously typing notes out to various contacts in Minneapolis with whom he was working on vague, open-ended initiatives. His phone was constantly blowing up with messages, almost all of them related in some way to his image or career. When I finally convinced him to take an afternoon off to sneak into a hotel pool downtown, he spent the entire time perched on a lounge chair with his notebook on his lap, trying to engage me in a "creativity brainstorm."

"Sweetie, you know I have to hustle," he said every time I called him out on working too hard or tried to get him to spend quality unstructured time with me. "You and I are different. You're further ahead in your career. I still need to make a name for myself."

"But you want to be a comedian," I sulked. "All this other stuff is extra."

"And if I were home working on comedy, I'd be going to open mics every night of the week," he said. "But this is what I'm doing right now. I need to do it well. I need to get ahead."

Who, exactly, he was getting ahead *of* remained a mystery to me. All I knew was that Santiago was wired to want to be the best at everything he set out to do. And not only the best, but recognized and celebrated for being so. Part of that included having a partner who was also the best, so he constantly encouraged me to push harder in the name of going after my dreams, even though I was already working full-time to design a media curriculum, recruit students, and develop Ico-Inna's marketing strategy. He gently nudged me to reach out to news outlets with pitches for freelance articles about my experiences in microfinance. He pressured me to cultivate a dreaded "personal brand," teaching me how to build a website showcasing my work, challenging me to come up with catchy taglines to describe myself and my goals. Any downtime was spent spitballing about what we might become and how we would get each other there.

I *did* manage to publish a couple stories on well-known news sites as a result, and it felt good, sure, but I would have rather spent my time moving at the pace I was accustomed to. Keeping up with Santiago felt exhausting, the tasks he laid out before me burdensome. Though I'd always been ambitious, and shared Santiago's penchant for fantasizing about my future, I had gone about it a bit differently. I knew how to lean on my natural abilities to get my work done faster, how to play off my strengths to maximize my free time. While Santiago's resting state was restlessness, my resting state was rest. I loved to sleep and relax, and I relished unstructured hours. It had always been a bit of a paradox: my drive for success juxtaposed with my inherent desire to just hang out and chill. Five intense years at one of the world's largest news outlets, constantly devising ways for my name to rise higher and higher on the masthead, had burned me out. By then, if I allowed myself to be honest, I actually sought a life that maximized space and flexibility, filled with travel and connections and unique experiences instead of a constant drumbeat of deadlines and obligations.

But my deep personal truth directly contradicted the image of ourselves Santiago and I spent so much quality time curating. And so those two versions of success constantly dueled in my mind: success based on how the world saw me versus success based on living life according to the terms I instinctually wanted. Since I spent all my time with Santiago, the public-persona version most often won out. And because I didn't have the capacity to keep up with Santiago's relentlessness, and because the depression was starting to drip, drip, drip into my consciousness, I began to feel inferior beside him.

I felt guilty for not maximizing my hours the way he did, paralyzed by my free time, unable to enjoy anything because nothing was ever enough. It was a vicious cycle: The more my untapped potential crushed me, the less motivation I had to do anything. The sparkly dreams I'd been coasting on since I'd first arrived at Ico-Inna felt small in comparison to Santiago's limitless capacity for producing. His charming, charismatic personality, his easy ability to make anyone he encountered smile and laugh while I stood lamely beside him, only furthered my growing sense of inadequacy. As he barreled ahead of me, I became terrified of losing him.

My splintering relationship with Coco added to my unease. He never lost his temper at me outright, and we still had our marathon drug sessions from time to time, but with the arrival of Santiago, I noticed he'd begun to ice me out of big Ico-Inna decisions. When I first arrived, Coco had made it clear that I was one of his most trusted advisors, the highest-paid employee, a star hire from the American media world. My responsibilities spanned every facet of the organization's communications and marketing needs, and he frequently confided in me, everything from company strategy to gossip about the staff.

Then one afternoon, my suspicions that he'd lost faith in me were validated. Coco sent me a WhatsApp message asking if I could pop by his apartment in the city. When I arrived, he and Olivia sat at the dining room table like we had done so many long nights before, but this time, there was no plate of cocaine as the centerpiece. Coco motioned for me to take a seat across from them.

"Media Mogul," he said dismissively as I pulled out a chair for myself. I felt nervous, my confidence drained. Coco had *never* made me feel nervous before. If anything, he ignited my hubris.

"Hey, you two," I said lamely, and Olivia shifted her eyes toward the ground. She had become one of my closest friends; a natural rapport had developed between us, so I knew something was up.

"Let me just get right to it," Coco interjected before I could make small talk. "I don't think we're seeing eye to eye on everything."

"Excuse me?" Heat rose up my neck and flushed my cheeks.

"That last marketing video you made, for example," he said. "It was all wrong. The music, the B-roll footage. Olivia and I stayed up late trying to fix it, trying to infuse the Ico-Inna magic."

I knew exactly what video he was talking about. It was a quick piece for our Facebook page, some student testimonials to the soundtrack of one of our New Year's guests playing "In the Jungle" on his banjo. It had been fluffy and relatively insignificant, and I hadn't thought anything of it at the time when Coco edited the background music and switched around some shots.

I couldn't think of a confident-sounding response, so I just nodded stupidly. When had I become so afraid of what Coco thought of me? Where was the sassy powerhouse who moved down here to shake things up just a few short months ago?

"You've got a lot on your plate with the upcoming semester," Coco continued. "The media program is our highest-profile track. I'm personally invested in its success. It's what I've wanted for Ico-Inna from the very start. We can't have you screwing anything up."

My heart pounded faster. By that point, I'd fully developed my curriculum, and I was excited to test it out on my first batch of students. But I didn't realize I'd be watched so closely. I thought I'd have the freedom to experiment, to make mistakes and correct them during future semesters.

"You know I won't screw it up," I managed to say. "Coco, I care about this so much—"

"And that's why I'm clearing up some time and space for you," he interrupted. "Olivia will take over all the other marketing duties from now on."

"So you can focus on your program," Olivia added shyly, looking at her hands. I knew she didn't want to betray me, but I also knew she'd been gunning for more responsibilities. She'd recently confided in me that the role of Coco's First Lady was getting tiresome.

With Olivia there, I couldn't protest. She was my friend, and I didn't want to betray her, either. An earlier version of me would have told Coco to fuck off, that of course I could juggle multiple responsibilities, that I was brimming with ideas just like he was. But I felt too defeated to fight back. I wasn't used to getting negative feedback. I wasn't used to failing in someone else's eyes other than my own. All my life, I'd taken my accomplishments for granted, my internal monologue the only thing convincing me I wasn't good enough. Now, someone agreed with that voice.

There was nothing left to say. Plastering on a stoic expression to hide my humiliation, I nodded and gathered my things. "Okay. That makes sense. I gotta run; I'm late for a dinner thing."

"Text you later?" Olivia called after me, and I nodded again and made my way to the door. I took a taxi straight back to my apartment and crawled into bed. I was still lying there when Santiago returned hours later. I told him I had just lain down for a quick twenty-minute power nap, forced a smile, and kissed him hello.

A week later, the entire staff quit.

Apparently, Coco had gone on yet another drunken rampage, storming around the jungle criticizing everything and yelling at anyone who got in his way. At dinner, he threw his empty plate across the table and told Chef Lola he was sick of eating "Costco peanut butter." He yanked off a dead branch from a plantain tree and threw it at Farmer Jesse, telling him that he was useless at his only job. He screamed at Isa for letting the property "run down into a shithole," and where the hell was he supposed to bring his VIP guests? He continued to stomp around his land, bottle of Seco in hand, until everyone had been insulted.

Santiago and I had been in the city that evening, thank goodness, but we heard about it the next day from DeLong, who rode a Diablo Rojo from San Miguel back to the Panama City headquarters to gather his things. After Coco's tantrum, the staff had come together in their rancho, talking and venting until late into the night. They were done with his abuse. Ico-Inna was nothing but a farce, an idea Coco sold to all his powerful friends because he was well-spoken and well-read. In reality, there was nothing sustainable about its operations, nothing "town-like" about the town. "We're a glorified campsite with a really good salesperson," DeLong said, beads of sweat forming along his hairline. "A salesperson who treats us like trash. And we're done."

The spring students had already departed, and the summer ones wouldn't arrive for another month. It was the perfect time to make a coordinated exit. The staff had gone to bed that night agreeing to leave all together, a unified crew. Everyone slept on it, and the next morning, nobody backed out. They packed their belongings and cornered Coco at breakfast to quit as a group. Then they made their way up Suicide Hill, one after the other, like ants marching up an anthill, until the only two people left in the jungle were Coco and Olivia, blindsided and sipping watery coffee. Just like that.

"Welp," I said as DeLong finished telling us the story. "We're totally fucked."

It was true. Our community, transient as it already was, had dissolved overnight. Ico-Inna couldn't function without a staff. Students would arrive in a little less than a month, and there would be nobody to teach them anything. How would we even eat?

"Don't say that, babe," Santiago said gently, then turned to DeLong. "Look, man, do what you have to do. We'll miss you, but we'll be just fine." He clapped DeLong on the back, and DeLong headed downstairs to hail a cab to the airport.

My mind raced through worst-case scenarios, the weight of having to solve this problem too big for my body to comprehend. I felt like a sock filled to the brim with pennies. Santiago seemed almost maniacally chipper, and if my dread showed on my face, he didn't acknowledge it.

"Maybe this is an opportunity," he said. "The staff was starting to feel all wrong, anyhow. They didn't want to keep up with the pace of our growth. They just wanted to drink wine and play guitar and hang out."

"But they *ran* the place," I protested. "It took Coco *years* to find people crazy and brave enough to live in the jungle. We'll never be able to do that by next month."

"We can, we can!" Santiago said, pumping his fist toward the ceiling like a dictator, his voice accelerating and amplifying. "I know we can. I'll get to work on this right away. Post jobs at all the universities with sustainability programs. Reach out to recruiters in the space. Take over Facebook groups. Yeah, this is a huge opportunity to take Ico-Inna to the next level. Huge."

"I'm just not so sure," I sighed.

Santiago paused and put his hand on my shoulder. "Sweetie, your negativity isn't making this situation any better," he said, in the same tone a kindergarten teacher might use to address a five-year-old refusing to participate in nap time. "I said we can do this. I always do what I set out to do. Me and Coco—we could be unstoppable together. But not with your attitude, we can't."

It was all I could do to keep from crying. I felt helpless and overwhelmed. I couldn't tell Santiago, though. I couldn't bring down the mood any more than I already had. Right now, Santiago was my only lifeline, a raft in the middle of a tumultuous sea just barely keeping me above water.

Swallowing back tears, I smiled and nodded. "You're right. We can do this."

Santiago and I were playing gin rummy and drinking Seco with Olivia and Coco when Max, the filmmaker, called a few days later. Exciting news! She was inches away from inking a deal with a major network for a documentary series about Ico-Inna. Coco put her on speakerphone.

"Are you ready to be famous?" she barked. It was more of a command than a question. I watched Coco's eyes flicker, his grin stretching across his face.

"I'm so ready for you," Max continued. "A full civilization being built at the mercy of the forces of nature. It's too good."

Santiago nodded along enthusiastically, even though she couldn't see him through the phone. He looked elated; I knew his neurons were firing rapidly, making all sorts of connections about how this show would be good for his comedy career. Though I had been in a slump since the staff quit, even I couldn't help but feel a pang of excitement. If we handled this gracefully, it could mean huge growth for my media program.

"So what happens next?" Coco asked. "How do we make this reality show—a reality?" He chuckled at his own bad joke.

"*Docu*series," Max corrected. "We're not making a reality show. Reality TV is trash. This is going to be classy and serious. An episodic documentary. I want you to know I'm taking Ico-Inna seriously."

"Who said you weren't?" Coco replied. The question hung in the air for half a second, but nobody acknowledged it.

"I'll be down in a couple days to film some promo interviews," Max said. "Be ready to tell your stories. All you have to be is yourselves. I want Coco, Santi, Carly, all of you."

I perked up again at the sound of my name being associated with a TV show. This was exactly what Santiago had spent the past several months convincing me we wanted for ourselves. If it actually happened, it might distract me from being such a downer. Maybe things were going to be okay, after all.

My depression had become a consistent hum in the background of everything I did, but I still experienced pockets of feeling better, like a turbulent plane ride that suddenly stumbled upon smooth air. Putting the finishing touches on my curriculum excited me, as did late nights out at the bars in Casco Viejo with the few remaining staff. One night, returning home from a night of clubbing with some local friends, I felt that same surge of energy and brilliance that overtook me when I first had the idea for my media program. I stayed up until dawn scribbling ideas in my notebook while Santiago snored softly beside me.

A few weeks earlier, I'd asked Devon to arrange for her doctor friend to send me a new supply of antidepressants. I began taking it diligently again, at the same dosage, but I'd yet to notice any lasting effect. I knew, deep down, that I needed to see a real psychiatrist and explore my options with a professional. But every time I started to feel better, I held on to the idea that maybe the meds had started working again, maybe I just needed a little more time for them to reintegrate into my body. And in any case, we had so much to do to prepare Ico-Inna for the summer semester that navigating Panama City's mental health industrial complex remained squarely on the bottom of my to-do list.

Max came down and interviewed us, just as she said she would, and we managed to successfully shield her from Ico-Inna's tumultuous state. When she asked why the jungle was so quiet, we told her most of the staff was traveling between semesters and that the rest of us were staying in Panama City to work on "strategy and operations." When it came time to tell my story, glimmers of that empowered woman who first moved down here reappeared. As I recounted my career in New York, the risks I was willing to take to live an unconventional life, I even felt kind of proud of myself.

Max wanted me to repeat the whole story of how Santiago and I met for the camera, and she followed along with a big smile, coaxing me to share all the details about our airport conversation, our platonic hotel-room sleepover, our first kiss by the river. Gushing to her made me feel closer to Santiago, reminded me why I fell in love with him, why we were good for each other, consistent sources of motivation and encouragement and unbridled attraction.

"This is just so great," Max cooed when she turned her camera off. "I wanted a romantic storyline, and you two are going to deliver."

She invited me to fly back to Brooklyn with her to meet the production staff and film a couple interviews in my "old stomping grounds." Even though I had to cover the cost of the plane ticket myself, and my credit card bill was steadily rising higher than my bank account balance, I went. During a series of interviews that took place at the base of the Williamsburg Bridge, I spoke candidly with Max about my past struggles with depression, only glossing over the fact that recently, those feelings had returned. She filmed a few minutes of particularly embarrassing B-roll footage of me staring wistfully at my bottle of antidepressants and staged another mortifying shot of Santiago greeting me at the Panama City airport upon our return.

I don't know how they did it, but Santiago and Coco managed to hire an entire new staff in two weeks' time. Santiago poured himself into the recruitment search, funneling candidates to Coco, who then got on the phone and charmed them with his vision. Because of this, I saw my boyfriend even less, and my mood continued to fluctuate—some days, I was excited about the semester ahead and unstoppable with my impending curriculum; other times, I felt lonely and empty and just wanted to hang out in bed. Though my sex drive was waning, I forced myself to make seductive advances toward Santiago nearly every night, a futile attempt to reignite our initial intoxicating passion. Mostly, I just wanted my program to go well, so I trudged ahead, doing my best to ignore my slowing body and accelerating mind.

The new staff arrived two weeks before the semester began, and Santiago hosted an orientation in the city. He'd hired a similar crop to the prior crew, attractive, wide-eyed outdoorsy types who romanticized the idea of living in community in an eco-paradise. A couple of them were Panamanian, but most had come down from the US, like me. I watched their faces form expressions similar to mine when I arrived, demurred by Coco's magnanimous greetings, in slight disbelief that they'd upended their lives for this crazy experiment.

Santiago ran orientation like a five-day comedy routine, teaching the group the ins and outs of experiential education and sustainability peppered with loud jokes and ukulele performances. It was all it took for him not to dance around like a monkey with miniature cymbals. I watched him win over the rest of the staff as he performed, their easy laughter encouraging him to act even more outrageous, and I felt simultaneously proud and jealous. *That man is all mine,* I thought. Immediately followed by: *I'll never be as funny or charming as him.*

Then we got down to the jungle. It was exactly how the former staff had left it—total disarray. Empty bottles and wine boxes strewn all over the place, a barely functional kitchen stacked with dishes crusted with old food, moldy hammocks and deflated air mattresses in the living structures, a soggy and collapsed tent encampment left over from the thought leadership summit. Only this time, I couldn't relegate cleanup responsibilities to anyone else. I was merely a member of Santiago's army, boots on the ground tasked with whipping the property back into shape.

Surveying the mess, I felt sluggish and overwhelmed, any traces of residual motivation sapped. I craved the comfort and safety of my warm bed in Panama City, the covers pulled tightly over my head. I needed a mundane task, to go hide somewhere and not make small talk with my new colleagues, my lack of charisma stark against the contrast of my beloved, magnetic boyfriend.

"I'm going to go clean the toilets," I told Santiago, who was busy directing traffic by the decrepit tent city. He nodded and patted me on the back and went back to whatever he was doing. I grabbed a roll of paper towels and some cleaning spray from the supply area and trudged toward the bathroom, a wooden outhouse-like structure with a row of toilets Coco had installed a few years back when he started hosting fancy conferences on the property.

I sank down onto my knees and began wiping down the first toilet. It was covered in a thin layer of green mildew, spiderwebs collecting at the base, mysterious brown blobs that I told myself were dirt caked around the lid. A putrid smell wafted from the bowl. My limbs felt so weighted that I could barely move my arms in a scrubbing motion, but at least I was alone. At least I could hide back here during today's episode of "The Santiago Show."

As I moved from toilet to toilet, feeling heavier and heavier, my mind began to spiral. The confident, strong leader who came down here wearing my clothes and hauling my big blue backpack was now completely lost to me. It was clear that my feeble efforts to restart my medication regimen hadn't paid off, but in my current state, I certainly wasn't equipped to summon any motivation to try something different.

When you're feeling depressed, it's impossible to remember that there was ever once a time you didn't feel that way, impossible to empathize with the feelings and emotions of your former self, even though you know intellectually that she existed. The same happens when you're not depressed: The depressed version of yourself feels like nothing but a storyline, a sad relic of someone else's past, a personality type you can merely describe but in turn feel nothing for.

Memories of my early days at Ico-Inna flashed through my head, and I tried to invoke the mindset and energy of that person, but she was a stranger, a mythological character, certainly not anyone who had inhabited my own body. *You've failed at this before you've even started,* was all I could think. *Coco demoted you, your boyfriend is outshining you, and pretty soon, all your students will learn that you're nothing but a fraud—that you've never taught a class in your life, that you're completely unqualified to be here, that all your ideas are bullshit.*

Those thoughts grew louder as my limbs entangled themselves among the disgusting toilets, their overpowering smell almost knocking me over. For the first time in nearly a decade, a terrifying thought flickered through my head: I had the power to end this all, if I wanted to. I could turn off my thoughts for good. I could spare Santiago from the burden of being with me; I could put a stop to my suffering.

A vision of myself waking up, disoriented, in the hospital a decade earlier crystallized in my mind. I felt as helpless and desperate now as I had then. I slumped against the cold porcelain and let the tears come.

Through my muffled sobs I heard someone approach the entrance to the bathroom. I recognized Santiago's mud-smeared tennis shoes.

"Oh, no. Sweetie. Are you okay?" He rushed over and squatted down beside me.

I buried my face in his T-shirt and dampened the cloth with my tears. Just being near him was a comfort, but I knew the relief would be snatched away from me as soon as he turned his attention back to the rest of the staff. I wrapped my arms around him and cried harder, desperate not to let him go. As disconnected as I felt from Santiago when he was in his performance mode, he was my lifeline, my anchor. Without him I'd be alone and adrift, even more lost than I already felt. I clutched his body to mine and held on for as long as I could.

My dark, limp mood became my daily burden, a near-constant plague, kept at arm's length only when I was working. My media students arrived, even more wide-eyed and wanderlusty than the new staff, each of them eager to learn from me and impressed by my résumé. In their presence, I was able to turn down the volume on my internal chatter, but as soon as I was back alone with my thoughts, those thoughts grew louder and uglier. It took all the energy I could muster to teach my classes, which I poured myself into. But after a long day of mentoring young people, I was sapped, and I almost always went straight home to collapse into bed. The bulk of my media program took place at Ico-Inna's Panama City outpost, my students sleeping in those same sagging bunk beds I inhabited when I first arrived, with overnight "field trips" to the jungle once a week. Because of this arrangement, Santiago, who was mainly based in the jungle, had no idea how much time I was spending in bed. My depression was mine and mine alone to deal with.

Not that it would have made much of a difference if he spent more time in the city. If I thought Santiago worked too much before the semester started, now I was lucky to see him for a quick kiss in passing on the weekends. It was just as well; I didn't want to be a burden, didn't want him to know how much I was quietly suffering. But all the while, my resentment grew. I resented the new staff for being so dependent on him for direction, resented Coco for inviting Santiago to his apartment for the same long "strategy sessions" I used to be a part of, and most of all, resented Santiago for spending so little time with me.

It felt complicated and contradictory to push someone away and need them so desperately at the same time. In the limited time I had with Santiago, I wished he'd leave me alone, and while he was gone, I yearned for him to be close, to stroke my hair and tell me it was all going to be okay. Because I knew he was incapable of giving me the kind of attention I needed, and because I knew I would never be honest with him about my feelings anyway, what I longed for remained nothing but a fantasy. When you're depressed, fantasy is the safest place to escape, and when you return to your same sad reality, it's like the world is telling you that you deserved it all along.

Compounding my resentment of Santiago was the fact that he was now my boss. And he acted like it. When I brought my students down to the jungle, he frequently gave me "feedback" on my leadership style, urging me to take a firmer stance with them when they showed up late to my workshops, reminding me that it was more important to be respected than liked. The decorated career woman inside me couldn't believe I was allowing my boyfriend, who was nearly seven years my junior and had never worked in an office, to teach me anything about management. But my confidence was nowhere to be found, and thus my younger lover got the final word. Even positive reinforcement barely resonated. I knew I was doing a good job, that my students were learning from me, that they felt invigorated by my storytelling exercises. "Hey, Media Mogul, I hear you're slaying it," Coco had even offered in passing. It didn't matter; the depressive mind is only capable of focusing on failures.

Then the rain came. I had braced myself for the rainy season: Coco and his former employees had been joking about it all year. I had a pair of knee-high rubber Muck boots for the mud, and Santiago and I had attached a rain fly to our tent, so I figured I was as prepared as I could be. Besides, it had been so hot in the tropics, a cool drizzle sounded like a welcomed relief. But nothing could have prepared me for the torrential monsoons that raged throughout the Central American rainy season. The rain came in freezing sheets that soaked our bones, making it impossible to see, to talk, to breathe. It pooled in our tent, defying our pathetic little rain fly, and weighed down the wooden slabs holding the ranchos together. Mud caked up in piles that tripped us when we walked around the property. Everything smelled like mold, our clothes cold and soggy and sticking to our skin, our minimal equipment drenched.

Because we couldn't function in the jungle during storms, students and staff alike ended up huddling in the ranchos for shelter and passing bottles of Seco and boxed wine around. In those moments, I was grateful to be based in the city, where the rain barely had any effect on our daily lives. But I was also jealous of the camaraderie that came from the jungle residents' survival mode, creating yet another reason to feel isolated from Santiago's intimate experiences with everyone else.

Max marched in with a camera crew on a rainy day a few weeks into the semester. I was facilitating a lecture on "scene setting" at Ico-Inna's Panama City headquarters when they arrived, weighed down with all sorts of equipment, stacking black hard-shell suitcases in the front hall. One of her minions came straight into my classroom dangling a boom microphone.

"Wait, what's going on?" one of my students, a twenty-two-year-old aspiring social media influencer, shrieked excitedly. "Are we being filmed for something?"

Flustered, I told the class to do some free-writing and ushered the microphone guy back into the front hall. He practically collided with Max, who was swinging her signature boxy camera onto her shoulder.

"Max, what are you doing here?" I hissed. "We're in the middle of a session."

"Just getting some warm-up footage," she replied breezily, easing her way around me and approaching my classroom.

"Wait—so is this reality show happening?" Nobody had said anything to me about Max's series since she came down earlier in the summer to film those scenes for her final pitch.

She whirled around and placed her camera on one of the side tables. "*Docu*series, Carly, docuseries. And yes. What are you talking about? Coco didn't tell you?"

It turned out that the series on Ico-Inna had been green-lit by network executives the week prior. Her production crew, many of whom I'd already met in Brooklyn, had rented two floors of an apartment building in Casco Viejo, not too far from my own place.

Once the staff and students signed their stack of release forms, we'd be off and running.

Before I could ask any more questions, the front door opened again, and in trotted my boyfriend. His face practically radiated neon light at the sight of Max and her crew, his eyes and smile both enormous.

"There he is!" Max wrapped Santiago in a big hug, and the rest of her team surrounded him. He wore his aspiring theater-owner expression, shaking everyone's hand presidentially, cracking amusing side comments as he greeted each crew member by name.

I stood a few feet away, watching the scene unfold with my mouth agape, trying to make sense of whatever was going on in front of me. Had Coco and Santiago finalized a deal to film a television show about our lives—without telling me?

Santiago's big brown eyes finally locked onto mine. I raised my eyebrows and mouthed, *What the fuck?* He peeled himself away from his gaggle of admirers and came over to me.

"Sweetie, isn't this exciting? I thought you'd be excited. You really wanted this show to happen."

For what felt like the trillionth time in recent weeks, I fought to keep myself from crying. "Why didn't you tell me any of this was happening?"

He shrugged sheepishly. "Coco made me promise not to say anything until Max was down here in person. He didn't want to jinx it."

"But I'm your *girlfriend*," I protested. "We're supposed to be partners. I'd say this is a big piece of information not to share with your partner."

"And he's my *boss*," Santiago said. "And anyway, the deal is done. Me telling you a couple days before they got here wouldn't have changed that."

Before I could respond, Max barged over to us holding a pile of papers. "I need you two lovebirds to sign these, stat," she said. "We should get a head start on your storyline."

Santiago's gigantic smile reappeared, making it clear my whining was no longer welcome in this situation. "Let's do it!" he agreed.

"The rain should clear up this afternoon, if you want to grab some footage before dinner."

Cameras became a near-constant presence. Max's minions lurked in the corner of my classes and accompanied me on my Diablo Rojo rides to Casa Roja. They followed me up and down Suicide Hill as I trudged in and out of the jungle for long weekends with my students, and they greeted me as I exited my tent in the morning and shuffled over to the coffee station. Santiago and I played the part of a sunny, happy couple each time Max pulled us aside for an interview, his arm around me as I nuzzled into his chest, forcing a smile. Turning on charisma for the camera came relatively easily to me—my journalism and management experience lent itself nicely to this performative task—and sometimes, I almost started to believe I felt better during filmed confessionals. But as soon as the crew put the caps back on their lenses, I was left with my own thoughts again.

Partying in Panama City became the only activity that made me feel like any small semblance of my former self. In spite of my demanding curriculum, my horizontal marathons in bed hating myself, and the omnipresent production crew around the perimeter, I still made time to get drunk and high. Drugs and alcohol were my only escape, the sole tool for producing anything that even slightly resembled the joy I felt during my earliest months at Ico-Inna. I had Coco's dealer on speed dial, and he paid me regular visits. I barely noticed the hangovers; they were just an extension of my depression, another way to experience the misery I already dealt with daily.

I trudged through one such hangover on my way to Coco and Santiago's first all-staff meeting since the semester began. The night before, I'd watched the sunrise from my roof with some guys who ran a local hostel chain and finally forced myself into bed when the coke ran out. I managed to bank a couple jittery, fitful hours of sleep and then splashed some water on my face and dragged myself to

Ico-Inna's Panama City outpost, where the staff meeting would be taking place. Its stated purpose was to gather the team for an "early semester check-in," but I knew for a fact it was just because Max needed some B-roll footage of the staff working together in the city.

Everyone was already there when I arrived, the TV crew fiddling with their cameras and boom microphones, Santiago setting out boxes of pastries and jugs of orange juice, Coco and Max drinking black coffee and laughing in the corner. The rest of the staff was situated around the big wooden conference table in the main classroom, so I slunk into the one remaining seat.

"Alright, alright, everyone," Santiago bellowed, clapping his hands together to get everyone's attention. "I'm bribing you all with baked goods, but I promise I also have some pretty cool stuff to say, okay?"

A bunch of people chuckled, and I forced myself to laugh along, too, like a dutiful sidekick. One of the camera guys zoomed in on Santiago's face and I watched his expressions grow slightly more animated as he described a series of "getting to know each other" games we'd be playing. Something involving writing our goals for the semester on a series of Post-its, trading with a partner, and devising plans for how we might help each other achieve them. Though I'd arrived that morning with some residual party adrenaline, all the leftover energy was draining from me, fast. As Santiago continued to deliver instructions for the Post-it exercise, his hands flailing for the cameras, that all-too-familiar heaviness returned, pressing down on my skin like a magnetic force field. I started nodding off, jerking my head back and forth to force myself to stay awake.

I couldn't focus on anything Santiago or anyone else was saying. The room started to spiral around me like a toilet getting flushed. The lights were too bright and too dim at the same time. I felt trapped, glued to my chair, desperate to flee and reactivate my senses but incapable of movement. Like a ghost who traveled through walls, I managed to rise from my seat without feeling anything and make my way toward the door. I think I muttered something about needing to use the ladies' room. A camera swung around to point at me and I ducked my head and made my way out.

Outside, the humid tropical morning felt even more suffocating. It smelled like garbage and salt water. Still unable to think or feel anything, I allowed my feet to carry me across the park, through the crosswalk, and down to the Cinta Costera promenade along the ocean. I turned left and headed farther into the cluster of downtown skyscrapers. All I could hear was white noise, my mind scrambled into nonsense. The only thing I knew for certain was my misery, my dull and leaden body. I'd do anything to yank myself out of this state. I wanted to die. The one foolproof way to turn it all off.

Maybe I could jump off a building. Would anyone even notice? Santiago probably didn't even realize that I hadn't returned to the conference room. I channeled all the physical strength I had left and heaved myself into a revolving door. Now I was in the lobby of a hotel casino. Panama City was full of cheap casinos. The digital chimes of slot machines echoed in the back of my head, like I was hearing them from inside a fishbowl, as I clambered past the gambling equipment and into an elevator. I hit *T*, for *terraza*. Made it to the roof. A pool, a bar, a few lounge chairs. I could barely see any of it. I headed straight for the rooftop's edge, which was guarded by a cool steel railing.

I peeked over the side of the building. God, I was high up. The sensation of height made me feel even dizzier. Below me, a Latin American city went about its business: The hotel marquee flashed, a couple loitering guys smoked cigarettes by a stoplight, a taxi rolled by blaring reggaeton. I could jump. I could turn it all off. But something inside my body stopped me from doing it.

My breathing quickened as if I had just taken the stairs and not an elevator ride. I sank down to my knees and sat down with my back to the railing. If I was capable of feeling anything, it would have been panic. But the dullness persisted. It's a strange combination to want to do something as scary and violent as ending your life without feeling even a shred of energy to carry out the act. I wished my life was just a light switch I could flick off and escape, painlessly, into blackness.

I took out my phone and googled "how to kill yourself." On top of the results page was the phone number for the suicide hotline. I didn't know what else to do, so I dialed it.

A kind-sounding woman picked up, her voice caramelly and soothing. "This is Mary. And to whom am I speaking today?"

"Hi—uh—this is Carly." My mouth formed words, but I couldn't feel myself saying them.

"Hi, Carly. Thank you so much for reaching out to us today. It's really wonderful to speak with you."

"Thank you." The steadiness of our interaction, formal as it was, allowed me to notice the breaths that were still, miraculously, flowing in and out of my lungs. I suddenly wanted to tell her everything. I let the words tumble out, recounting my history of depression and the night I threw out my meds. My living situation, back and forth to the jungle during monsoon season, and my relationship, an absent but well-meaning boyfriend who was also my boss. Our shared commitment to an "eco-community" that was probably a scam. My intensifying misery.

"That sounds extremely challenging, Carly. A very unique situation, and a very hard one, at that."

I liked hearing Mary say my name—I felt listened to. So I kept going. I told her about suicide feeling like the only way out. The perverse comfort I felt thinking about never having to live inside my head again. "Sometimes I just want to turn off my thoughts for good," I admitted.

Mary and I spoke for another fifteen minutes, and by the time our conversation was over, I had traveled back inside my body and felt like I could think coherently, control my movements. I didn't feel better, exactly, but I felt human. I headed back downstairs and hailed a taxi to my apartment, where I got right into bed and fell asleep. My safest space.

It was dark out by the time Santiago returned. "What *happened* to you?" he said, flipping on the lights in our bedroom. "We're about to head out for a team dinner, are you okay? I've been texting and texting."

I was relieved to see there were no cameras behind him. "I had a really bad migraine," I lied. "I didn't want to bother you on such a big workday."

He climbed into bed beside me and kissed my forehead. "Sweetie, you never bother me," he said softly. "I'm always here."

I wanted to believe him, so I let myself relax into his embrace. His touch was warm and comforting. "I'm not going to make it to dinner," I said. "Could you stay with me?"

"Of course I'll stay with you," he said. "Let me text Coco and tell him to cover for me."

For one night, I had his full attention. I fell asleep in Santiago's arms, relieved I hadn't done anything to hurt myself, convinced that tomorrow would be better. Hopeful. Every new day was a do-over, right?

But the next morning, I woke up with that familiar anxious pit in my stomach. It was a jungle day. The thought of hauling myself out to San Miguel and up and down the mountain felt impossible. Teaching my students sounded even harder. The heaviness was back, but I wasn't allowed to sleep forever. I hadn't actually turned anything off, after all. I'd just put an ellipsis in my unbearable consciousness.

I had no choice but to make the journey out to the jungle, to follow Santiago. The more difficult it felt, the more I berated myself. I couldn't focus on anything but the voices in my head telling me I'd failed at the most important project I'd ever taken on in my life, failed at the best relationship I'd ever been lucky enough to find myself in. I gave my students a half-baked writing assignment and shuffled around the jungle in a daze.

Luckily, the TV crew was busy with some other storyline. I snuck off to Santiago's and my tent unnoticed. I'd only planned to curl up in my sleeping bag and pass out for a few hours. But on my way over to the tent, I noticed a discarded plastic bag.

I took the bag with me into the tent. Put it over my head. Willed myself to breathe in and out.

PART TWO

chapter nine

I shuffled into the San Francisco Airport baggage claim concourse in a pill-induced haze, shouldering a messenger bag that may as well have been filled to the brim with rocks. My mother waited for me by the carousel wearing burgundy yoga pants. She held a leash that culminated in her energetic Boston terrier, Layla, who spotted me before Mom did and lunged in my direction.

"Oh, Carly," Mom said as she approached me. "You're way too skinny."

I could barely keep my eyes open. The day before, after I ripped the plastic bag off my head and Santiago evacuated me from the jungle, Coco's drug dealer met us at the airport with the Panamanian equivalent of Xanax to help me get through the long flight. He gave me two bright-yellow discs the size of horse pills and told me to save the second one for later. I downed them both on the tarmac before the plane took off, chasing them with warm sips of boxed wine I bought at the airport.

For some miraculous reason, Santiago and I successfully evaded Max and the reality-show producers on our way to Panama City. I imagined them getting stuck in the mud on the mountain. Tires flailing, equipment shattering. A satisfying fantasy if I hadn't been so miserable.

Suicide Hill was never even meant to be traversed by vehicles during dry season—let alone in the rain—but Santiago had navigated the potholes and sharp turns with the confidence of someone who hadn't just learned to drive a stick shift a couple months prior. It was one of those things he dedicated way too much effort to mastering while I wallowed in my worsening mood.

By the time we made it out of the jungle and into San Miguel, the rain had receded to a light drizzle. Santiago stopped at Mónica's food cart and bought an order of patacones and a red Gatorade as I stared out the window in a trance. *It might be my last time driving through the little village, the bridge to Ico-Inna.* I tried to take a mental picture: the concrete basketball court, the tiny school with the peeling paint behind the bamboo-stick fence, a few pieces of trash gurgling down the river. But my mind couldn't focus on anything for more than a few seconds.

"Here," Santiago said as he slid back into the front seat of the truck, handing me a greasy Styrofoam box. "You really should eat something."

I nibbled on the side of a patacon. The shards of green plantain traveled down my throat in a bland, starchy blob, as heavy as everything else. I felt like I was going to puke.

As the city skyline came into focus an hour later, its empty office buildings and sizzling casinos, Santiago had already worked out all the details for me. First, he called Copa Airlines and booked me on the red-eye to San Francisco. Then, he dialed Coco and explained that I had an unexpected family emergency and needed to be back in the States as soon as possible. No, it was unclear when I'd return. Santiago would take over my lesson plan himself in the meantime. Finally, he made me ring up my mother, who lived in Oakland, just to the east of the San Francisco Bay. Mom had been based in California for the past several years, a long-standing dream she'd been able to actualize once she separated from my father and ran out of reasons to remain in Connecticut.

She was the last person I wanted to speak to—to admit my defeat to. But her voice was like velvet in my ear, a visceral comfort. I felt like an infant whose mere survival hinged on the care of a maternal figure.

Through my pharmaceutical stupor in the airport terminal, I wrapped my arms around my mother's slight frame. I still had a good twenty-five pounds on her.

"You know," she said, Layla nipping at my ankle, "I never trusted this Panama thing. I knew it sounded sketchy from the start."

I was too tired to reply, to defend my life choices. All of yesterday's will to want to die had drained out of me. I didn't even have the energy to hate myself. I just wanted to sleep, to turn off my bad decisions, to erase Ico-Inna and everything that came along with it.

"I'm glad you're home," Mom continued as she ushered me out of the terminal. "You needed to get out of there. Conrad what's-his-name . . . what a fraud."

I stayed silent as I hauled my big blue backpack, smeared with jungle dirt and other filth, into the trunk and flopped onto the passenger seat. It was almost a relief to just let someone else decide what would happen next. Almost. I still didn't feel much.

She wound her Subaru up the 101. San Francisco's familiar spine unfurled, a pastel flip-book. The Bay Bridge loomed ahead before giving way to the East Bay. My mother was saying something about the suspiciousness of trust fund kids as she pulled onto the 580, but I could barely register her words. I leaned my cheek on the cold car window.

"Mommy," I said. "I'm tired. I'm so tired."

Mom made me thick-cut toast slathered with plum jam and vanilla tea. During my childhood she was always fixing me a cup of English tea; she drank it more than water. I blew on the steaming liquid and took a small sip, and asked her how long I was asleep for.

"Oh, I'm not keeping track," she replied. "But it's four in the afternoon."

Her voice was soft, but I pictured her judging me as hard as I was judging myself. I didn't know how many days I spent in her guest room, in and out of consciousness. The sadness had been coming in tidal waves, jolts of stomach tightenings that eventually dissipated with the relief of more sleep.

During one short stretch I'd been awake, staring out the window at the foreignness of a fully functioning world, I managed to video chat with Santiago. He called me from what was once our shared tent, his eyes deep brown pools of concern.

"Sweetie," he said. "I'm so worried about you."

My face in the tiny rectangular box on the lower right-hand corner of the screen looked pallid and dull, the bags under my eyes the size of grapefruits. "I'll be okay." My voice sounded like tires on gravel. "I miss you."

I really did miss him. In spite of everything, he'd shown up for me the past few days—and the entire year. My longing for our relationship was the only thing reminding me I was still human.

He didn't say it back. He stared at the camera long and hard, then stuck out his tongue and made a silly face. Giggled nervously. "Everything's the same here. You're not missing much."

I thought of my students, blurry and abstract, clutching their notebooks and sneaking sips of Seco when they thought I wasn't watching. "How are my kids?" I asked him.

"Oh, they're fine." Santiago brightened and gave a thumbs-up. "I led them through some improv games. It was fun. It was dorky. We had a good time."

Improv games. My brilliant, meticulously conceptualized media school of the future had been reduced to summer camp. *This is all my fault,* I thought.

Greg, the on-site nurse, appeared in the video frame behind my boyfriend, jogging and out of breath. "Santi! *There* you are! We've been looking everywhere, man. We've got a bit of a situation."

There was always a situation, always an emergency, and Santiago was always appointed to fix things. "Coming, coming, I'll be right there," he shouted as he turned in Greg's direction. "Babe, I gotta—"

"I know. You need to go." I wanted him to tell me he missed me. That everything would be okay. That he still loved me, even though I was so broken.

Instead, he made another silly face. "We'll talk soon."

"I miss you," I tried again. "I love you."

"I gotta go. I gotta go." His face popped off the screen, the "call ended" icon glaring its bright-red finality at me. I buried my face in the pillow. Just six months ago, Santiago's lust for me was so palpable that we could barely peel ourselves out of bed.

I squeezed my eyes shut and let myself slip back into blackness, the only place I felt safe from my own mind. I didn't wake up again until Mom knocked on my door with another cup of tea.

Devon came to visit me a few days later. "I'm here to do nothing but love on you," she said as soon as I opened my mother's front door, folding me into an enormous hug. Her golden hair smelled like Pantene, just like it always did.

"Dev. I missed you so much." At the sight of my best friend, something inside me stirred. For the first time since coming home, I didn't want to go back to sleep. I wanted to tell her everything.

Her eyes surveyed my rumpled pajamas. "You look . . . cozy."

She was the only person in the world I'd never feel ashamed in front of, never bend the truth in my favor, even a little bit. Judgment never tainted Devon's limitless curiosity. She genuinely wanted to know things, and she almost always met whatever she uncovered with compassion. "I haven't gotten out of bed in a few days," I admitted.

"Then let's get your body moving. Can you borrow your mom's bike? We can BART back into the city and then cruise out the beach."

The thought of biking around with Devon woke me up even more. When we first became friends in San Francisco in our early twenties, we biked all over the city together, two-wheeled adventures taking us to new neighborhoods and parks and bars. I hadn't yet comprehended the fact that being back in the Bay Area meant I got uninterrupted time with my closest friend for the first time in years.

"Sure. Ugh. I desperately need a shower."

Mom emerged from her bedroom holding Layla under one arm like a football and offered Devon some tea while I headed to the bathroom. I heard Devon telling her about the live classical music performance she and her housemates hosted in the living room of the Avalon last weekend. They were planning a camping trip to Grass Valley in a giant retrofitted school bus that belonged to one of the new residents.

The scalding water guzzling from the showerhead washed away the last few lost days. As I scrubbed my limbs, I noticed the muscles that had formed up my calves and thighs and forearms. My body had carried me through so many terrains and experiences the past year. It may have been a vessel for my darkness and pain, but it also trekked up and down a giant mountain in the Panamanian jungle each week. It planted coffee bushes and hacked at banana leaves with a machete. It went dancing until sunrise and still made it in front of my students the next morning. My body was brave even when my mind was weak.

When you're in as fragile a mental state as I was, navigating the aftermath of a suicide attempt, it's so easy for your thoughts to pivot instantaneously, to vacillate between extremes. Even just a moment of gratitude, of recognizing a shard of positivity, can fill you with hope. So what if I was back in San Francisco? Maybe I escaped an impossible situation. Maybe my depression would melt away if I started laying the groundwork for a normal life again, if I let San Francisco embrace me the way my best friend just did.

I patted myself dry feeling a new sense of resolve to rebuild my life. What you never realize during those fleeting moments of optimism is that they can recede as quickly as they pop up.

Devon and I pedaled down JFK Drive, Golden Gate Park's main artery. Soldiers of eucalyptus trees flanked us on both sides as we glided under their canopy. I had traveled this path so many times: meandering LSD journeys to the beach, speed-walking to summer festivals, the last drunken stumble of the annual Bay to Breakers race, and that one time in history I managed to run an entire four miles. The coalescence of natural splendor and human joy often made me feel invincible.

"I have something to tell you," Devon said as we whirred past Speedway Meadow. She glanced over at me. "I'm in love."

"Well, duh," I replied. Devon had been dating the same guy, Yusuf, since before I left for Mexico. She met him at a renegade party inside an abandoned water tower and he moved into her bedroom at the Avalon five days later. He was short and bald and always looking for his next business hustle. "It just makes sense," she told me when he became her live-in boyfriend after less than a week.

Whether Yusuf liked me was up for debate. Before I left for Mexico, he and Devon went camping in the redwoods with me and Robbie. Robbie and I spent the entire drive in the back of Devon's Westfalia making turkey noises at each other, giggling, and kissing with too much tongue. When we stopped for gas somewhere outside Ukiah, Yusuf was so annoyed that he walked away. Devon followed him to the freeway overpass and convinced him to come back and endure the weekend with us.

She insisted that Yusuf had been quite fond of me since I got rid of Robbie. But I was still a little intimidated by him.

Now, balancing on her bicycle seat with no hands as we rode through the park, my best friend shook her head and grinned. She looked like a yellow lab drying itself off after a walk in the rain. "It's not Yusuf."

Nothing about Devon's love life ever surprised me. "Oh?"

"His name is Nico. He's amazing, Carly. He might be perfect. He was on the Glass Shark crew with me. We just, like, lived together in the desert for three weeks. He's—have you ever felt like someone's soul might actually be born from the same place as yours?" She sighed and grabbed her handlebars.

While I was being evacuated from the Panamanian jungle, Devon was returning home from this summer's Burning Man. She and a crew of a few dozen builders had toiled away in the sun, creating a life-size great white shark out of recycled stained glass—the most revered art piece that year.

Nico was an architect, and he was five years her junior, she told me. "Just like you and Santiago!" she said. "You're right, there's something so refreshing about a younger guy."

"It's edgy, too," I agreed, thinking of how forbidden and sexy it felt when Santiago told me he wasn't even yet twenty-five. "But how did Yusuf take it?"

"Oh, he's fine," Devon replied, shrugging as if I had just asked her how he felt when she forgot to bring the mail inside. "We're still together, of course."

Yusuf wouldn't be leaving the Avalon or even moving out of her bedroom, she explained. He was cool if she stayed a couple nights a week with Nico. That gave Yusuf time to hang out with the dreadlocked astrophysicist he met at a machine learning conference a couple months ago.

As much as I failed at nonmonogamy, Devon had always seemed to make it look like an uncomplicated pursuit. I tried to imagine Santiago spending a few nights a week with a dreadlocked astrophysicist, and I felt nauseated. After my unsavory experience with Robbie, I never again wanted to imagine my significant other touching another woman.

The thought of Santiago made me wonder what he was doing right in that moment. Scheming with Coco in Panama City? Giving the students a pep talk after a particularly ferocious storm? I'd been gone for less than a week, but Ico-Inna already felt like mythology. Golden Gate Park smelled like home. Devon and I rode all the way to the beach and ran straight into the Pacific Ocean. The freezing water reminded me I was still alive.

A few days later, Devon invited me over to the Avalon for an afternoon of live music in the garden. Since our bike ride, I'd been feeling more like a woman who could exist in the world again. I was ready to see old friends, ready to start figuring out where to go from here.

The blustery San Francisco weather was no match for the tropics. But my unpaid credit card bill was quickly accruing interest—without any viable source of income, I was in no place for a shopping trip. So I chose my outfit carefully based on my limited selections: a sequined tank top with a see-through lace back, the one I wore for my first interview with Max. Denim shorts even though my legs were certain to get goose bumps. Mom let me borrow her leather jacket. I traced my lids with eyeliner for the second time that week, something I otherwise hadn't done for months. My tan hadn't faded yet. The person staring back at me in the mirror looked healthy and ready for something as normal as a day hanging out in her best friend's yard.

Henry, a longtime Avalon resident and founder of a successful cloud computing startup, was greeting guests beside the large wrought iron gate that separated the house from the sidewalk when I arrived. Henry had gotten his startup off the ground using the money he made designing a Facebook widget that was ultimately acquired by Facebook itself, and according to household lore, he'd sketched out his new company's earliest prototypes while perched on the couch in the Avalon kitchen. Devon, Henry, and Henry's twin sister, Theodora, had come up with the idea for their communal home four years earlier and convinced its first batch of residents to move in.

Theodora, whose real name was actually Tiffany Greenberg but who believed herself to be the kind of person better off with an exotic mononym, was chief marketing officer at her brother's startup. She'd appointed herself the company's official spokesperson and frequently jetted around to conferences and TEDx events to talk about how cloud computing mimicked the forces of nature. She lived in the biggest room on the Avalon's top floor and treated herself to an all-you-can-eat buffet of attractive lovers. (Henry, for his part, preferred a more modest and under-the-radar lifestyle, occupying one of the house's smallest rooms and driving the beat-up Toyota Camry he'd owned since high school.) I didn't care for Theodora all that much, but Devon kept trying to convince me that once you got to know her and she dropped the "self-satisfied demigoddess" act, she was actually pretty cool. After all, it wasn't easy to make it as a female leader in tech; every woman who ascended to those ranks needed some sort of protective armor around her personality.

"Henry!" I exclaimed as I approached the gate, leaning in for a hug. "It's been so long."

He squinted at me behind his wire-rimmed glasses before awkwardly returning my hug. "Oh, wait. Do I—*Carly*? I didn't even recognize you."

I blushed. Had I been away from San Francisco that long?

"Did you lose weight or something?" Henry blurted out, then tried to backtrack. "I mean, sorry, can I even say that?" I glanced down at my body. It was true; I was nearly twenty pounds thinner than the last time I'd visited Devon at the Avalon. I'd always had a voracious appetite, but these past few months of depression combined with a rugged part-time lifestyle in the jungle must have whittled down my figure. My mother also couldn't stop pointing it out.

"No, it's all good, you're right," I said. "I'm choosing to take that as a compliment." I grinned at him and made my way toward the garden, where I recognized several of my old pals from my San Francisco life, plus a handful of Avalon residents. Devon hadn't yet told anyone that I was back in town, and everyone seemed excited to see me. I made the rounds like a politician, feeling confident and full of stories and genuinely delighted to be back in a familiar place among friendly faces. That afternoon, too distracted by the novelty of returning to my former city to even think about the past few weeks, I felt as charismatic as Santiago.

A jazz trio played under the gazebo, and I recognized the bassist as one of Devon's roommates, a handsome Vietnamese American guy named Tommy who kept a music studio in the basement. The *New York Times* magazine had written about his band a few years back, much to this social circle's amusement. I ambled over to the makeshift bar in the corner of the yard.

Drue and Eliza, a couple affectionately known as "Druliza," were serving drinks. They had lived at the Avalon since its inception, and I'd never seen one of them without the other. Eliza was a dancer with San Francisco's most famous contemporary dance troupe, and Drue directed music videos, including several for Tommy's band. I didn't know them well, but they both greeted me with warm smiles as I approached.

Eliza ladled a yellowish concoction from the punch bowl into a mason jar and handed it to me while Drue asked what I'd been up to for the past year. "A little of this in Mexico, a little of that in Panama," I ad-libbed, realizing that I'd need to figure out a way to sharpen up my elevator pitch sooner than later if I wanted to find a job. At the mention of Panama, I felt a familiar jolt of anxiety, and for a moment I was zapped away from the party and back inside my suffocating tent in the jungle. I downed my drink, which turned out to be vodka and lemonade, in one gulp and asked Eliza for a refill.

Wandering back toward the music, I stopped to say hi to Trevor, a lanky computer scientist with whom I had a one-night stand after the Avalon's inaugural Halloween party, and Gregoire, a large-scale installation artist who was currently designing a piece for the public transit station down by the Civic Center. Over his shoulder, on the other side of the yard, I spotted Ari. She sipped a beer and laughed with a friend, tossing her wavy hair behind her shoulder, her infectious smile lighting up her face. I barely knew her, and I hadn't seen her since Robbie's and my disastrous breakup at Burning Man the summer before. What would I say if we crossed paths that afternoon?

Devon grabbed my elbow and snapped me back into the present moment. "*There* you are," she said. "I'm so glad you're here! It's almost like you really live in SF again."

I clinked my mason jar of vodka lemonade against her mason jar of red wine. She pulled me toward the front of the gazebo and twirled me around dramatically, and we both giggled.

"Speaking of," Devon continued, "have you decided what's next? I know you don't wanna stay in your mom's guest room forever."

I hadn't made any decisions about anything—hadn't thought further ahead than waking up the next morning since I'd arrived. I could go back to New York, where I'd been living before I moved to Latin America. But something about that idea felt chaotic and frenzied, singed by the memories of my dysfunctional relationship with Robbie and my cutthroat job in the media. And I sure as hell wasn't going back to Panama or Mexico anytime soon. The Bay Area seemed as decent as anywhere else. My mom's condo was rent-free, and she made me tea every day. Why *couldn't* I stay in her guest room forever, let myself get taken care of like a little girl? Or if not forever, at least for now?

I shrugged in response to Devon's question. "I guess I'm just taking it one day at a time," I said. "I'm pretty good at my mom's."

Devon sipped her wine and stared at me over the rim of the jar with a familiar look—the look she had anytime she was scheming. Devon loved to scheme; she was always tossing out big ideas, coming up with get-rich-quick arrangements. It was one of the reasons she and Yusuf, who was always hustling one thing or another, got along so well. Last I heard, they were starting an Etsy shop that exclusively sold hats bedazzled with rhinestones.

"Dev, stop giving me that look," I said. "I know you're thinking about something."

She did another little twirl, her flowy skirt flaring out to the sides. "I just think it would be good for you to be settled somewhere," she said. "You know, a real home base. Then you can figure out everything else in your life from there. From somewhere comfortable."

"But I am comfortable," I said.

"You're also thirty-one years old. You should get your own place."

I sighed and rolled my eyes. "Alright. Yeah. With all the money I have saved." I deliberately hadn't checked my credit card balance since returning to the United States. "I don't suppose you know of anything?"

Devon smiled. "I suppose I do," she replied. "In fact, there just so happens to be a room opening up here at the Avalon."

Me? At the Avalon? I'd never even considered it. This was always Devon's turf—an entertaining place to visit, a mansion full of moderately intimidating people, the venue for the best Halloween party in town. Could I see myself living here? I knew getting a room was damn near impossible: There was a long waiting list of potential residents, and even then, the housemates liked to recruit rather than accept people who directly expressed interest. And besides, I had been part of a commune of sorts in the jungle, and it turned out to be a disaster.

"I don't think so, Devon," I said, shaking my head. "I mean . . . I couldn't even afford it if I wanted to."

She grabbed my hand and twirled me around again. "Well," she said. "Good thing I already paid your first month's rent."

chapter ten

Dr. Violet Sage's office was located on the sixth floor of a nondescript beige office building in downtown Oakland. There was no elevator, so I hoofed it up a half-dozen flights of linoleum stairs. Yellowed paintings of flowers did a poor job hiding the cracks in the walls. I found Suite 602 and entered a windowless room with more linoleum flooring and cracked walls. Sat down on a torn leather chair and picked up an outdated copy of *People* magazine while I waited for my appointment to begin.

The other day, I'd managed to successfully navigate the bureaucracy of Covered California, my state's answer to universal health care. Because my annual income currently amounted to $0, I was eligible for a plan that only cost me $92 a month. After my tumultuous experience in Panama, I needed to reevaluate my treatment options under the care of a professional—I'd been back on my regular antidepressants for a full month before my incident with the plastic bag. So I enrolled in a health plan and promptly scanned a list of in-network psychiatrists, choosing the one located closest to my mother's condo.

But here's the thing: Anyone who's ever received thirty seconds of mental health care knows that the in-network providers are never as good. Shelling out $200, even $300 for a high-quality private-practice psychiatrist is almost always a better option, if you can afford it. And even if there *is* a decent doctor in your insurance network, shopping around until you find that particular unicorn can be an exhausting process. You see shrink after shrink, resynthesizing your life story into a few sentences, trying to identify someone you feel comfortable enough with to bare your innermost traumas to.

Until then, I'd always taken my health care privilege—my easy access to the best doctors and most effective treatments I could find—for granted. I was too focused on my own inner world to consider all the structural inequities at play and all the benefits my upbringing and steady paycheck afforded me. My personal problems consumed me; my depression felt insurmountable when it blossomed and blocked out almost everything else, rendering any good fortune moot. But this time, while still better situated than the vast majority of suffering humans, I didn't have the same luxuries I'd gotten used to with a full-time job. So I selected an in-network psychiatrist based on another attractive metric: proximity.

"Carly?" A woman with a comically high ponytail greeted me and ushered me into the back office. Her hair spouted from the crown of her head like a spiky, bleached-blond fountain. It must have taken a lot of gel to style in such a strange, specific way. I started thinking about my middle school cheerleading competitions, the Dippity-Do we used to shellack our hair into foam curlers that we then slept in, waking up with aching scalps and impenetrable ringlets. I was still picturing pom-poms and stiff dance moves when the blond woman with the funny hair said my name again.

"Yeah, hi." I shook myself back into reality and sat down on her lavender velvet couch, avoiding the conspicuous brown stain that sliced it down the middle. I looked around the room. Orchids of various shapes, colors, and sizes sat atop almost every surface, along with an impressive collection of crystals. The doctor picked up a small pink rock and rolled it around in her hands.

"I'm Dr. Violet Sage," the woman said, peering at me over thick lavender glasses frames that matched her couch. She passed the crystal from palm to palm. She wore an oversize gray sweatshirt with the collar cut off over a pair of bright patterned leggings adorned with sunbursts and other celestial patterns. A diploma from Cal State Fullerton was framed on the wall behind her, covering up another crack. "Can you tell me a little bit about why you're visiting me today?"

I took a deep breath and laid out my story. I tried to be concise, but it was hard. There was a lot to cover. My college suicide attempt, my journalism career, my move to Mexico, my doomed project in Panama. My abrupt disposal of an antidepressant that had actually been working, and my attempt to resume taking it when things got tough again. My rendezvous in the tent with the bag over my head. My return to San Francisco to figure out a way to get better.

As I spoke, I watched her eyes widen behind her glasses. "And that's why I'm here today," I concluded. "I need to find a medication that works for me. The nortriptyline doesn't seem to be doing its job this time around. What do you think?"

Dr. Violet Sage placed the pink crystal back on her desk and uttered a low whistle. "Well, just . . . wow," she said. "What a story. Your life—it sounds extraordinary. It's safe to say I have never had a client like you before."

I knew it was frowned upon for a professional psychiatrist to weigh in on my personal story like that, especially when I was coming to her in such a broken state. But I couldn't help but feel flattered. I sat up a little straighter.

She went on to explain that the nortriptyline probably wasn't working for me anymore because I'd stopped taking it so suddenly; my receptors were likely rejecting it. She recommended I start with Zoloft and see how I felt from there. She'd had some patients react well to that medication recently. Why shouldn't I give it a shot, too? Because I couldn't think of a reason not to, I agreed.

"Okay, let's try Zoloft," I said. "Hopefully it helps. I mean, I've been feeling better lately, but I don't think I trust it."

"It's normal for moods to fluctuate, especially since you just made such a drastic change in your environment," Dr. Violet Sage said. "Have you ever tried spreading magnesium lotion all over your skin? I find it works wonders for mood stabilization."

I had never heard of magnesium lotion before. She went on to suggest vitamin D supplements, omega-3s, and an ultraviolet lamp that I could order online and sit in front of for ten minutes in the morning and ten minutes at night. "We depend so much on these pharmaceutical solutions," she said. "But there are other, more natural remedies out there, too."

I'd never considered anything other than a pharmaceutical solution before. I was intrigued. Dr. Violet Sage was quirky, but I kind of liked her. She certainly had the most personality of any mental health practitioner I'd ever met before. I took out my phone and jotted down a list of all the alternative medicines she'd suggested.

Then she asked me a series of questions I wasn't prepared for. "And substance use? How often are you drinking? Anything else you're using?"

I thought about my longtime marijuana habit. Though I didn't smoke as regularly down in Panama, I'd started up again in San Francisco, where acquiring a cannabis prescription was as easy as getting a library card. In fact, I'd ridden my bike to a dispensary a few miles from my mother's house just the other day and returned home with a brand-new vape pen and an array of cartridges. I pictured Coco's drug dealer tooling around Panama City in his Range Rover, hawking baggies of cheap, pure cocaine. I hadn't done coke since I'd come home. Not by choice, more by circumstance. I wasn't seeking it out, but I certainly wouldn't say no if someone offered me some. And then there was my drinking. For months, I drank red wine from a box every night before bed. I'd eased up on that at my mom's house, but again, that was more my environment than anything else.

I decided to cherry-pick a few grains of truth with Dr. Violet Sage. I knew, deep down, that being completely honest would better serve me. But at that point, I also genuinely believed I didn't need to curtail my substance use, and somewhere in my subconscious I was fiercely dedicated to keeping that belief alive. If I told her everything, she might try to convince me to stop. Stopping certainly wasn't an option, not when drugs and alcohol were my only respite from my demons, even if the escape was temporary and the comedown was a struggle. Trying to explain that to my doctor might complicate things. Besides, whatever I said aloud would further solidify whatever I was willing to believe about myself. If Dr. Violet Sage thought it to be the truth, then maybe it was actually true.

"Sometimes I smoke pot . . . medicinally, of course," I said. "And a glass of red wine here and there. Oh, and on special occasions . . . maybe a couple times a year . . . I'll try cocaine."

The doctor nodded and picked up her pink crystal again, rolling it between her fingers. "Alright. Well, none of that sounds particularly problematic to me."

That was not the response I'd anticipated. "Not even the coke?"

Dr. Violet Sage paused and considered my question. Shook her head. "You know, I could lose my license for saying this," she began, and then lowered her voice. "But I think in small doses, there's nothing wrong with it. Look at the history books. Cocaine was regarded quite differently during Freud's time. As long as the indulgence doesn't spiral out of control, you might even think of it as a tool for accessing different parts of yourself."

In my many years of professional psychiatric care, prior to and since meeting Dr. Violet Sage, it's safe to say I've never heard a provider say anything that even slightly resembled what she told me that day. Even though I knew that her response to my substance use represented a radical departure from conventional understandings of intoxicants and mental health, I took it as a full condoning of my behavior. As validation that I didn't have a problem. At least not when it came to drugs and alcohol.

Before I left, Dr. Violet Sage plucked a smooth green stone from one of her piles of crystals and handed it to me. "It's malachite," she said. "Malachite helps to reveal and heal emotional pain. I can tell you're a strong woman. You just need to reacquaint yourself with that inner strength."

I put the malachite in my pocket and thanked her. She wrote out a prescription for Zoloft on a pad and told me to come back and see her in a month so we could evaluate my progress.

The following week, I loaded my big blue backpack into an Uber and crossed the Bay Bridge from Oakland into San Francisco. I lugged the bag up the front steps of the Avalon and into my new bedroom, a small space off the first-floor parlor that only had one window in the closet but made up for it with its own private bathroom. The house was eerily quiet when I arrived. The frilly, turn-of-the-century parlor furniture was vacant, nobody sitting at the piano plunking on keys like usual. I took my shoes off in the foyer and placed them inside a cubby labeled "Carly"—everyone had their own designated footwear receptacle at the front of the house, not unlike something you'd find at a nursery school.

After Devon's offer, I spent a few days thinking about what it might actually be like to live at the Avalon, and the more time that passed, the more attractive the proposition became. Unlike Ico-Inna, it seemed like a pretty thoughtful operation: The house was always sparkling clean, everyone who lived there involved with interesting pursuits. Plus, fifteen people was a lot smaller and more manageable than the eighty or so who lived in the jungle when school was in session. Devon had happily made the Avalon her home for more than four years, and her day-to-day life, albeit unusual, was far from unruly. My decision solidified when her boyfriend, Yusuf, and I met up for coffee on Valencia Street and he immediately launched into strategically approaching my myriad issues as if I were one of the business ideas he was constantly scheming up.

"Look, right now, everything's a little unstable for you," he observed. "No job, nowhere to live, a relationship that may or may not last."

"Thanks for reminding me," I replied with exaggerated sarcasm. The fact that everything was so uncertain had begun to feel mildly amusing when I told my friends about it—the immediacy of real-time conversations distracted me from the anxiety of the unknown.

"All I'm saying is, you have the perfect opportunity to solve one of the three," Yusuf continued. "If you move into the Avalon with us, you've got a floor under your feet and a roof over your head. A solid foundation to hold you while you figure out all your other stuff. Plus, I'm beta testing a new medicinal tea out of the kitchen. Drink that shit every morning and you'll feel like Wonder Woman. I think there's a pretty big opportunity in the turmeric space."

Yusuf's pitch made a lot of sense to me, wacky tea startup and all. I thought about it for a few more days and then told Devon yes, I'd take the room, and I'd pay her back for the rent as soon as I figured out a way to amass some resources. My mother told me she would miss having me around her condo but was pleased my life seemed to be progressing in a positive direction. I kissed her dog Layla goodbye on the way out.

The silence in the Avalon upon my arrival was surprising and made me feel like I had to move gingerly around my new home. I tiptoed through the parlor, past the dining room with its handsome wooden table and fourteen uniform chairs, into the back living room, where blankets were strewn out on a pile of memory foam, which I knew the housemates had dubbed "the fluff." The projector screen was pulled down, and a half-eaten bowl of popcorn sat on one of the coffee tables. Must have been the remnants of a movie night. I'd heard that Eliza and Drue were widely regarded in the community for film screenings. It made sense, given that their perfectly curated aesthetic—from their fashion to their bedroom decor—resembled a Wes Anderson scene.

The extravagant, kaleidoscopic wallpaper kept catching my attention. It was different in every room but just as ornate: long, creeping vines up the walls in the foyer, a vibrant purple floral pattern in the parlor, birds carrying crisscrossing branches in their beaks across the dining room, a border of strutting peacocks below the living room ceiling. It looked like something out of grandma's psychedelic fantasy. Devon told me once that the landlord, a mysterious woman named Sally whom nobody had ever met in person, hired a professional "wallpaper artist" in the mid-1990s when she was still using the Avalon as a single-family home. The wallpaper was sacred: Nobody was allowed to defile it with tape, nails, or pushpins. That stipulation was actually written into the lease.

I wandered into the kitchen for a glass of water and was startled to see Ari in there, chopping asparagus on a big cutting board on the counter, a podcast playing softly in the background. I'd assumed I was home alone. Aside from glimpsing her across the garden party, I hadn't interacted with her since my breakup with Robbie. This was certainly the first time we'd ever been together without anyone else present. And now we were roommates.

"Hey, you!" she said brightly as I entered the room, setting down the knife and reaching her arms wide for a hug. "We're so excited to have you here."

I tried to match her enthusiasm, but the thought of her sleeping with my former boyfriend in our Burning Man tent was still lodged in my brain. "Aw, thanks," I said. "Well, I'm just as excited to be here."

I felt self-conscious talking to Ari. I'd never found out how much she knew about Robbie's and my split or if she still had some kind of a relationship with him. I felt both intimately connected to her and extremely guarded, hyperaware of my every move. Neither of us spoke aloud what was clearly on both of our minds.

"What are you making?" I asked instead. "Devon tells me you're such a good cook."

"Oh, nothing," she replied, waving away the compliment. "Just a little Nicoise salad. I'm going to blanch the asparagus first so it's nice and crispy on the outside. I can make you a plate if you're hungry."

"Sure," I said, even though I still hadn't fully regained my appetite since returning to San Francisco. I grabbed a mason jar from the shelf and filled it with water, sipping it, studying Ari as she chopped, rustled around with some pots, and poured a sizzle of olive oil into a cast-iron pan. She had an ease in the kitchen that made it look like she'd been cooking her whole life. Come to think of it, she had an ease about everything she did. An intrinsic comfort in her skin, comfort moving through the world. Her warm mannerisms seemed to make everyone around her just as comfortable.

Maybe that's why I found her so disarming—because I didn't know what it felt like to be so self-assured.

Ari explained to me that everyone at the Avalon shared groceries and that she was in charge of shopping for food and making sure the kitchen was always fully stocked. A portion of our rent money went to the grocery budget each month, so we could eat as much as we wanted to, anytime. On Mondays, everyone gathered together around the big dining room table to share a meal, a tradition known as "family dinner," but otherwise, eating was a free-for-all. She pointed to a whiteboard attached to the industrial-sized fridge with a list of ingredients on it: nutritional yeast, almond milk, cilantro, bananas. "Anytime you want something, just write it up there," she said. "I'll do my best to have it in the fridge within a day or two."

As someone who ate almost all her meals at restaurants when left to her own devices, I liked this setup. With unlimited access to healthy ingredients that I didn't have to purchase myself, I might be able to change some of my habits. "Are you sure you don't mind buying all that food all the time?" I asked.

Ari shook her head and grinned. "I love it! I love being in the kitchen; I love feeding people."

"We'll be good roommates, then," I said. "I love eating, but I hate buying groceries."

Ari giggled and tossed a handful of chopped asparagus into a pot of boiling water. "I can see why you and Devon are such good friends," she said. "Dev always brags about how she hasn't gone grocery shopping in four years."

I looked around the rest of the kitchen. Spices with handwritten labels on a shelf, an empty sink next to a drying rack full of dishes scrubbed clean, clearly marked garbage cans for trash, recycling, and compost. I could already tell that the Avalon had its shit together in ways Ico-Inna never would. I smiled in Ari's direction, but at nobody in particular, as I watched her perfectly orchestrated salad-making process.

Things got better for a while.

I started to integrate at the Avalon more. Devon and I went back to being inseparable like our first years in San Francisco together. We kicked Yusuf out of their bed to curl up and watch *Project Runway*, and we went out to long meals in the middle of the day like a pair of housewives. I got to know the other residents better, too. Henry taught me how to play chess. I helped Theodora edit her keynote speech for a conference downtown. And Gregoire took me to a party previewing his newest art piece, where I stayed after the reception to schmooze with his biggest investor. "You ask such sharp questions," Gregoire observed in his matter-of-fact way as we headed home together. It felt good to be recognized for something I'd thrived at earlier in my career. Like my inner lights were turning back on, one by one.

I even started to feel more comfortable around Ari. The more time we spent together, the more I could understand why Devon had always liked her. She was so easy to talk to that my self-consciousness began to disintegrate around her. We discovered that, as people who both came of age on the East Coast in the early aughts, we both loved Grateful Dead cover bands and appreciated a healthy dose of cynicism. We made tuna melts together and ate them on the front porch. She even confided in me that the guy she'd recently started dating struggled with depression, and I opened up to her about my own experience.

After we'd lived together for several weeks, I decided to broach the subject of Robbie. As soon as I said his name, we both started giggling. The giggles morphed into full-bodied laughter and we collapsed together onto the kitchen couch. Our shared experience had allowed us to understand each other without reducing it to words.

When Ari finally *did* have some words to share, they weren't particularly complimentary. "Ugh, God. What a fucking asshole."

Her comment made both of us laugh even harder. She wiped tears from her eyes with the sleeve of her sweatshirt.

Once we got to talking, I learned Ari's side of the story. Robbie had pursued her pretty aggressively after I got to Mexico, had turned on his signature charm. He told her I was perfectly okay with our nonmonogamous arrangement and that as a member of our "shared community," she was a safe choice for him to begin a second relationship with.

"After I heard about you guys splitting at Burning Man, we went for a walk around Dolores Park," she said. "I told him I didn't want to see him anymore. He never once mentioned that being in an open relationship was hard for you. I'm so sorry to have played a part in causing you pain."

Hearing her say all that was a kind of closure I didn't even realize I wanted. I'd long since buried Robbie's and my relationship, but something about my time with him had always felt a little unresolved. It was so common for our society to portray the other woman as a devious snake, hell-bent on snatching up your man, while the male in question got away with his behavior unscathed. Toxic female competition was a tired, overused trope.

Addressing everything head-on with Ari freed me from any lingering intimidation of her. She was no longer my adversary. She was my equal. Robbie could be a relic of our shared past, but here she was, right in front of me, part of my present, the possibility of friendship ours for the taking. I reached over and pulled her in for a hug and we sat there on the couch, holding each other and rocking back and forth, until we both started giggling again.

Drue and Eliza invited me into their shared bedroom for a Judd Apatow movie marathon. I sat between them on their couch, amused by the funny asides Drue made after almost every scene. About halfway through *The 40-Year-Old Virgin,* Eliza took a familiar baggie filled with white powder out of the top drawer of her desk and dangled it in front of me.

"Do you indulge?"

I hadn't done cocaine since leaving Panama, and my body felt activated by its familiar sight. I craved the drug immediately just looking at it. Eliza cut lines for the three of us on top of a coffee-table book featuring the art of Roy Lichtenstein.

Pretty soon, nobody was paying attention to the film. We'd erupted into a flurry of protracted sentences and exaggerated hand movements. Eliza began working through a dance sequence from her upcoming show and lifted me off the couch to join her. We thumped around the room as I clumsily tried to emulate her moves, Drue watching from the bed and laughing at us.

"So tell me," Eliza said as she picked me up by the waist and whirled me around. "Are you in love with anyone these days?"

Santiago and I were still regularly in touch, and while I didn't miss much about Ico-Inna, I still missed him, almost achingly so. Our video calls had grown more frequent as I settled into my life at the Avalon and started feeling like my old self, the gregarious woman he first fell for in the Panama City airport. We hadn't overtly discussed our relationship status yet, but I wanted us to work things out. I had a feeling his workaholic, performative tendencies wouldn't be much of an issue when I wasn't dealing with crippling depression and my own self-doubts—when I had the confidence to keep up with him again.

I recounted Santi's and my love story for Drue and Eliza: our first night in that airport hotel, our first kiss by the river. How we'd quickly become enchanted by each other's minds and ideas.

"What a dreamboat," Drue said. "He sounds pretty perfect."

"Well . . . not exactly," I replied. "Santiago's complicated."

"How so?" Eliza asked.

I thought about it. "Well, for one thing, he's always the center of attention," I said. "I get jealous of that. Jealous he's going to outshine me in some way."

Drue studied my face for a moment. "Well . . . no offense, but that sounds like a 'you' problem."

You're right, I thought. *It is most definitely a "me" problem.*

After that night, I channeled all my effort into trying to win Santiago back. I brought my laptop over to my favorite coffee shop in the Lower Haight and wrote him long letters, crafting my wisest-sounding prose, pontificating about the state of San Francisco compared to Latin America and drumming up entertaining observations of life in the "well-oiled commune," a term I'd begun to use that tickled the other Avalon residents. If anything reminded Santiago of how much he admired me, it was my writing. I tried to give him his space, to not interrogate him about what was going on down at Ico-Inna, to not act possessive during our limited phone conversations or paranoid when I hadn't heard from him for a while.

It worked. A couple weeks into my time at the Avalon, an email arrived from Santiago declaring that he wanted to double down on investing in our relationship. "I love seeing you thrive from afar," he wrote. "I'm advocating for the two of us. I'm advocating for you. I love you."

I love you. Those three simple words kept me moving forward, motivated me to design a new life for myself buoyed by the comfort and assurance of knowing I wasn't going at it alone. With Santiago's security cradling me, I applied for an editorial job at one of the biggest tech companies in the Bay Area, a global Goliath rife with inflated salaries and colorful perks. If I was going to get back into the working world, I reasoned, I may as well go for the place that has the best health benefits. Then maybe I'd be able to address my depression once and for all without going broke in the process. I landed an interview almost immediately.

Life moved on without me at Ico-Inna, too. Santiago hired one of our Panama City friends, an expat from Florida who ran her own digital marketing firm, to take over my media program. She happily stepped into my role, and I sent her over a detailed curriculum and reading list so she'd be able to pick up right where I left off. Max and her team kept filming, and chaos kept ensuing: Santiago steered the staff through an organized student revolt, a food shortage, and the endless onslaught of rainstorms. Coco maintained his status as the egomaniacal overlord, making appearances in the jungle only when he felt like bossing people around and otherwise reigning over his kingdom from the comfort of his apartment. I never heard from him again after I left.

Ari and Devon had jobs that afforded them the luxury of going to a midday yoga class with me, both in part thanks to Henry and Theodora. Theodora had dreams of building some sort of "Avalon 2.0" in the woods, an even bigger communal situation where people could live together in nature. She'd appointed Devon chief executive of the project and paid her a solid living wage from Henry's bank account, so Devon no longer needed to find work as a freelance graphic designer. Avalon 2.0 was still in the research phase, so Devon spent most of her time on the phone with various real estate agents and housing lawyers, learning vocabulary words like *subdivision* and *easement* and sifting through plots of land on the market for the types of astonishing prices that contributed to the Bay Area's reviled reputation.

Ari, for her part, had recently left a job in the marketing department of Henry's startup. I still couldn't figure out exactly what the company did. (Their tagline: "We make space for your data to free up space in your consciousness.") Working under Theodora on the marketing team, Ari had made a bevy of contacts in the local design world and was in the process of launching a boutique branding agency with another former colleague. So Devon and Ari spent their days working flexible hours out of the Avalon's living room or their own bedrooms, and I benefited from their unorthodox schedules as I looked for ways to fill my time in the many hours between bouts of job searching.

We wandered down Valencia Street with yoga mats slung in bags over our shoulders. The city had changed since I last lived here. Compared to Latin America or even Brooklyn, San Francisco in late 2016 felt like residing in the future. Everything was all clean lines and sepia tones and one-tap credit card scanners attached to iPhones. A friend of Gregoire's was opening up a burger joint in the financial district completely run by robots. Not only were the trash and recycling collected reliably and regularly, but the county also boasted a fully functioning municipal composting operation. And everything was *so* expensive: You paid $8 for a piece of toast lathered with farm-fresh jam, or $80 for a straight-razor shave and a can of artisanal IPA, or $800 for a sleek fixed-gear bicycle. ("What's next, an $8,000 gourmet meal plan for your dog?" I joked in one of my emails to Santiago.)

Contrasting sharply to all the shiny tech excess was an acute humanitarian crisis playing out on the streets. Though I'd encountered some of the most sobering poverty I'd ever seen during my time in Latin America, homelessness in the region was virtually nonexistent. People looked out for each other; families and friends stuck together, even if it meant a dozen people living in a couple concrete rooms. But the American Dream was built on the premise of fierce independence, and nowhere did that "every man for himself" reality feel more poignant than on the streets of San Francisco.

During my daily three-block walk to the coffee shop, I passed by several unhoused people huddled under shabby blankets or draped over stoops. Individuals in the middle of drug-induced psychotic episodes wobbled down the sidewalk screaming to themselves, sometimes phrases so menacing that I had to cross the street fearing my safety. On the BART train one day, I switched cars when a seemingly innocuous man in stained cargo shorts began shouting violent obscenities. You couldn't leave so much as a box of Kleenex in your car without risking having the windows smashed.

Living in a comfortable home with nice people as I witnessed human suffering on a daily basis spun up a confusing combination of emotions: sadness, gratitude, guilt, responsibility. At both Ico-Inna, where our jungle bubble existed in one of the most remote areas of Panama, and the Avalon, where fifteen people cohabitated in defiance of San Francisco's housing shortage, we constantly engaged in dialogues about how to improve the lives of our neighbors, how to mitigate the problems on our doorsteps. How to "own our privilege," as Coco sanctimoniously put it.

But this all struck me as more of the same "make the world a better place" doctrine that I'd always been turned off by. Did our abundance of resources give us a right to decide how society should function? Or conversely, did our relative wealth make us responsible for fixing the corrupt systems that we'd inherited?

So far, all I'd encountered in both of these spaces were enthusiastic debates and creative brainstorming sessions. Nobody seemed moved toward meaningful action beyond the sounds of their own voices. And those voices were loud with righteous indignation at dinner tables and on Facebook pages. Could it be that we were just so paralyzed by the size of the issues that small, everyday actions were no longer worthwhile? That we had to rewrite the laws of civilization on a plot of land in the jungle or within the four walls of a San Francisco mansion in order to make any sort of tangible difference?

That afternoon, on Valencia Street, every block seemed to exemplify San Francisco's heartbreaking dichotomy. Ari and Devon and I were in the middle of a heated discussion about the availability of local social services, and how so many nonprofits competed for resources rather than coordinating their efforts. A despondent-looking man loitered in the doorway of a $15 smoothie place, and a pile of discarded syringes littered the ground beneath a high-tech trash can decked out with a separate compartment for recyclables.

"Do you guys ever feel bad about all this?" I asked, gesturing to our surroundings. We paused on the corner of Seventeenth Street.

Devon sighed. "Of course," she said. "I think about how horrified I was when I first got here and how numb I am to all of it now. It's crazy how we just accept it as normal."

"I don't understand how a place with this much wealth can't figure it out," Ari added. "Like, I get that it's a really complicated problem. But is it more complicated than all the other stuff coming out of Silicon Valley?"

I thought about the fortune Henry had amassed inventing some sort of nebulous digital storage solution and the pledge he'd recently signed to donate the majority of his wealth to philanthropic causes. Even figuring out which organizations to allocate what funds to was a full-time job, and he'd hired a small team of financial advisors to help.

Some of that money would likely trickle its way down to social-impact programs like the one I worked on in Mexico. I pictured Dominika's simple home, her magnanimous personality, her ease living in harmony with her own land. Dominika and I had stayed in touch since I left Mexico—despite her community's dearth of most modern amenities, she and all her neighbors had Facebook accounts that they updated regularly with pictures of their families, their harvests, their church services—and she often left little affirmations underneath my own posts: "que hermosa, Carly," or "muchas bendiciones" (how beautiful, many blessings).

Getting to know people like her, learning from them rather than prescribing solutions they didn't ask for, felt better to me than throwing money at issues we couldn't fully understand. In Dominika's hometown, though, nobody struggled like the people we walked by daily in San Francisco.

chapter eleven

Seeing Santiago for the first time since leaving Panama, folding my body into his after he cleared customs at SFO, was a sweet release. He'd be staying with me in my tiny bedroom at the Avalon for the entire first two weeks of December. I paraded him around the house, showing him off to the other residents like a gold medal.

Our first few days back together were almost as heated and energetic as our earliest moments at Ico-Inna's New Year's party. It was hard to believe we'd only met eleven months prior; a lifetime had unfolded in between. I brought him with me to social events around town: movie screenings at our friend's art warehouse and live music at the piano bar on Market Street. He practiced new comedy material on me and I threw my head back and laughed, grabbing his hand and dragging him into the kitchen so he could perform for my roommates. Ari chopped onions as he told jokes, and I stood behind him, gleaming like an overbearing parent whose child had gotten the lead in the middle school musical. I was so excited to introduce him to my new, vibrant life in San Francisco, to demonstrate my resilience and prove I'd gotten well.

Things weren't so rosy down in the jungle, he told me. Filming for Max's show had finally come to an end, but not without causing a few scars. The cameras caught the entire "student revolt" that had given him such a big headache earlier in the semester, and he was worried about how that might be framed on TV, about what its portrayal might do to Ico-Inna's reputation. Santiago had also overheard Coco give a few on-camera interviews and didn't like how he came across. "He knows how to play a pompous ass to a T," he said. "He didn't even try to memorize the talking points I outlined for him."

I raised an eyebrow. "And that surprises you why, exactly?"

He shook his head. "I just really believe in the spirit of Ico-Inna," he said. "Coco or no Coco, it doesn't matter. The idea is good. The intentions of the staff, of all of us. I want to transform education. I really think we can do it. But not if Max somehow screws us over."

I didn't reply that beyond transforming education, I knew he wanted to use Ico-Inna as a springboard to whatever successful public-facing career would come next. Nor did I reply that he should have known the reality show was a huge risk from the start, but he was too distracted by the big-name network and shiny lights. Instead, I wrapped my arms around him and leaned my head on his chest. Listened to his heartbeat. "I know you have good intentions," I murmured as he kissed the top of my head. "I believe in you, too, I really do." But did I actually? Or did I just believe that without him, I'd be cast off and lonely, in danger of falling into another deep depression?

One thing was clear: During those first few days of Santiago's visit, my depression was far at bay. I'd had a decent couple months living at the Avalon, making new friends, mapping out a stable future. I was on a steady diet of Zoloft, and it may have started working. It's so hard to tell with antidepressants. You evaluate the state of your mind with that same fucked-up mind that created all your issues in the first place. But I *was* capable of noticing how quiet my inner critic had gotten. She was still there—I didn't know an existence in which she didn't play some sort of role in my life—but it felt like I had power over her, versus the other way around. When my depression got really bad, the strength she wielded over me was impossible to overcome. Yet here I was, living out my days feeling some semblance of happy, and the presence of my cherished boyfriend only served to reinforce that.

Santiago even encouraged me to lead a writing workshop at the Avalon while he was visiting. "You're such a good teacher and mentor," he coaxed. "And the Avalon is so dynamic and vibrant. You should share your gifts with your housemates."

And so one evening, I gathered a couple dozen people in our living room. I made vegan stuffed mushrooms, a new recipe I'd discovered while perusing the aisles of a nearby organic food co-op with Ari. I passed around the warm mushroom caps and filled empty mason jars with red wine. I doled out my best writing tips ("tell the stories you know," "nouns over adjectives," "lean into specific details") and led the group through a twenty-minute free-writing exercise. Afterward, everyone shared what they'd come up with aloud.

I'd facilitated a similar exercise for my students under a gazebo on a rainy afternoon in the jungle, but I'd been feeling sick with despair that day. It was nice to have a do-over within the comfort of a warm new home I'd grown attached to. Sitting in front of my friends with my notebook open, offering feedback and praise for their writing efforts, I felt like a productive member of society with a useful talent to contribute.

But mostly, I felt like I'd made Santiago proud. I watched him as he slept soundly in my bed that evening, journaling my thoughts beside him like I'd done during those nights I felt stable and healthy in our Panama City apartment. "If everything I did today was only for you," I wrote, "then it will have been worth it." I kissed his forehead and nuzzled my body into his, drifting off into a satisfied sleep.

Within a few days of his arrival, Santiago threw himself right back into that same hyperproductive mode that made me feel so alienated the past summer. I wanted us to experience the magic of San Francisco together—I secretly hoped he'd fall in love with the city and decide to move here. I had big ideas that I'd bring him around to amateur comedy clubs, to prove to him that he might be able to get his own career some traction by my side. I wanted to take him to museums and parks, on a bike ride across the Golden Gate Bridge. Henry had given me a few tabs of what he described as "mind-blowing LSD," and I thought it would be fun for me and Santiago to take it together and go off on some sort of adventure.

Santiago made it clear that we weren't, however, on any sort of romantic vacation. How could I possibly have thought otherwise? At this point, I knew full well who he was, how he preferred to move through the world. Yet I kept fighting to bring out a version of him who didn't exist.

"Let's go hike to the top of Twin Peaks," I said one morning, holding out the tabs of acid in a ziplock bag and dangling them in his direction. "The view is absolutely epic."

Santiago, who had just stepped out of the shower, rubbed a towel over his wet hair. "Sweetie, I really want to work on my application to Hendrick's network. I told you that."

In addition to organizing events in fancy destinations, Hendrick curated an exclusive, year-round community of alums from the conference we'd attended in the jungle. It wasn't enough to have been to one of the summits; you then had to formally apply (with a hefty application fee, no less) to be invited into Hendrick's invite-only Facebook group and WhatsApp channel. Official members of the network got first access to buy the expensive tickets to future events, along with invitations to gatherings of other members in various cities throughout the year. I couldn't imagine that anyone who applied *wasn't* accepted, but Santiago seemed to be taking the process very seriously. Yesterday, he'd made me film him on the Avalon roof talking about his "one big vision for making the world a better place."

"How hard could that application possibly be?" I said now, rolling my eyes. "Get it done, and then we'll go to Twin Peaks."

Santiago sighed. "I've also got some emails to write. And a standup routine to work on. And I wanna get a head start on the itinerary for next week's retreat." Now that the semester was over, Santiago and Coco planned to gather the Ico-Inna staff for a postmortem of sorts in the jungle. Santiago supposedly wanted everyone to take a detailed, organized look at how they might learn from this semester's mistakes and shortcomings, while Coco wanted everyone to bond by playing drinking games. Hearing things like this made me grateful I was no longer there.

"Do you have to do that all *today*?" I whined. I pressed my body against his from behind and tousled his wet hair. "I was hoping we could spend some time together."

Santiago gently removed my hand from his head. "Yes, I need to get it done today. Wasn't there a fun coworking space you were telling me about? Doesn't that sound fun?"

Thinking about Santiago working all day made my heart pound faster. My body was seized by the feeling of needing him to pay attention to me. "No, that doesn't sound *fun*," I protested, imitating his hollow double use of the word *fun*. "What sounds *fun* is getting some quality time with my boyfriend in beautiful nature. Henry says this acid is life-changing."

Santiago shook his head. "I'm sorry, sweetie. Today I'm going to work."

"Fine," I scoffed, anger rising inside me. "Squander one of our last days together sitting at a desk with your computer. You're really going to *make the world a better place* by joining that exclusive Facebook group." I was ranting, but I couldn't stop myself. "Fight oppression! Fight for your people!"

Santiago's face fell. He was quiet for a minute. "That was really mean," he finally said, quietly, his lower lip trembling. "You know how much I care about fighting for my people." He gathered his clothes and marched toward my tiny bathroom, slamming the door behind him.

And that's how I ended up spending the next three consecutive days in a coworking space by the Ferry Building, watching Santiago work, scrolling the internet, and making up things to do. I could have passed the time applying for jobs, but I had just advanced to the fourth round of the interview process at the big tech company, and things were looking good for me there. I wanted to go to yoga with Devon and Ari, or hang out chatting with my roommates in the Avalon's kitchen. But mostly, I wanted to be with Santiago—to savor our limited time together, even if it meant doing whatever he wanted to do. So I opened my laptop and pretended to keep myself busy, counting down the minutes until he was finished for the day.

I drummed up the courage to approach Santiago about his future plans on his last day in San Francisco. He was scrambling around my bedroom, gathering the T-shirts and boxer briefs strewn around and shoving them into his suitcase. I was due to walk him to the Twenty-Fourth Street BART station so he could catch a train to the airport in an hour.

"So . . . Santi," I began. "Did you have fun this week?"

He paused with a pair of underwear dangling from his hand and pecked me on the lips. "Of course, sweetie," he said. "I love being with you. Love to see the life you've created."

"What do you think of San Francisco?"

He shrugged. "Seems like a cool city. You've got a big community here at the Avalon."

"Could you . . . do you . . . what about for you?" I couldn't find the right words to tell him I wanted him here with me. I nervously awaited his reply.

He shrugged again. "I don't know. I need to get through next semester first. But you know how much I've been thinking about Los Angeles." Did I? He'd never mentioned LA before, but of course it made sense for him. I wasn't sure how much patience I had left for a long-distance relationship.

"I didn't know that," I said flatly.

"Oh, well . . . yeah. I figured I'd do one more semester at Ico-Inna, see what kind of positive impact I could have down there, and then head back to the States. Check out the comedy scene in LA. My friend Bear, from college? Him and I were talking about getting a place together, maybe in Venice? Or I heard Echo Park is pretty cool."

I glared at him. "*He* and I," I said. "Not *him* and I."

Santiago zipped his suitcase. "Sweetie, are you upset at me about something?"

I fought back tears and tried to keep a straight face. I was never going to win him over by being a brat. "No . . . no," I began, trying to keep my voice measured. "I guess I just, maybe, wanted to start thinking about what it could look like to build a life together. You know, come home to each other at the end of the day. Make dinner. Curl up with a movie, maybe get a dog. Didn't you like being here at the Avalon? Wasn't it exciting? Aren't my friends well-connected? Maybe they could help you get where you want to go."

He sighed and pulled his suitcase upright, moving the wheels back and forth as he passed the handle from hand to hand. "I mean . . ." he started. "I think I never thought about that option. I mean, it sounds fine, but . . ."

Tears continued to prick through the corners of my eyes, but I did my best to stop them from coming. Swallowed and blinked. He couldn't see me cry; he'd been through enough of that this summer, and I'd managed to prove I was an independent, ambitious woman after all. "So," I said instead, trying to keep my voice from cracking. "How would I fit into all of this?"

He pulled me in for a hug and kissed the top of my head. "I'm not sure," he admitted. "I guess I always assumed we'd be one of those cool California couples. I'm in LA, you're in San Fran, and, you know, we jet back and forth to see each other on the weekends. The flight's not that far."

"Don't call it San Fran," I said into his chest, muffling my words so he wouldn't hear them trembling.

He sighed again. "Sweetie . . ." he started, then paused. Took a deep breath. "Look, your life here at the Avalon? It's *good*. It's what you've always wanted for yourself. You get to have fun with your friends, the social scene is exciting. You've got a great résumé, much better than mine, and you're about to land a job at one of the biggest companies in the world. I just know it; I know you're gonna get that job. It's a job so many people would want. That's why I'm so impressed by you."

I shrugged. I was sick of hearing him say how allegedly impressive I was. None of that mattered to me. I continued talking into his T-shirt, my tears starting to form a wet mark. "I don't even care about that job if I don't have my boyfriend with me."

He ran his fingers through my hair and I relaxed into his touch. "Our lives, sweetie," he said. "They just look a little different. I don't want to watch movies at night or get a dog. I want to chase my dreams. In LA, I'd go out to open mics five, maybe six nights a week. I gotta hustle right now. And travel. Max says she can maybe hook me up with a guy who reps young comedians, someone she knows from the network. If I can link with him, I wanna fly around the country for gigs; I don't care if they're in small towns or big cities or what. I just need to get my name out there. So . . . yeah."

He paused and took a deep breath. "I guess I hadn't really put it to words yet, but yeah. That's the kind of life I want once I'm done down in Panama. Comedy nights, gigs, whatever I can get. And then we'd see each other on weekends; you could come out to wherever my shows were, or I could come up and visit you here, plug into the Avalon for a couple days. We'd be independent, we'd be working on ourselves, on our dreams. But we'd be there for each other. We'd always be there for each other. We'd talk all the time, and when we got together, we'd . . . we'd be unstoppable." He kissed the top of my head again and squeezed me tighter. "That's what I've always loved about you: your independence. Your fierce independence. That's the kind of woman I need to lift me up."

At this point, I was shaking. I couldn't help myself. His little speech, his fantasy plan for his future, sounded nothing like what I wanted. My subconscious already knew that it would never work. But I also knew I couldn't lose him. Not now. Not when I was finally starting to feel better.

I hugged him tighter and sniffled, no longer trying to stop myself from crying. He stroked my back. "We can do this, my love," he said. "You and me. You don't need me here with you. You've got everything else you need. I'm just a phone call away, and with you always in spirit."

I pulled away, close to sobbing. "I just miss you so much when you're gone!" I said. "I love you; I want you near me. Is that too much to ask?"

He squeezed my shoulder and sighed again. "Maybe . . . for right now."

My chest felt tight as I walked him to the BART station, my footsteps Frankensteinian. Dread stirred in my limbs. I was terrified my depression would return, but it felt inevitable.

"Hey, I love you," Santiago said as his train pulled up to the platform. "We can do this. I know we can."

I managed to nod. And yet, when he stepped onto the train and the doors shut between us, as he blew a kiss through the grimy window, as the BART carried him away from me and off to his different life, I knew, deep down, that I had already lost him.

No amount of self-control could suppress my tears after that. Monsoons poured from my eyes like the jungle in the rainy season. I cried in bed alone, in the shower, on the roof staring down at the city. I cried on the way to yoga and in Devon's room to a patient audience. I grew increasingly sluggish, increasingly numb, but couldn't stop crying even as my feelings subdued.

Christmas came, and I relocated to my mother's house and cried some more. I sobbed on her couch as I opened presents, wailed as we ate Chinese takeout together. When I wasn't crying, I curled up like a snail shell on her couch, my face buried into her throw pillow, Layla donut-shaped on my shoulder. Dogs always seem to know when something's wrong. Something was very wrong.

Santiago and I continued to communicate, and to him, I pretended everything was normal. I sent him heart emojis and responded to his questions of "How was your day, sweetie?" with positive, albeit very brief, overtures. I pretended I was busy when he tried to call, made up extravagant social events that I couldn't miss even though my only socializing for days had been letting my loved ones watch, helplessly, as I reveled in my anguish. At a certain point, I didn't even know why I was crying so much. I just knew I felt useless, that the future seemed untenable, that I was all alone and even so much as brushing my teeth or taking the dog around the block to pee felt like summiting Kilimanjaro. It didn't even occur to me to think about trying a new antidepressant; my tears distracted me from pursuing any possible solutions.

Somewhere in that blurry stretch of time, the big tech company offered me a job on their editorial team. I managed to pull myself together long enough to accept a verbal offer and sign some paperwork and push my start date out as far as they would let me. I posted the news on Facebook ("Time for a 'big-girl job' once again!") and sat idly by, blank-faced, as hundreds of likes poured in from acquaintances around the world, a long tail of shallow congratulatory missives below my status update. The praise felt as hollow as my own body splayed out on the couch, as empty as my heart. I couldn't feel anything except the wetness on my cheeks, which still wouldn't stop, even as I was devoid of absolutely everything else.

The day after Christmas, my mother approached me on the couch, holding an old pair of my beat-up sneakers. She thrust them in my direction. "Put these on," she said. I didn't move. "*Now,*" she added, for emphasis.

"Mom . . ." I groaned and rolled over, sticking my face in the crack between the pillow and the couch cushion.

"This behavior stops today. No more wallowing. We're going for a walk. The fresh air will be good for you."

I groaned again and pulled myself up to a seated position. Moving even a few inches took all my strength. I heaved an enormous sigh and put my fingers on my temples. I'd been in the same position for so long that any sort of abrupt change made me dizzy.

Mom watched me as I put one shoe on, then the other, as if I were submerged in a giant jar of honey. She held out her hand and helped me off the couch. My mother had always been good at tough love, a testament to her Waspy East Coast upbringing. What she lacked in touchy-feelies, she made up for in lead-by-example motivation.

We walked a few blocks down to Lake Merritt, the large body of water smack in the middle of Downtown Oakland. When Devon and I first became friends, we'd both been working in offices on the Oakland waterfront—I at the campaign headquarters of the leading candidate for California governor, she at a rapidly expanding solar-energy startup. After work, we'd walk around the lake and talk about music and climate change and Latin American politics, and I'd smoke a joint while she watched, never tempted for some. Our friendship solidified that summer, and we'd been inseparable ever since. I couldn't help but smile at the memory as I trudged along behind my mother holding Layla's leash. It was the first time I'd smiled, really smiled, since Santiago left.

After my despondent time in the jungle, I didn't believe what experts said about nature and movement being good antidotes to depression. But a half hour of chatting with my mother as we speed-walked around the lake, beneath fairy lights strung across the trees, watching the ducks as they skimmed the water's surface, looking so chilled out and peaceful . . . led me to not feel so terrible anymore. I had a stable new job on the horizon at a company most people would sell an organ on the black market to get into. A warm house full of new and old friends. A mother who watched out for me, a cute dog to snuggle with. By the time we made it back to her condo, all those tears felt like someone else's story. I was ready to pick myself up, dust myself off, and head back to the Avalon. I packed up my backpack and made my way home.

chapter twelve

To describe my change in mood like something as abrupt as flicking on a light switch might be disingenuous. It was more like one of those dimmers where you can control the speed at which a room illuminates. By the time I was lying on the Avalon's fluff pile that evening, deep in a conversation with Henry about how the construction of cities mimics the behavior of leaf-cutter ants, the dimming switch had been elevated to its brightest setting—a slow, steady awakening of my senses over the course of the afternoon, from my invigorating walk around the lake with Mom to my meditative train ride back into San Francisco to my bustling dinner with housemates. That night at the Avalon, the depression was just: gone. Poof. Not a trace of it weighing down my mind or body. Replaced, instead, by that creeping invincibility that had overtaken me when I first arrived in Panama.

Coming in and out of depression sort of feels like what I imagine it's like to experience multiple personalities. When you're in the midst of a depressive episode, it's impossible to empathize with that other side of you, the side that isn't always suffering, that doesn't want to crawl into a hole and wallow in misery. When you're out of one, on the other side, all of that depression seems like nothing but a story you told yourself about someone else. You know, intellectually, that you felt that way. You can remember moving through the actions of someone who might have felt that way. But you can't remember the force of the feelings themselves. The crippling sensations of hopelessness. You can't imagine that those feelings might ever return, because you're better, and all that betterness drowns out everything bad that came before.

I was so relieved to be freed from the grips of my own mind that I could have grown wings and flapped my way up to the ceiling along with all the decorative birds on the Avalon's wallpaper. I spent that night composing a long email to Santiago, replenished with new versions of old thoughts about all my hopes and dreams. My big tech job represented the next phase of a continually interesting life. "Our stories don't always unfold as we plan them, but they still unfold, and we can adapt to the plot changes along the way and shine even more brightly than we'd imagined," I wrote to him, pleased by my wisdom.

Giddy with these revelations, I couldn't sleep. I wrapped myself in a blanket and crept up to the Avalon's roof, watching my beautiful city shimmer below. I gazed at the skyline for what felt like hours, my mind racing like the twinkling lights, until the first traces of sunlight peeked over Potrero Hill. Still not even the slightest bit tired, I headed back downstairs to brew myself a cup of tea and roll a joint. As I puttered around the kitchen, my roommate Gregoire appeared in the doorway wearing a pair of neon patterned leggings.

"I've never seen you up this early," he mused.

"Good morning," I replied, smiling wide. "I guess I just had an unexpected surge of energy."

"Feel like channeling that into a vinyasa class?" he said. "My favorite guy teaches at Buddha's Revenge over in the Castro at six thirty. I'm headed that way now."

I never exercised early in the day—was never even *awake* at this hour unless I was coming off a long night of partying—but suddenly, a yoga class sounded delicious. "Let me just change real fast!" I said, trotting over to my bedroom and yanking on a pair of workout pants. The neighborhood stirred to life through various phases of dawn as we crossed Dolores Park. I was delighted. Maybe I could get used to a daily morning-yoga routine. I could be anything I wanted to be!

I wasn't yet sleepy when class was over, so I made a French press pot of coffee and knocked loudly on Devon and Yusuf's door. "Go away," I heard Yusuf mumble from their bed. I entered anyway.

"Rise and shine!" I said brightly, bounding over to the bed with the French press in one hand and a pair of mugs in the other. "I made coffee. I want to talk to you guys about this crazy conversation Henry and I had last night. Did you know that ants elect their own president?"

Devon squinted up at me. "The fuck are you doing up?" she said hoarsely, checking the time on her phone. "You're never awake at this hour." She flung her head back onto her pillow. "And neither are we."

I pursed my lips into an exaggerated pout. "I'm bored; hang out with me."

"Do it somewhere else, if you're going to," Yusuf groaned.

Devon slowly put one foot on the floor and then the other. "This better be good," she said. "Something about insects? I don't even know what you're talking about."

Hearing her say that, and recognizing the absurdity of my entrance into their bedroom, made me laugh hysterically. "You know what," I said as I caught my breath. "Neither do I. But at least I have coffee!"

The activation energy continued to simmer inside of me as Devon and I drank our coffee in the yard. It persisted as I helped Ari make a big pot of soup for lunch. I was still wide-awake after we ate, and napping felt like a lost cause, so I decided to take a bike ride to burn through some of my excess fuel. My mind raced, a dizzying array of thoughts and ideas rattling around about how I might become a visionary tech thought leader in my new job, about Santiago's and my promising future, as I mounted my bike and cruised toward Golden Gate Park. I wound my way through the city, down my favorite path on JFK Drive, until I hit the ocean. I locked my bike and tore off my shoes and ran barefoot onto the beach, hopping around and luxuriating in the sensations, the textures of chilly sand and wind at my ankles.

A book! What if I wrote a book? I had so many stories to tell about my time in the jungle. Maybe I could tell an even better tale than Max and her reality-show team! What if I penned a bestseller? I could use my platform to have an earnest conversation about mental health, to destigmatize a subject that caused so many people shame. I flung open my backpack and pulled out my journal. Sat cross-legged on the sand and scribbled pages and pages of ideas until my hand hurt and my pen was almost out of ink. I wrote out a full marketing plan, a book jacket summary, and the first few pages of chapter one before pausing to catch my breath. I was utterly exhilarated, shimmers radiating from me in all directions, my mind dancing and my skin tingling. I biked home, triumphant, fantasizing about the speech I'd give on *The Today Show* once my memoir topped the *New York Times* bestseller list.

And I still couldn't sleep. I didn't sleep through takeout and a movie in the living room. That night, I lay in bed in my little room and stared at the ceiling, forcing myself to count my breaths. I may have dozed off for an hour or two, but I woke up bright-eyed and ready to conquer another day before the sun came up. So I snuck out into the parlor with my notebook and pen and kept writing where I left off. By the time the birds were tweeting, I had finished an entire chapter.

Two days later, when I still hadn't managed to have a full night's sleep, I finally realized that something was wrong. I felt better than I had in my entire life, like I'd taken the purest dose of MDMA and it had lasted, steadily, with no consequences or comedown, for seventy-two straight hours. I was buzzing and erratic and fully cracked out. It was thrilling; I was hyper and everything was hysterically funny and I never wanted the feelings to end. But I also knew, intellectually, that life didn't work this way. That this wasn't what a default human experience was supposed to feel like.

I left a message for Dr. Violet Sage. It was two days before New Year's Eve, and I knew I wouldn't reach her. "It's an emergency," I pleaded on her voicemail. "I haven't slept in three days. I can't turn my mind off and I'm scared. I don't know what's going on."

In the meantime, all of the Avalon was headed to a ranch near Sequoia National Park for a New Year's weekend extravaganza. The event would be rife with psychedelics, dance parties, delicious food, board games, and hot tub sessions. I didn't know what else to do, so I threw some clothes into a garbage bag. Walked down to the smoke shop and purchased a box full of nitrous oxide cartridges and a whipped-cream dispenser. Then I hopped in Devon and Yusuf's car and let them drive me to whatever magical dreamland was about to unfold, still amped-up and chattering away. Even though I knew something was wrong, I decided to bury my anxiety and just enjoy myself. After all, I still felt great. Who knew how long it would last, or what would come next?

The weekend party swirled around me, a colorful singsong of friends and revelry, but I just wanted to write. Still awake, I holed up on the bottom bunk of my shared cabin, inhaling nitrous and scrawling in my journal. The nitrous slowed my thoughts and calmed me down and zapped me, temporarily, out of my frenzied brain. I finished a box of cartridges in one sitting as I penned a long love letter to Santiago about our bizarre and emotional twelve months together. Exactly one year ago, we'd met in the jungle. Now, we were in very different places, but I still felt as close to him as ever. I took a photo of the letter and texted it to him. He was down at Ico-Inna, helping Coco get everything ready for the annual New Year's event. I was jealous I couldn't be there with them but didn't want to return to the scene of my mental breakdown so soon.

Midnight on the final day of 2016 came and went in a slew of bonfires and thumping electronic music, and I joined the other Avalon residents on the dance floor, our arms intertwined, moving as one giant, amorphous, fifteen-headed creature. I sank into their embrace. As we counted down from ten, I put in a video call to Santiago, but of course, he didn't answer. I let the call ring and ring, and as we reached the end of our countdown, everyone cheering and hugging and jumping up and down around me, I kissed my phone. Let my lips linger on the screen, sending pulses of energy down to wherever he was, hoping that whatever he was doing, he was thinking about me, too.

I finally fell asleep in the car on the way home from the New Year's party—one of those deep, unconscious, death-hole sleeps where you're too knocked out to even remember your dreams—and didn't wake up until Devon pulled into the Avalon's driveway. Groggy, I climbed out of the car and skulked through the foyer and into my little bedroom. Climbed into bed and pulled the covers all the way up over my scalp and curled up and passed out. I stayed that way, in one round, immobile position, for fourteen hours.

I finally woke up, feeling like shit, the next day. I hauled myself off my mattress and dragged my lumbering body into the kitchen. Moving even fifty feet took all my energy, and when I got to the big kitchen couch, I collapsed and hugged my knees to my chest. The morning unfolded in a daze, various housemates coming in and out, making eggs, brewing coffee, chatting over their chia smoothies. I stared into space, seeing them and not seeing them at the same time, transfixed on nothing. It was like zoning out in front of a movie version of my life without the sound on. Eventually, I picked myself up off the couch and shuffled back to my room and tumbled back onto the bed. When I opened my eyes again, it was dark out.

My mood soon followed the behavior of my body. I didn't understand how I could have been so excited about my life mere days before. I was too exhausted to ever care about anything again and was utterly alone in my exhaustion. Sleep was the only thing that allowed me to forget how lonely I truly was.

In the midst of my haze, after an arduous game of phone tag, I was finally able to reach Dr. Violet Sage.

"Happiest of New Years to you!" she said in a singsongy voice when I picked up, as if she were calling her great-aunt and not a mentally ill patient in crisis.

"Um. Thanks," I managed. "So . . . things aren't going super well?"

"Tell me more," she said, and at the invitation to explain what had been going on, I let it all spill: the sleepless nights, the frenzied brainstorming sessions, the feelings of invincibility. The paralyzing crash that had kept me in bed for the past several days.

She was silent for a few moments, but I could hear her breathing. "Well?" I prompted. "Do you have any idea what might be wrong with me?"

She exhaled very slowly. "You know, Carly," she began. "To me, this sounds like a classic manic episode. Now, mania can feel absolutely exquisite. It can be used as a tool for unlocking all sorts of inner genius. But it also has dire consequences on the other side—manic episodes are inevitably followed by depressive ones. Has anyone ever suggested you might be bipolar?"

Bipolar? I'd known all my adult life that I had a crippling brand of depression, but I'd never considered myself to be bipolar. I didn't know much about the condition. Sometimes you were up, sometimes you were down. I'd always just assumed my bouts of energy and excitement were because, in spite of my problematic inner critic, I could also be smart and motivated. "You are an idea machine," my supervisor at the media company once told me. That it might be linked to some sort of mental illness was a whole new paradigm for me to think through.

". . . many of us associate a bipolar diagnosis with bouts of behavior that might be considered acute psychosis," Dr. Violet Sage was saying. "But *hypo*mania . . . a more subdued form of mania that can masquerade as energetic feelings in our everyday lives . . . that's a more common symptom of what we call *bipolar two*. It might not feel like an urgent condition, or perhaps less of an emergency than an all-encompassing, destabilizing manic episode. However, the depressive effects in the aftermath are often just as bad."

I listened to her without listening. My mind replayed all those nights in Panama scribbling in my journals, the soaring freedom I felt when I was first building my program, the strength that had brought me to a 6:00 a.m. yoga class the other day. Was that all part of a medical condition? Something that felt good but had, as Dr. Violet Sage described, "dire consequences"? Were my only moments of happiness now forbidden? I let the realization that something might be horribly, horribly wrong—something I'd never even considered before—wash over me. I wanted to go back to sleep. But I also felt a glimmer of relief. If I was able to name the problem, then perhaps I was one step closer to fixing it.

"Okay . . ." I replied to the doctor. "Alright, okay. Let me try to make sense of this. Can you see me soon and we can talk about how we might begin to attack this? Maybe try me out on some new meds? I'm free tomorrow. Or even later today."

Dr. Violet Sage sighed. "I'm sorry, dear," she said. "But I'm afraid I don't have any openings in my schedule until next month. They really work us to the bone over here. I've got a caseload of more than six hundred at the moment."

Next month? I didn't want to endure these feelings for thirty more *seconds*, let alone thirty more days. The weight of her unavailability crushed me. I started to panic. "Well, does this count as a meeting?" I tried. "Maybe you can get me on some sort of new medication, and when we meet in a month, I can tell you all about how it's going?"

She sighed again. "I'm sorry," she repeated. "There's nothing I can do for now. My license prohibits me from prescribing new medication anywhere but during an in-person session."

I wiped my sweaty palms on my comforter. "Please, Dr. Sage, please," I said. "This is clearly an emergency. I need help. I need help! I'll do anything. I'll meet you after hours. I'll—"

"There's nothing I can do immediately," she said again. "But I would be happy to refer you back to the list of doctors in our network, and perhaps one of them might be able to see you earlier."

The thought of poring through a long list of phone numbers, of calling a bunch of licensed strangers to tell them the most intimate details of my life story in exchange for a dubious pill prescription that might or might not work, was too much to bear. I wanted to hide from the task. I wanted to hide from *everything*. So I hung up the phone and did just that.

The email from Santiago could have come within a few hours or a few days. I had no idea how much time had passed. All I knew was that I only felt safe in my comfortable bed inside my dark little room, in and out of consciousness. I let text messages pile up on my phone, ignored Devon and Ari when they knocked on my door, and didn't tell anyone outside the Avalon where I was. When I saw Santiago's name in my inbox through my blurred vision, I tapped on it just to make sure I didn't owe him some form of urgent communication.

I skimmed his message and knew immediately. My eyes bounced from phrase to phrase: "I love you so much, but," "I just can't anymore," "Need to focus on my career," "Definitely moving to Los Angeles." This was it. Of course I'd known, on some level, it was coming—that nothing about our relationship was sustainable, that it wasn't ideal to kiss your phone goodnight on New Year's Eve—and perhaps that buried realization even contributed to my most recent crash.

I took a deep breath and reread the entire letter. He'd realized over New Year's that he was in no place to focus on a relationship, he said, and he couldn't give me what I deserved. What I deserved most was presence, and it was clear I wanted a form of partnership that he just couldn't offer. Reading his sentences made me feel like I was replaying a familiar tape; we had already had versions of this conversation several times. But now, our separation was real, and there would be no fighting to win him back. I didn't have the energy to fight for anything.

On top of everything else, my new job was starting the following Monday. Like a hungover morning after a night of partying, I had no choice but to haul myself out of bed and play the part of a presentable human. I managed to conjure just enough "first-day-of-school" adrenaline to pick out a decent outfit and splash some cold water on my face. I looked at myself in the mirror, hoping nobody would notice the dark tea bags under my eyes. No amount of makeup would hide the puffiness.

The tech company's headquarters was located in one of those South Bay towns that had once been nothing but flatlands and strip malls but now hosted palatial office parks rife with swimming pools and volleyball courts and arcades. To get there, I had to take a luxury bus that picked me up at a stop located about a ten-minute walk from the Avalon. The buses were fodder for much of modern-day San Francisco's ire. Activists thought that shuttling techies from the big city down the Peninsula served as a microcosm for the housing crisis, proof that rents were rising right alongside the inflated salaries. The more companies like mine beckoned workers to the Bay Area, the less room there would be for everyone else.

They weren't entirely wrong. But the debate was more complicated than targeting the sterile white buses that transported tech workers to and from their jobs; it involved a complex labyrinth of housing policies, "not-in-my-backyard" voters, and corrupt elected officials. Still, the buses made for an easy target: shiny, massive vehicles flashing marquees above their dashboards with mythological code names for office destinations such as "Crittendorf" and "Hertfordshire." The long lines of zombified white people in their mid-twenties and early thirties shrouded in fleeces, their headphones blocking out the rest of the world, tapping away on their screens as they waited to board. The opposite of concerned citizens engaging with their neighbors. In my days as a local news editor, at the peak of the tech-bus wars, I posted articles about how people threw eggs at their windows and barricaded their path holding protest signs. Today, though, I zipped up my own fleece jacket and joined the legions of zombies waiting in line.

With traffic, the ride took nearly two hours, and I was nauseous from the stop-and-go by the time we pulled into a big parking lot behind a nondescript tan building. "Welcome, Noobies!" a white banner hung over the entrance proclaimed. That's what they called anyone new who started working here: You were deemed a Noobie until the next crop of hires were deposited onto the campus. I knew this because I'd known at least a dozen other people who'd had jobs here; it was one of the biggest employers in San Francisco. Anywhere else in the world, it sounded really impressive to tell someone you had a job at this particular tech company—according to rumors, it was harder to get into than Harvard—but locally, it garnered about the same indifference as saying you worked at the mall.

A corral of fancy food trucks lined the other side of the parking lot. Breakfast burritos with smoked salmon and crème fraîche, Filipino pork adobo bowls topped with over-easy eggs, cinnamon-spiked cold brew from the hippest coffee shop in the South Bay. I wasn't hungry, but I couldn't remember the last time I'd eaten. I ordered a burrito, and when I reached for my wallet, the counter guy chuckled sarcastically. "You think they're gonna make you pay for this?" He rolled his eyes. "Give it a week or two, you won't be pulling out that wallet anymore."

I took the burrito apologetically, wanting desperately to tell him that I wasn't one of *those* people, when a cheerful-looking woman with curling-ironed hair bounced over to me. She shoved out her hand for me to shake. "Do we have a Noob here?" she asked, winking.

I nodded sheepishly, still making eye contact with the counter guy, as the curly-haired woman pulled a ridiculous-looking rainbow-colored cap, replete with tiny silver bells sewn onto the tip, out of her backpack. It looked like something a court jester would wear in a preschool production of *Robin Hood*. "Don't forget to put on your Noobie hat!" she squealed, jamming the cap on my head before I could smooth down my hair. The counter guy rolled his eyes again and took the next person's order, and I felt my cheeks grow hot. The bells made a little jangling sound as I followed the woman inside the building.

Orientation consisted of eight straight hours of company-branded slides with acronyms I couldn't decipher, like "OKR" and "KPI." I paid attention like a diligent student for the first forty-five minutes or so, and then my mind started to wander. I looked around the room at my cohort, searching for attractive men, feeling an impulse to identify a love interest now that I was single. But all I saw were nerds in hoodies and more women with perfect hair. I thought of Santiago and how I wouldn't be able to relay the details of my first day to him. Going from a vegetable state to a brand-new job had given me no time to process the fact that he was no longer my boyfriend. The realization crushed me. I excused myself to go to the bathroom.

Sitting on the Japanese-designed heated toilet seat, I allowed myself to cry. A few tears multiplied into tons, and before I knew it, I was sobbing with the same vigor I'd indulged myself in during Christmas on my mother's couch. Only this time, my fears had come true. Santiago was down there in Panama, entertaining his bevy of admirers, while I'd joined the ranks of a corporate dystopia in Silicon Valley after enduring what was probably a bipolar two manic episode. I spent the next hour in the bathroom stall, with increasingly warmed-up butt cheeks, scrolling hopelessly through Santiago's Facebook page. Staring at photos, that gawky body and those huge brown eyes, yearning for a version of him that never existed.

When I finally dragged myself out of the bathroom, I hid my worn-out eyes behind a pair of sunglasses and left the orientation building. I wandered around the tech campus feeling like I was underwater, past several identical office parks in a row, the blaring midday sun giving me armpit stains. By the time I made it back to where I had started, orientation was breaking for lunch. So I camouflaged myself among the swarm of my new coworkers, willing nobody to talk to me.

chapter thirteen

Each week, our three hundred–person communications team came together for an all-hands meeting, forty or so people crammed into a conference room and everyone else dialed in via video screen from various office outposts around the world. My first time at the meeting, the head of communications asked me to introduce myself to the team in the whimsical format they always used: Tell two lies and one truth about myself, and then everyone would guess what was true. I rattled off the first two pieces of nonsense that popped into my head, that I went to high school in Thailand and competed in Division I pole-vaulting in college. And then the only outrageous truth I could think of: "I'm going to be on a reality-TV show about the time I lived in the middle of the jungle in Panama." As soon as I said it out loud, I regretted it.

One of my coworkers leaned over to the person next to him and said, loud enough for me to hear, "*Please* let that one be true." My cheeks reddened as my teammates lobbed in their guesses. Only a handful of people raised their hands in favor of the reality show.

"Well?" the comms director asked me. She was a woman in her forties, wearing workout clothes, who started as an intern at this same company upon its founding nearly two decades ago. "Which one was true?"

"The reality show," I admitted, averting my eyes to the floor. The chorus of follow-up questions was instantaneous. "What's the show about?" "What channel will it be on?" "Can we watch it?" "Why did you ever leave?" "Was it just like *Survivor*?"

I shook my head and tried to deflect. Thinking about Max and Coco and Ico-Inna, and especially Santiago, felt somewhat perverse in the middle of a work setting. That jungle was thousands of miles away from this corporate one. I certainly wasn't about to tell my shiny new colleagues about my semipublic suicide attempt.

"Oh, it's nothing, I probably won't even get much air time," I managed to say. "I left because it was time for me to get a real job. And that's why I'm here."

In actuality, the series would be debuting on a major network in a mere two months, and I had no idea what to expect. Would my doomed love story with Santiago play out in front of a captive audience? How would Max weave my depression into the plot? Would I be publicly labeled "that depression girl" for the rest of my life? The prospects were excruciating. I sat down at the conference table, signaling the end of my introduction, and the head of communications moved onto a slideshow presentation about an upcoming gadgets conference in Vegas.

After a couple weeks, I moved from Silicon Valley to my company's San Francisco office. It was located on the Embarcadero, a picturesque boulevard that hugs the waterfront, and featured wraparound windows, Wi-Fi-equipped outdoor terraces, and a kitchen stocked with the fanciest collection of snacks I had ever seen: candied mango shavings, dark-chocolate-dipped almonds, cumin-dusted sunflower seeds, a bounty of fresh exotic fruit. There was even a fully loaded Italian espresso machine replete with four different kinds of locally sourced coffee beans we could grind ourselves and an array of nut milks to steam for lattes and cappuccinos.

I was still in "ramp-up" mode, which my boss, Michael, described as "meeting people and absorbing our work and culture through osmosis" but which felt more to me like hanging out and doing nothing. Most days, I posted up by the window near the snack kitchen, propped my feet up on an overstuffed ottoman, and stared out at the sweeping expanse of the East Bay, Oakland's ports in the foreground and Mount Diablo's peak in the distance, as I sipped coconut LaCroix and tried not to feel terrible.

Pretty soon, I became a semi-functioning human again. I went to one of those newly popular morning dance parties before work, dressed in a 1980s Jazzercise costume, with my friend Pixie from Burning Man. The workout got my endorphins firing to the point where I felt a surge of creativity at the office. I typed up a proposal for a new company-wide internal newsletter, a bit of a departure from the day job I'd been hired for, and sent it directly to the head of communications.

"Nice work," she replied, cc'ing Michael. "I think you're really onto something here. Mike: great hire!"

My small successes at work bolstered my mood enough to accept an invitation to a wild overnight party with some of my Avalon housemates.

"Here," Gregoire said, handing me a skin-tight cheetah-print bodysuit. "This is the right aura for tonight." He was wearing sparkly spandex shorts and a tuxedo vest and gave me the thumbs-up sign when he saw that his chosen costume for me fit perfectly. Then, he ushered me into an Uber with Eliza and Drue, who were dressed like a pair of twin cowboy strippers.

The gathering was hosted by the Third Eye Collective, a professional party-throwing organization loosely associated with the Avalon. Third Eye parties were known for extremely intricate large-scale art pieces, which often involved robots or lasers or other kinds of flashy toys arranged as sorts of staged political protests against various capitalist institutions—a confusing detail, given most of the attendees worked in tech. In addition to elaborate, sexy costumes, guests were encouraged to embody different personas and interact with one another "in character" throughout the duration of the event, which usually lasted well into the following morning. No drugs or alcohol were provided on-site, but if you weren't under the influence of *something*, you'd probably be pretty bored. At least, that's how Devon described it to me when I asked her what the big deal was with Third Eye Collective in the first place. People in our circles had been talking about this particular party for weeks, and Eliza had spent several days assembling an art piece involving discarded televisions in our yard.

"Who are these people and how do they have so much power over our social lives?" I asked Devon as I watched Eliza and her friends toiling away outside under the hot sun, stacking vintage television sets on top of one another in different configurations. "Like, doesn't Eliza have a job? Why is she putting so much of her creative energy toward a party that's only gonna last one night?"

"That's the magic of the Third Eye," Devon said with feigned drama. "Nobody knows who runs it. The people behind these parties are nameless and faceless. Except I know what one of their faces looks like, 'cause I made out with it on a ski trip once." She threw back her head and cackled but refused to reveal his name when I prodded.

And so Third Eye Collective remained a mystery to me, although I was still befuddled by how much time and energy went into planning and creating content for their events. That was the thing about San Francisco: The social scene was dominated by former outcasts who had grown up playing complicated games like Dungeons & Dragons in their parents' basements. Their nerdiness became an asset once they hit working age, when many of them built programs and engineered algorithms that powered some of the tech world's most successful startups. Only then, when they amassed a respectable amount of money and status, were they able to shed the geeky identities of their teenage years. Now, it was all sex, drugs, and rock and roll (or in their cases, orgies, psychedelic research chemicals, and dark techno). They threw social events even more exclusive than the ones they'd been left out from in high school—except here was proof that you could never actually escape the essence of who you were. After all, these parties resembled a real-life Dungeons & Dragons game on acid.

That weekend's Third Eye Collective party was taking place inside an abandoned shipping warehouse in a small industrial port town on the other side of the San Francisco Bay. The line to get in snaked down five flights of stairs and stretched across the parking lot and down the block. There wasn't another operating business in sight. As I entered with my Avalon crew, a woman decked out in a glittering flapper dress and a captain's hat hurried up to me, shoving a gold-painted wooden duck into my hands.

"Quick, fair citizen, you must rescue the Golden Duck from the harsh grip of Old General Morgenstern!" she shrieked.

It wasn't immediately obvious just how, exactly, I was supposed to play along. "Uh . . ." I stammered, looking over at Gregoire desperately for help. "What's this duck for?"

The flapper didn't break character for a second. "The Golden Duck! The Golden Duck! It's our only hope left for our people. Do *not* believe Morgenstern's propaganda. He'll try to sway you with lies. Lies!"

I didn't want to throw cold water on her enthusiasm, but trying to interact with this person was agonizing. I was way too sober to let my guard down. I reached into my messenger bag and pulled out a flask, taking a warm, soothing pull of whiskey. I held it out to the flapper.

"Uh . . . drink?"

"This is *hopeless*!" she cried, yanking the duck out of my hand and cradling it in her arms like a newborn baby. "Perhaps the ministry knows what to do!" And with that, clutching the duck, she traipsed away.

I took in my surroundings. The dark warehouse was punctuated by strobe lights and lasers. Electronic music thumped from speakers a full story tall. A massive replica of a rubber duckie with a Hitler mustache stood in a far corner—that thing must have been ten feet high, minimum—and a bunch of partygoers were trying to climb it. To my right, a woman dressed as a 1950s diner waitress danced around on roller skates, pouring shots of tequila into the mouths of passersby. Off to another side was a mountain of giant stuffed teddy bears. All over the pile of bears lay more partygoers, staring at the ceiling, cuddling, snorting white powders from tiny spoons, and generally lolling about. I didn't know which direction to walk in, so I took another swig from my flask and followed Gregoire to the bears. Eliza and Drue were already on the dance floor, spraying everyone around them with water from their plastic cowboy pistols.

Over by the bears, Gregoire plopped down next to a guy with a turn-of-the-century curled mustache and a gold septum piercing. They embraced, and the mustached dude handed a key to Gregoire, who immediately put it to his nose and took a big sniff. Exhaling pleasantly, he lay back into a bear and wrapped its plush arms around his torso in a "big spoon" cuddling position. "I'm Carly," I said to Mustache, because I didn't have anything else to do.

"Timothy, at your service," the guy said, bowing ever so slightly without moving the rest of his body. "Can I interest you in a bump of the finest ketamine on this side of the bay?"

I sat down cross-legged in front of him and took the key. The drugs stung my nasal passage. I had never done ketamine before, but it was a favorite in Avalon and Avalon-adjacent circles. Devon and Ari said they didn't get the appeal, but at every party we went to, there was always a lump of people in the corner, high on K, rubbing each other's appendages ever so slowly.

A fuzzy feeling blanketed my body, and I leaned against Timothy naturally, like he was an old friend. He stroked my hair and I stared up at the red laser beams crisscrossing the ceiling above me. The light put me in a trance, and soon, I forgot we were indoors. I forgot where we were entirely. I'm not sure how long we lay there like that, but when I finally sat up, Gregoire was gone.

"So how do you spend your days, Miss Carly?" Timothy asked, digging his key into a small baggie and extracting it, again, for me.

I took another sniff of ketamine and told him.

"Well, what do you know!" Timothy slapped me on the back. "That's my place of employment, too." He told me he was a senior software engineer working on a top-secret project involving customer-management software meant to mimic the human brain.

"Does that mean the robots are coming for our jobs?" I asked.

Timothy shrugged. "I think it'll create a whole new workforce dedicated to building the robots. At least, that's what I tell my wife at dinner to convince her I'm doing something meaningful."

"Is your wife at this party, too?"

Timothy chuckled. "No way. She hates Third Eye Collective. Says it's nothing but patriarchal white men trying to tire themselves out. She'd never go anywhere *near* these colonialists."

"Party colonialists!" This struck me as hilarious, and I erupted into a fit of giggles. "They *are* kind of party colonialists, aren't they. I mean, why is everyone I talk to trying to force me into some sort of bad improv game? Why do we have to do things *their* way?" I laughed harder and shoved my fist in the air. "Take back the party!"

I spent the rest of the night in a happy haze. I got in a water fight with Drue and Eliza, let Gregoire twirl me around under a canopy of more lasers, and joked around with Timothy. Before I knew it, the first signs of daylight peeked through the barred windows. I wasn't tired in the slightest. In fact, I wasn't much of anything. My body felt like it was operating independently from my feelings.

"After-party at the Avalon?" I said to Gregoire, whose black eyeliner had begun to smear under his eyes. He nodded enthusiastically, and we rounded up our friends. We piled into Ubers and headed back over the bridge and entered our big Victorian house like one long walk-of-shame parade, all messy-haired and costumes askew. Except it didn't feel like there was anything to be ashamed of—I was happy. That had to count for something, right? We spent the next several hours spread out over the living room, taking hits of nitrous and passing around joints and laughing about nothing in particular. The morning light hit the wallpaper like a zoetrope, and I let myself melt into the colors and patterns. I'm pretty sure I was smiling, but I could barely identify where my mouth was.

I nodded off in front of my laptop the following Monday at work. My fingers felt like miniature weights plunking on the keyboard as I attempted to write emails. I made myself two double espressos, and the caffeine caused my heart to pound and filled me with anxiety, but I was still exhausted. So exhausted.

Timothy found me on the company's internal employee database and sent me a direct message. "Lunch?"

It couldn't hurt to move my body a little bit, so I agreed to meet him in one of the cafes in our building next door. The company owned five large office buildings on the San Francisco waterfront, and each one had at least two restaurants that served up gourmet meals to employees for free. These weren't your average cafeteria pizza slices and fries. Menus included seared Arctic char on beds of garlicky spinach, Panang curry with shrimp and mussels, and sushi that chefs hand-rolled in front of you. The particular spot where I agreed to meet Timothy even had a build-your-own boba tea bar.

Timothy could tell something was wrong as soon as I slumped down across from him in the booth. He took a bite of squid-ink carbonara and chewed loudly. "Still recovering from the weekend, I guess?"

I sipped my milky boba tea—even more caffeine to try to jolt me into personhood. "Something like that," I said.

"Well, I was hoping we could have something like a 'business lunch,' if you're up for it," he replied. "I was thinking a lot about what you told me on Saturday—the storytelling platform you want to build for employees—and it's just such a good idea. I have all sorts of thoughts."

I'd forgotten that at the party, I told Timothy about the idea I pitched to my department head. When I felt normal, it sounded like the easiest task in the world: Create a newsletter that went out to every employee around the world at the same time every day, telling stories about the company's products and people. (That was my elevator pitch.) But now, weighed down into nothingness, even talking about building something of that magnitude felt impossible. So I just listened to Timothy talk instead.

". . . performance reviews are so fucked-up," he was saying. "How can we judge our abilities using such an archaic, binary system? You should tell stories that completely blow the lid off that process. In fact! There's so much to expose under the hood here. What if we worked together to start a revolution? Sometimes I get down on myself for being part of such a capitalist machine, but then I remember, I have the agency to try to change things from the inside."

With each of his passing words, I grew less engaged and more anxious. I wasn't trying to create any sort of uprising at this job. I just wanted to make it through the day, so I could make it through tomorrow, and the next. So I could be rewarded with my comfortable bed when all my responsibilities had been checked off my list, and maybe finally pay off my credit card bills. At that moment, though, even so much as walking back to my desk and sitting down at my computer seemed like a task I couldn't complete. I was so tired.

"Starting a revolution would be a lot of work," I managed. I leaned my head against the wall and closed my eyes for a beat.

"*Life* is a lot of work," Timothy said. And then, when I still didn't open my eyes: "Hey . . . are you sure you're okay?"

He was right. Life *was* a lot of work. Too much work. "I'm just so wrecked from partying," I lied. Partying may have temporarily drained my energy, but this felt more permanent than that. "Didn't you tell me something about a nap room? Do you know if they have one in this building?"

"Oh, yeah, totally, that's a good idea," Timothy said. "You should definitely go to the nap room. It's just through those doors, down the hall to your right." I apologized for not being able to stay longer, and he waved me away.

The nap room was dark, with five reclining chairs all lined up in a row. A calming scene from the inside of an aquarium was projected on the wall in front of the furniture. I heard soft snoring, and as my eyes adjusted, I noticed one guy in a hoodie curled up on the far left. So I chose the chair at the other end of the row and reclined it as far back as it would go. The leather was cool and soothing on my face. I closed my eyes and let myself escape, once again.

chapter fourteen

The bipolar clinic was a sparse, windowless room on the fifth floor of the hospital with a large folding table, uncomfortable chairs, and yellow concrete walls. Two doctors, both middle-aged men in glasses, blinked at me from one side of the table. I sat facing them on the other side, my hands folded nervously, knuckles white. They asked me what brought me to their mental health center that day, and I described the story of my past year as best I could. I hadn't talked to a medical professional since my frustrating phone conversation with Dr. Violet Sage a couple months earlier. San Francisco allegedly offered one of the region's best bipolar treatment programs, and with my new health insurance, I could finally afford it. I needed to find out if there was any merit to Dr. Sage's suggestion that my struggles extended beyond regular old depression.

"And tell me, Carly, about your relationship with substances," one of the doctors said. Bob, maybe, or Mark. I could barely tell the difference between the two of them.

I hesitated. Did I really want to get into my drug use? Since my all-night bender at the Third Eye Collective party, I'd significantly cut back. I was too drained to have any sort of social life, to seek out much of anything. Sometimes I drank red wine with Devon on the kitchen couch at the Avalon, and I still smoked weed a decent amount. Though lately, marijuana only made me feel worse. What used to spark creative thoughts and bursts of productivity now had me spiraling down those all-too-familiar ruminating paths.

I decided to focus on the present and ignore the binges of hard partying I sometimes indulged in. I admitted to the interchangeable doctors that I drank wine from time to time and used cannabis medicinally. All the Panamanian cocaine, the benders with Robbie in New York, the MDMA dance parties, remained my little secret. I was already feeling so ashamed of my mood that I didn't want to give them another reason to judge me. And, like the similar decision I made with Dr. Violet Sage, choosing my words carefully allowed me to continue believing that my behavior wasn't actually cause for concern.

"You know, alcohol can counteract the properties of your antidepressants," Dr. Mark-or-Bob said. "Even two glasses of wine can interrupt the serotonin-reuptake process. I would recommend abstinence as long as you're taking medications."

Psychiatrists had been telling me this since I first started taking my meds in college, and I never listened. Most of the time, the pills still worked, at least somewhat. Abstinence, on the other hand, seemed all but impossible. I couldn't imagine a life that didn't involve alcohol in some form. Socializing would be so boring—anxiety-inducing, even, and excruciating. So I did what I usually did when I heard this line of logic from a doctor: I smiled, nodded, downplayed, and said I'd think about it. Then I dismissed their cautionary words so quickly that it remained easy to forget I'd ever heard them.

"... there isn't enough reliable research out there on the effects of cannabis as it relates to psychopharmacology," the other doctor was saying. "I'd be careful with that, too."

Smile. Nod.

After my interrogation, the doctors asked me to leave the room and wait in the hallway while they talked through all the information I'd given them and considered next steps, like I was auditioning for *American Idol* and not a medication plan. I sat down on the shiny linoleum floor and leaned back against the wall, opening up Facebook to look at Santiago's profile for what was probably the eleventh time that morning. Checking Santiago's social media had become almost a nervous tic; I did it every time

I had an idle moment. I still missed him, my aching a permanent condition of sorts, like an extra finger I wasn't quite sure what to do with but had to accept was a part of my body. Cutting it off would just leave a nasty, bloody scar.

One of the doctors opened the door and poked his head out. "Alright, Carly, we're ready to see you again."

I reentered the stark, dreary room and sat back down at the table. Dr. Bob-or-Mark shuffled around some papers—they'd been taking notes the whole time I talked—and cleared his throat.

"Based on everything you've told us, Carly, it is clear you are suffering from type-two bipolar disorder," he said. "It's a very cut-and-dry case. The good news is, scientists have developed very effective medications to address this condition. Have you heard of lithium?"

Lithium? I didn't know much about lithium, except that it seemed like a very, very intense drug. There was a Nirvana song called "Lithium." And wasn't Kurt Cobain even worse off than I was during his short life? No, I couldn't take lithium. I didn't want to risk dulling my senses more than they'd already diminished. After all, lately, what these doctors were calling "mania" was my only path to feeling good. If I took it away, would I ever be able to feel anything again?

"I'm . . . worried about lithium," I responded carefully. "I'm a writer. I'm worried it will sap all my motivation and creativity. Doesn't it do that sort of thing?"

"We work with many people in creative disciplines who have had extremely successful responses to lithium," said one of the doctors. "What they report is that, while they don't necessarily binge on making art or indulge in erratic behavior, their pursuits are much more steady. Lithium is the tried-and-true method for treating bipolar disorder."

I *loved* the feeling of binging on my creative pursuits, so to speak. It made me feel alive. But I also knew my current state was completely unsustainable. And I had yet to try to address it with any sort of "tried-and-true" antidote.

"Alright," I said slowly. "Okay. I'm in. Let's try lithium."

My housemate Eliza organized a "girls night out" to Lipstick Society: a ladies-only, sexually charged party for bisexual and "bicurious" women. I was neither bisexual nor bicurious, but I hadn't been out of my house for anything but work in weeks, and I still wasn't anywhere close to being over Santiago. By then, I'd been taking lithium for two weeks, and my mood had barely shifted, if at all. Forcing myself out to the Lipstick Society seemed like the jolt in routine that I needed, and every once in a while, acting like a stable person in the presence of others allowed me to escape my thoughts for a bit—even though I knew they'd be right there waiting for me when I was by myself again, like an angry mob inside my mind.

"This is ridiculous," Devon said as I looked through my closet for an outfit. *Should I don something butch?* I wondered. *A blazer and button-down shirt? Or lean into my feminine side?* I selected a little black dress. Devon and Ari were lounging on my bed, flipping through a dumb celebrity-gossip magazine Devon had stolen from the dentist's office earlier that day.

"You've never been attracted to women," Devon continued. "Not once. Remember that time Pixie's friend tried to kiss you at that random music festival in Humboldt? You freaked out."

Devon was right, of course. But I really needed to leave the house. And fantasizing about a woman as my first rebound hookup since Santiago felt exciting amid weeks of not feeling excitement about anything. Plus, what would Santi think if he found out? I smiled as I pictured the look on his face, those wide brown eyes, if he scrolled through my Facebook and discovered a photo of me and my new girlfriend.

"There's a first time for everything," I retorted, pulling the dress over my head. "Are you *sure* you guys don't want to come?"

Devon and Ari looked at each other and rolled their eyes. "No, thank you," Ari said. "I've been to exactly one sex party in my life.

Theodora's creepy 'pajama night' or whatever. I shared a cab home with Devon five minutes after we got there."

"Yeah, we're 'stay-home-from-the-orgy' people," Devon deadpanned. "But I respect your decisions and wish you all the best." She and Ari devolved into a fit of laughter.

Sex parties were just as common in our San Francisco social circles as nerdy immersive art gatherings. They were usually frequented by that same "Dungeons & Dragons" brand of reformed geek, on the less attractive end of the spectrum. After all, getting laid was all but guaranteed when you paid an entry fee. Aside from the waiting room of the Orgy Palace at Burning Man where Robbie and I broke up, I'd never come close to any sort of party. If I were being honest with myself, I was like Devon and Ari: a "stay-home-from-the-orgy" person. But I'd do anything to get my mind off Santiago, and no matter how depressed I was, I still relished a good story. So off to Lipstick Society I went, in my little black dress.

Eliza ushered me into an Uber full of her female friends, who were all, incidentally, wearing lipstick. They chatted enthusiastically as the car made its way downtown, swapping stories of past same-sex encounters, escapades at orgies, and amusing incidents from their long-term relationships. I listened from the back seat, squished between two beautiful women, feeling sheltered and uninteresting and very, very single. My mood was bleak by the time the Uber pulled up in front of Butterfly House, a dance club near San Francisco's Civic Center on a particularly unsavory block. An unconscious body sprawled beside the club's entryway, and nobody acknowledged it.

Butterfly House was dimly lit by candles inside, a sultry female voice singing over a synthesizer. The room by the bar was filled with women—feminine women decked out in high heels whose lipstick matched my car mates'. Eliza and her friends disappeared into the crowd. I looked around for someone to talk to. Everyone stood in flirtatious, inviting postures, rubbing each other's arms, leaning close to hang on to every word of conversation. I, on the other hand, felt awkward and stiff, unsure of what to do with my body, of how to interact with these gorgeous strangers whom I wasn't even remotely, in the slightest bit, attracted to.

I headed straight for the bar and ordered a mezcal margarita. The smoky liquor reminded me of Mexico, of another time in my life when I did something far outside my comfort zone. I downed the drink in a few gulps and ordered another one. I had just begun to slightly relax when an olive-skinned, long-haired woman with pouty lips materialized next to me and called out to the bartender for a dirty martini.

Her arm brushed against mine and she left it there. I didn't dare move a muscle. "I'm Sam," she said confidently, meeting my eyes with hers. Her silk blouse was unbuttoned enough to see her black lace bra underneath.

"Hey," I managed, unsure of what to do next. Was I supposed to hit on this person? Lean in for a kiss? Was *this* my ticket to either making Santiago jealous or moving on from his memory entirely?

Sam pressed her forearm more firmly into mine and told me she worked in marketing; her office was in the Salesforce Tower and she'd walked here after a happy hour with some coworkers. She'd never have the guts to come to something like this sober, she said, and her admission put me more at ease. She and her boyfriend were looking for a "unicorn," meaning a woman they could have meaningful-yet-casual threesomes with, no expectations, mutual respect, that sort of thing. He suggested she come to Lipstick Society to find that person. As I downed my third mezcal margarita and wondered if I could be a unicorn, I heard a tinkling noise. Sam and I turned to look and saw a woman in knee-high tights and a corset standing on a banquette and ringing a bell.

"Come on, sexy ladies," she purred. "It's time to play spin the bottle!"

"Ooh, fun!" Sam said, grabbing my hand and pulling me toward the corseted woman. We sat cross-legged in a circle, some on the banquette, others on the floor, an empty Veuve Clicquot bottle positioned atop an ottoman. Corset spun first, and the bottle landed on the woman on Sam's other side, whose hair was shellacked back into a severe-looking ballerina bun. Corset took Ballerina Bun's chin in one hand and softly pecked her on the lips. Then, to my surprise, and to the resounding giggly cheers of everyone around me, Ballerina Bun grabbed Corset by the back of her neck and pulled her in for a steamy make out session. The group whooped and catcalled.

A few more rounds, and then the bottle pointed at me. I locked eyes with the spinner: perfectly blow-dried hair with blond highlights, more lipstick. Sam squeezed my shoulder. "That's you," she said. And then the girl with the blow-dried hair was crawling toward me, and then her lips were on mine, and they felt soft, and as I wondered whether her lipstick would rub off on me, I hoped the encounter would be over soon.

It was my turn to spin, but I got up to leave instead. "I have to go to the bathroom," I lied to Sam, and then beelined toward the ladies' room.

The circle of women continued giggling and kissing. I stayed in the bathroom stall for just long enough. Then, as stealthily as possible, I tiptoed past the spin-the-bottle game and slunk out the door, almost tripping over the body that was still beside the entrance. I hailed the first taxi that passed by and climbed in, sinking my relieved body into the leather seat.

If I was going to get over Santiago, clearly, I had to find another way.

After several more weeks with no improvement in my mood, the bipolar clinic doctors encouraged me to take a monthlong leave from work to attend an intensive outpatient therapy program. My company's extremely generous health plan included the option of paid medical leave, and while I still had a hard time feeling grateful for much of anything, I *was* able to recognize, even then, that not everyone who struggled like me had such easy access to potential treatments. As hard as it was to keep seeking help, I knew I was luckier than other people who shared my struggles. But what if, on the other hand, mental illness served as some sort of perverse equalizer? If my insurance covered the most expensive doctors and medications and treatments, and none of them made getting out of bed any easier, then what was the point of even trying? As I grappled with these questions, something inside me chose to keep trying.

I'd only been at my job for three months, though, so informing Michael, my manager, of my impending plans to take a medical leave was humiliating at best.

"So . . . you have depression," he repeated back to me as I sat in his office, wiping my clammy palms on his red IKEA couch, the day I broke the news.

"Yeah," I replied lamely. "My doctors think it would be best if I got some professional help. Like, more-than-a-therapist type help."

"But . . . what does that mean? Can you tell me more?"

I could tell Michael was just curious, but his questions made me extremely uncomfortable. Trying to describe the day-to-day details of living with depression felt like giving him carte blanche access to my bedroom and letting him rifle around in my most personal possessions. Michael had a long and impressive career as a speechwriter for a former senator. He was a naturally inquisitive, deeply intellectual guy with permanently imprinted circles under his eyes from his years of pulling all-nighters writing talking points on private jets. I couldn't quite tell what, exactly, he did at work besides cheerlead our editorial team and send funny Twitter links to our group chat.

"It's hard to explain," I said to him, trying to put my darkness into words that felt office-appropriate. "I just don't have any energy. To do anything. I'm drained all the time, physically. And nothing feels good to me. All I can think about are the ways I'm failing at life. I just want to stay in bed." There. Hopefully that was enough for him to leave me alone and grant me access to my outpatient program.

He plodded ahead. "But your work has been excellent, Carly," he said. "This is really confusing to me, because here, you are totally on top of your game."

My face grew hot. It was true I was performing well at work. The job was relatively easy—after five years in an all-consuming online journalism grind, I was seasoned enough to apply those skills to a less-demanding industry. I didn't want to explain this to Michael. I wanted to sprint for the door. I imagined my unmade bed waiting for me at home. All I had to do was finish this conversation.

"Work is . . . a good distraction," I said. "Sometimes it helps. It's not, like, sustainable or anything, though. I don't think I want to keep going along like this."

Michael nodded slowly through his perpetually exhausted face. "Well . . ." he looked down at his lap as I silently prayed to be dismissed. "I'm sorry, Carly. I'm sorry things are so hard for you. I never would have guessed it, and I hope you can get the help that you need. Let me just think about a coverage plan for our team while you're gone. I'm sure we can make it work."

The room on the sixth floor of the mental health treatment center reminded me of the bipolar clinic: harsh lighting, concrete walls. A thin layer of oatmeal-colored carpeting covered the floor, and a dozen or so folding chairs were arranged in a circle in the middle of the room.

I arrived on time, but most of the chairs already held people when I got there. Average-looking people of all ages, fidgeting and making small talk. I grabbed one of the open seats, between a teenager with green hair and a middle-aged woman wearing a peacoat buttoned all the way to the top. I smiled wanly at the teenager, then turned and offered the woman the same expression.

A lady with frizzy hair pulled away from her face with bobby pins sauntered in and took the last remaining empty chair. Her commanding posture made it clear she was the top dog around here. She wore an oversize flowered blouse that hung, boxlike, over her slight frame. She clapped her hands once and cleared her throat, and heads snapped in her direction.

"Good morning, my friends," she said. Her voice was one of those high-pitched, soft-spoken baby voices, as if her body had matured throughout the years but her vocal chords remained in kindergarten.

"Good morning, Dr. Alice," the group droned in semi-unison.

When I first registered for the program, the intake coordinator explained to me that, because we were only mandated to come three times a week but groups took place every day, the composition of each session would be slightly different. People also came and went on their own timelines, so there was no clear beginning or end.

Every session began with a brief "check-in" from each of the participants. I surveyed my compatriots as each of them spoke. The green-haired teenager discussed her struggles navigating PTSD after years of sexual abuse in a foster home. The woman in the peacoat talked about how the death of her husband had left her feeling alone and purposeless. Another person was navigating a violent eating disorder, and someone else had recently been discharged from in-patient care after enduring an acute psychotic episode in which he thought he'd been communicating with angels.

As their stories unfolded, a creeping feeling began to blossom inside me that I didn't belong there. That my problems were of my own making. Here I was, an employee at one of the world's most coveted companies, living in a beautiful home full of interesting people, nothing particularly noteworthy about my upbringing or coming-of-age story aside from the fact that my brain chemistry made me hate myself.

When it was my turn to check in, I tried to explain the burden of my inner monologue, my perpetual exhaustion, and I felt like a fraud. I felt guilty. Why was I wasting my time among a group of individuals who had real reasons for their suffering, when my own life should have been nothing but charmed? If I couldn't appreciate my good fortune for what it was, I reasoned, then that was my own damn fault. While I was familiar with the feeling of impostor syndrome in the workplace, experiencing the phenomenon around my depression was new and equally unpleasant.

This line of thinking accompanied me for the rest of the day, as we watched a Brené Brown TED talk and discussed the role shame played in our lives. The facilitator, Dr. Alice, was in the middle of describing how she first experienced shame as a child—something about eating a tuna sandwich; I'm not sure what the point was—when I began to spiral on my own shame. My depression made me feel so ashamed, its mysterious origins and senselessness. I left that first session feeling worse than when I arrived.

To console myself, I bought a bottle of wine at the corner store on my way back to the Avalon. I drank the whole thing in bed when I got home, still feeling guilty and ashamed and, most of all, sorry for myself.

On top of everything else, the reality show about Ico-Inna premiered that same week, on a streaming network popular with hipsters and college kids. There was no television at the Avalon—only a huge projector we could plug our laptops into—so Devon had to buy a subscription to the channel, where we could watch all the episodes in one go.

Ari made a special popcorn on the stove with nutritional yeast and sea salt, and the three of us piled onto the mountain of living room fluff to watch my Panamanian dream turn into a Panamanian nightmare on national television. I held Devon's hand as the opening credits rolled: an aerial shot of Ico-Inna from above, all the thatched hut roofs and slivers of river. Then Coco's smug face appeared, some canned sound bite about building his own version of utopia from the ground up. B-roll footage of pretty girls laughing and swaying in their hammocks.

As soon as I saw these familiar images fill the screen, I knew I wouldn't be able to watch the show. All of it was too raw. I felt sick.

"Guys, I can't do this," I said. Devon paused the video—a shot of students ascending Suicide Hill mid-hike. "I'm not ready."

Ari rubbed my back. "That makes total sense," she said. "You don't have to."

Devon tossed a piece of popcorn into her mouth. "But can we still?" she asked. "I am so, so curious about your life down there. What if we watched it for you and reported back?"

"You actually want to do that?" I said incredulously.

"There's nothing I'd rather do!" she replied. "We can watch it later, though, if you want to do something else now."

After seeing even the shortest few minutes of footage, the only thing I wanted to do was hide in my bed. "No, no, I'm going to catch up on some work," I lied. "Go ahead, watch the show. Tell me what you think."

I backed out of the living room as Devon restarted the episode, hearing another one of Coco's cringey one-liners ("We're using our abundant resources to create exponential impact!") as I made my exit. I crawled back into my bed, safe from the world once again. I'm not sure how much time passed, but eventually, my phone dinged.

I checked out the text message. A college friend I hadn't heard from in years. "I'm watching you on TV right now!!!!" he wrote. "You look so thin!"

I shuddered and tossed my phone onto the edge of my bed, burying my face back into the pillow, hoping if I squeezed my eyes shut tightly enough, the ensuing darkness might erase it all.

Eventually, a soft knock on my door pulled me out of that liminal space between sleeping and hiding. Devon entered my room and sat down on the edge of my bed.

"You okay?" she asked. "I know that must have been hard."

"Fine," I mumbled without sitting up. Devon curled her knees against her chest and leaned against the wall.

"Honestly, Carly . . ." she began. I could tell she was choosing her words carefully. I lay there and waited for her to continue.

"Honestly, Carly, you did the right thing. Coming home, getting out of there—that was the right thing to do. I think you know that. I think you'll really *own* that one day. I mean, that place?"

I braced myself for what she might say next. *That place seemed like paradise, but you needed to get well. That place was amazing, but it's a really alternative lifestyle. That place was only for a certain kind of person, and you're not that.*

What she did say surprised me: "That place looks like a total disaster."

Then she started laughing. Quietly at first, and then harder and harder, until laughter shook her entire body. "God, it just seems like a *hellhole*," she said when she finally caught her breath. "That's some real *Lord of the Flies* shit right there. You were so, so smart to leave before that show made you look really stupid. You got out just in time." She started laughing again.

I was so taken aback by my best friend's straight talk that I couldn't help but giggle, too. Soon we were both laughing, and I sat up, and the room was a blur, and I was sucked into a momentary vortex of hysterics at the absurdity of it all. Wiping away tears, Devon gave me a big hug.

"This is what I love about you," she said through a few residual chuckles. "You'll try anything once, even if that means joining a weird jungle cult."

"I'll try anything *twice*," I corrected her, recalling how I'd made the same quip during one of my more confident moments in Panama. "I could have gotten out of there so much earlier, I guess."

I leaned against her and exhaled. There was still no way I'd be watching the show. But Devon's preliminary review did make me feel like I was right where I belonged. Even just for that moment with her, even though I knew our laughter would eventually pass.

chapter fifteen

My month in intensive outpatient group therapy barely had any effect on the state of my mood, and because of that, I would later recall only a few details. Details like arriving late almost every day and feeling bad about it. Like struggling to make small talk with the other patients during our lunch break. Like ordering venti vanilla lattes at the Starbucks across the street and getting caffeine jitters when I tried to focus. Like staring out the window at the vast expanse of eucalyptus trees—the hospital bordered one of my favorite places in the city for urban hiking when I was up for it—and wishing I could be outside feeling the breeze on my face instead of breathing stale hospital air. But most of all, I would remember not feeling any better after it was all over.

The program focused on dialectical behavior therapy, a form of cognitive training that includes intensive exercises on emotion regulation, distress tolerance, self-soothing, mindfulness, and interpersonal relations. The problem was, I already knew about all of that. I'd first encountered these coping mechanisms after my college suicide attempt, and at the time, they seemed groundbreaking. When I put them into practice, most of them actually worked.

But college marked a very different era in my life: I'd been coming to terms with the reality of my mental illness for the first time, and even naming it with professionals allowed me to feel seen and understood in a brand-new way. I'd been on a different antidepressant regimen, and a successful one, at that. The meds lifted my mood to a place where I could fully function, and that functioning gave me the motivation to put dialectical behavior therapy tactics into practice during my everyday life.

This time around, I was too depressed to do almost anything besides my basic obligations. I was still taking lithium, which had no effect aside from making my hands shake at awkward times. Sure, I could peel myself out of bed and go through the motions, but my brain felt so disconnected from the present moment that it felt like I was acting out all the exercises on behalf of someone else. Dialectical behavioral strategies can work great if you're motivated enough to try them out. But when you're in a place where almost everything feels numb—when it takes far too much effort to form entirely new habits that serve to rewire your brain—then this kind of training is basically irrelevant. You have to get to a place where you're capable of changing before you're able to make any meaningful changes.

After thirty days, my leave of absence from work came to an end, and the doctors at the outpatient program begrudgingly discharged me, but not before adding a new antidepressant to my daily regimen: Wellbutrin. Wellbutrin has activating properties, and can sometimes be used as a substitute for Adderall, so I guess they figured including it in my daily routine might jump-start something inside me. I took it dutifully, of course, still hoping to land on a new combo of meds that might actually help. But other than that, the program had no lasting impact on my day-to-day life. Back to work I went.

The next several months passed in a blur—or maybe a smudge. The sun inevitably rose every morning, even when I prayed for it to remain nighttime forever so I could keep sleeping. I rose along with it in order to collect my paycheck and stellar health benefits, spending most of my remaining time in bed. Monday-night family dinners at the Avalon provided a rare, entertaining respite, but after an hour or so around all my buoyant housemates, I almost always got up to excuse myself.

I knew this was no way to live, but I wasn't sure what else to do. Yet still, somewhere inside me, I wasn't ready to give up on getting well. After all, like I told Devon, I'd try anything twice. That person still existed, somewhere. I was walking around in her body every day. In the meantime, life continued to sputter its way forward, and I waited to discover the next thing I might try.

Every year, Theodora hosted what she called a "conscious conflict resolution" in our living room. She brought in an outside facilitator, and each resident committed an entire Saturday to using nonviolent communication skills in a public forum to process various interpersonal issues that had come up over the past year. This was one of those activities that veered a bit too far on the New Agey spectrum for me to take fully seriously. Though Ari and Devon shared my New England–bred cynicism about the Avalon's woo-woo tendencies, even they defended traditions like conscious conflict resolution, which had kept our home successfully operating since its inception. It's not easy to balance the interests of fifteen strong-willed people and keep all systems flowing with minimal drama. Nonviolent communication, or "NVC" as it was known by experts who studied mediation, remained a staunch value of everyone who took up residence at the Avalon.

The facilitator, a nondescript woman with strawberry blond hair and a purple hoodie hugging her slight frame, gathered us in a circular formation where we'd sit, uninterrupted save for a bathroom break, for the next three hours. Her commanding voice contradicted her otherwise-ordinary appearance: This woman meant business. Theodora, perched to her left in perfect, cross-legged yogic posture, nodded along as the woman outlined the rules for the day: No topic was too uncomfortable for discussion, we must communicate using "I" statements, and please avoid "below-the-line" behavior. I'm not quite sure what she meant by "below the line," but I gathered from context clues that she meant no hurling of insults, placing outright blame, or acting otherwise immaturely. We were a group of consciously minded adults, and conflicts arose in almost every group of adults, so let the conscious conflict resolution *begin*!

The day mostly consisted of going around the circle naming various issues that had triggered us recently. I wasn't involved in almost anything that was mentioned—I'd been too flattened to participate in many activities that got heated enough to turn into conflict—so I watched from the sidelines, a cement gargoyle perched on a building surveying the interesting happenings of his city's living, breathing mortals below. I still felt somewhat shy when all the residents got together: Everyone's personality was so outsized already; collecting them all in one room almost felt electric. I had never yearned to be a part of conflict—in fact, I went to great lengths to avoid it in my own life—but I couldn't help feeling a little left out as everyone lobbed their complaints. These complaints, after all, signified the comings and goings of people leading interesting, dynamic lives.

Theodora went first. She was irritated that we hadn't yet converted to a fully vegan kitchen. If we were going to live out our collective values of sustainability, how could we deign to pour cow milk into our morning coffee? The agricultural industrial complex was an abomination on our society, and those poor animals had no say in whether or not we could use their byproducts for our own benefit. "Imagine how the slaves felt when they first came to America, forced into labor that wasn't of their own choosing," she said evenly, with a straight face. "That's how chickens feel when we eat their eggs without their consent." Eliza, the Avalon's other militant vegan, nodded along emphatically, her eyes wide with support.

"Excuse me, did you just compare eating eggs to owning slaves?" Devon interjected. Unlike me, Dev was never one to avoid conflict at the group level; my best friend remained confident in all her convictions. "That's fucking ridiculous, Thea. I'm sorry, but it just is. Not to mention offensive."

The facilitator chimed in in her measured voice, calm but stern. "This is starting to sound like below-the-line communication," she said. "Now, Theodora, perhaps it makes sense for you to describe how it makes you *feel* when you see others in the house eating eggs?"

And so the meeting unfolded with similar issues brought to the surface, all of which were discussed at length. Eliza and Drue, who were experimenting with opening up their relationship for the first time, asked for more privacy and discretion when they invited their lovers over. They were currently dating another couple as a two-some and also "engaging in intimate playtime" separately.

"I saw someone gawking at Christopher and Jade when we were all making tea in the kitchen," Eliza complained. "I'm not going to name names, but it made me feel like some sort of exhibit. I'm not an animal at the zoo. These are my personal, private relationships."

The gawking person in question was probably me. I folded my arms and tried to look invisible. Eliza and Drue's relationship was something of a soap opera, and even though it seemed hectic and exhausting from the outside, I couldn't help but feel a little envious. My experience with Robbie had proven to me that polyamory was not something I wanted any part of, but at the very least, Eliza and Drue's experiences were fascinating and energizing and so, so far beyond my current state of being. And the two of them seemed closer than ever today, sitting next to each other like one attached unit, Eliza rubbing her toes on Drue's ankle.

Then it was Devon's turn to voice her grievances. In contrast to what was happening with Drue and Eliza, Devon was now in a monogamous relationship with Nico, her younger soulmate she'd met at Burning Man last summer. Her former live-in boyfriend, Yusuf, now inhabited the room next door. In typical Devon fashion, she and Yusuf had seamlessly transitioned to platonic best buds. In fact, in that very moment, Yusuf sat across from her in the circle, wearing one of Devon's signature bedazzled trucker hats backward on his bald head. Devon maintained close, nonsexual relationships with all her exes. It was one of the many things I admired about her.

"I hate how everyone seems to be poking around in my and Yusuf's business," Devon said. "Everything's fine. We're *great*. We don't need anyone to weigh in or take sides. Right, Y?"

Yusuf nodded from beneath his trucker hat. "Yeah. It's chill."

Gregoire cleared his throat. "If I may," he began.

"You may *not*," Devon replied.

"It sounds like Gregoire has something to say to you, Devon," the facilitator calmly cut in. "Would you like to receive it?"

Devon sighed. "I guess," she sulked, slumping backward against the couch.

"Gregoire, it's your turn to speak," the facilitator said.

"I just feel the way you treated Yusuf was unfair," Gregoire said. "Going from an open relationship with him to a closed relationship with someone else feels like a bait and switch."

"Again, this has absolutely nothing to do with you," Devon snapped. She had a hard time controlling her temper when she got pissed off, which was rare. But when it happened, I never wanted to be on the other side of it. Luckily, I was always on her side. We'd only gotten in one argument over the course of our nearly decade-long friendship. It was back when I lived in San Francisco the first time around, during the Avalon's huge annual Halloween party. Devon's bedroom was closed to the public, and I'd brought a couple friends in there to do shots of tequila. When she opened the door and found us sitting on her bed, shot glasses in hand, she screamed at me. The next day, over mimosas at brunch, we both apologized and everything was instantly okay again.

As the tension continued to escalate between Devon and Gregoire, and the facilitator did her best to keep their interactions "above the line," I zoned out. What could I possibly say to this group of lively, engaged, sexually active people when it was my turn to speak?

My turn eventually came, of course. Conscious conflict day was a "radically participatory" event. After several more disagreements were brought to the surface ("The dishes have been piling up in the sink," Ari pointed out. "I'm not going to invite my Midwestern siblings to our Halloween party if there's an 'orgy room,'" warned Trevor. "All the late-night jam sessions on the piano have been fucking with my circadian rhythms," said Henry), the facilitator ended our session with a final prompt. "What is it that you really wish the group truly understood about you?" she said.

A few people said some things I didn't register. I was too busy rehearsing in my head what I knew I had to tell everyone. Then, all eyes were on me. In spite of months of isolation, my fondness for this group of people and our shared home motivated me to be honest.

"I really wish you all truly understood my depression," I ventured slowly. "It's something I have to live with every day. It affects everything I do. It makes moving through the world harder, so much harder."

I fought back tears as I continued, feeling vaguely cathartic. Maybe there was some truth to this whole conscious conflict thing, after all. "I don't expect you to know what it feels like, but I want you to know that I'm struggling. All the time."

My confession pulled some sort of internal release valve. I continued, the words tumbling out more quickly. "Getting out of bed is the hardest thing I have to do, and I have to do it every single day. So if you see my door closed for long periods of time . . . I'm probably inside. Probably in bed. Probably trying to figure out how I'll possibly get myself to keep going, yet again, when everything hurts, all the time."

I hiccupped back a few tears. Ari moved over and put her arm around me. Then Devon crawled across the circle and gave me a big hug. Gregoire followed suit, wrapping Devon's hug in his own. Eliza and Drue circled their arms around Gregoire and Devon. Pretty soon, everyone in the house had piled around me, squeezing me tight. Even Yusuf, who hated physical affection, was patting the throng of humans with his hand. The facilitator beamed from inside her purple hoodie. "This is what community is all about," she said. "This is unconditional love."

Someone knocked softly on my door later that evening. I opened it and found myself face-to-face with Theodora. Though I'd been in her presence many times, we'd never interacted one-on-one before. I'd always felt a bit intimidated by her, with that perfect posture and propensity to steer any conversation into abstract, philosophical ideas. Now, she smiled at me beneath her wispy magenta-streaked bangs, which she'd dyed for Burning Man one year and now remained her signature style. She had a charming gap between her front two teeth.

"Theodora?" I said, even though it was obvious. She nodded anyway and made her way over to my bed, where she sat down, cross-legged, on top of my pile of rumpled sheets. Since the conscious conflict session earlier that day, I'd just been lying around, not really sleeping, but not doing much else, either.

"I wanted to thank you for opening your heart to us today," she began by way of introduction. "It was very brave."

One of my biggest pet peeves was when people called me "brave" for talking about my depression. It further underscored the fact that something was wrong with me. Like talking about my basic lived experiences required courage because they were something to be ashamed of. But I didn't tell any of that to Theodora. She still made me uneasy, so I remained on high alert.

"Thank you," I replied instead.

"One of our core values here at the Avalon is helping people to reach transcendence through personal growth," she continued. "I would like to help you overcome this affliction."

I sighed. Was depression really something I could "cure" entirely? Or would it just be a condition I'd need to find tolerable ways to manage forever? "I don't know if depression is the kind of thing you just get rid of," I said. "I think it's something you figure out how to live with."

Theodora nodded slowly, a perfect vertical line connecting her head to her torso. "I hear you," she said. "And also, I fear you might be resolving to accept the status quo. Have you heard of ketamine infusions?"

I had indeed heard of ketamine infusions. Recent research had suggested ketamine might be emerging as a potentially groundbreaking treatment for persistent depression. I'd read all the news articles and parsed all the "miracle patients." But I'd also snorted K at parties a few times since moving back to San Francisco, and it never gave me any form of depression relief. If anything, it just extracted me from my current state of mind momentarily, making everything feel distorted and alien before my surroundings dissipated back into a disappointing reality. I told Theodora as much.

She shook her head just as slowly and deliberately as she'd nodded. All her bodily movements seemed intentional and premeditated. "This is different," she said. "An infusion is when they inject the substance directly into your bloodstream. I'm on the board of a nonprofit that funds the studies of therapeutic psychedelics. The research around ketamine has been simply breathtaking."

I knew what nonprofit she was talking about—I also knew that Henry had donated a hefty sum to its coffers last year. When I'd first moved into the Avalon, the twins hosted a fancy fundraiser for its other biggest benefactors right in our parlor. Gregoire had played the piano and Eliza made fancy cocktails. I'd been impressed by the Avalon's connection to such a forward-thinking organization. It was part of what made living here so exciting. At the mention of this nonprofit, I started to perk up.

"I'm familiar with what you're talking about," I told her. "I'm just skeptical that it'd work for me."

"You never know until you try," she said. She pulled her phone out of the pocket of her flowy pants, which were adorned with an elaborate pattern of cat faces floating through the galaxy. "I'm going to text you the name of an integrative medicine clinic in Mill Valley. They're doing experimental infusions, totally aboveboard. Give them a call, and tell them I sent you." From my desk, my phone vibrated with her message.

She stood up as gracefully as she'd sat down. "I've got to go now," she said. "I have an intimate friend waiting for me upstairs."

Theodora's revolving door of lovers entered and exited our home with the same cool, aloof confidence she exuded.

With that, she glided out of my room, leaving me alone with my disheveled bedding and a glimmer of hope.

I took a train and then two separate buses, over the Golden Gate Bridge and out a mountainous stretch of Highway 1, to get to the Tree of Life Holistic Health Center in Marin County. The head physician had signed me up for a series of five intravenous ketamine therapy sessions after I called him up and dropped Theodora's name. As long as I paid for each session in cash, since the treatment was still considered "under the table," the doctor said I sounded like a prime candidate and would likely feel relief almost instantly. I was able to schedule my appointment close enough to the end of the workday that, in spite of the long journey on public transit, I wouldn't have to explain myself to my boss again.

The clinic was as sterile-looking as any other doctor's office, with a big wooden reception area and a matching wooden floor. A portly nurse greeted me in the waiting area and ushered me into one of the back rooms.

"I'm Miriam," she said matter-of-factly. Her demeanor was neither warm nor particularly off-putting, and her movements were brisk. I followed her into a room with five reclining chairs all in a row, side tables separating each one from the other. Two of the chairs were occupied by people in business attire, wearing eye masks and leaning back, tubes connecting their arms to bags of fluid hanging from poles.

"This is the IV Lounge," Miriam informed me plainly, as if we'd just entered a dive bar. "You're in seat number three. Keep your voice down; as you can see, we have therapy sessions in progress."

I hadn't said anything, and I continued not to speak as I climbed into the third chair from the door. Miriam handed me an eye mask and a pair of headphones. "We'll play you some calming sounds as you receive your dosage. Just sit back and relax. You might feel a little out of it when it's over, but it shouldn't be too strong. You have someone picking you up, right?"

I nodded; my mother would be meeting me here after her own workday came to an end. I wriggled a little in my seat and tried to get comfortable as Miriam held on to my left wrist and jabbed a needle into my vein. I lowered the mask over my eyes and put on the headphones and leaned the chair back. And waited to feel something. And waited. And waited.

The music sounded like something I'd hear on the sound system of a store that sold incense and crystals. Beneath the mask, I shut my eyes. It wasn't like an acid trip; I didn't see anything visual. Just darkness upon darkness as my ears filled with Enya. I must have fallen asleep, and eventually, someone squeezed my shoulder. I lifted up my eye mask; the shock of fluorescent office lighting jolted me back to the room.

"Time's up," Miriam declared, all business. I stumbled a little as I rose from the chair. Maybe I *did* feel kind of high. Nothing crazy, just looser in my limbs and warmer in my chest. A bit like finishing a first glass of wine. But that feeling always wore off pretty quickly unless I poured myself a second.

I handed the receptionist an envelope with $200 cash and wandered outside. Daylight savings had recently passed, and it was still light out. I spotted my mother's Subaru parked across the street, and I got into the passenger side.

"So? Did it work?" she asked, pulling the car onto the main road.

I shrugged. "Don't know yet." But I knew. I knew in my heart that it didn't work, and it wasn't going to. That hopeless feeling carried me back to her condo in Oakland, where I stretched out on her couch with the Boston terrier curled up in a heap at my feet.

"I think I'm just going to sleep here tonight," I said, too defeated to move or even think about how I'd eventually migrate back to the Avalon. "Right here on this couch." I buried my face in the crack where the throw pillow met the backrest.

Mom came over and rubbed my back and gave me a kiss on the top of my head. Her affectionate gestures made me want to act even more infantile. To just give up and let myself be taken care of. "You'll get through this," she told me, stroking my hair. "You've always been a fighter."

But I was right—ketamine therapy didn't work, and it wasn't going to. I went back to the Tree of Life four more times, and after each session, I hardly felt a thing. Certainly no lingering cognitive effects. Ari and Devon picked me up the second time, and we drove to Muir Beach and walked along the rocks at sunset. The majesty of the Pacific Coast stirred something inside me, but not enough to make me feel better in any lasting way. The third, fourth, and fifth times, I took the buses and train back home, alone, just as I'd gotten myself there. I stared out the window and watched the cars whiz by on the 101.

I didn't email my doctors at the bipolar clinic until I noticed clumps of my hair coming out in the shower. Lithium already caused frustrating tremors—I'd had a mortifying experience trying to eat soup with a colleague at one of our office cafes, and the couple times I'd summoned enough energy to attempt yoga, I could barely hold triangle pose. I sent the doctors an angry note through the hospital's patient portal, complaining that I couldn't eat anything that required a spoon, and now, to make matters worse, I was losing my hair.

Their generic response came a few days later, instructing me to be patient and reminding me that the lithium was doing a solid job in preventing another dreaded manic episode. I nearly threw my laptop across the room like I was having one of my childhood temper tantrums. I felt like I was coming unhinged.

I started looking around for a new therapist, anyone who might be able to advocate for a different regimen of pills, hoping that it was just a matter of tweaking my meds. I ended up cycling through a motley crew of psychological professionals, all of whom were covered by my company's health insurance, none of whom jived with my needs. There was the woman whose conversation style was so clipped and awkward that I had a hard time making it through my personal story without questioning its accuracy. The older lady with the puff of curly hair who looked so appalled when I revealed a few casual details about my drug use that I almost relished the shock value. The handsome man only a few years older than me, to whom I was too embarrassed to confide the intimate details of what felt like an increasingly pathetic existence.

Finally, Devon's now-ex-boyfriend Yusuf suggested I go see his therapist, who had recently helped him discover he might be on the autism spectrum—a revelation that had transformed his understanding of himself. She was out of network, and cost a cool $200 a pop, but Yusuf insisted she was worth every penny. Kristina had started out as his and Devon's couples therapist, back when they were still trying to patch together their relationship, and she'd helped them navigate their seemingly effortless transition to friends and roommates. Yusuf had decided to keep her on just for himself after he and Devon ended their relationship.

Kristina had shoulder-length hair streaked with elegant shades of gray and a kind, welcoming face. I loved her from the minute I met her. She patiently listened as I recounted my adult lifetime of depression, my romp through Latin America that had failed so spectacularly. When she asked about drugs and alcohol, I told her that I drank socially and smoked weed for creativity, a line I'd gotten used to reciting. Though my partying had grown more frequent in recent months, and sometimes served as the only motivating force to get me out of bed, I still wasn't willing to explore its relationship to my mental health. I didn't want to believe that my only form of temporary relief might, paradoxically, prevent me from experiencing permanent relief.

Kristina led me through relaxing visual exercises and suggested a long list of meditation and mindfulness practitioners to read. She also suggested I look into TMS therapy, or transcranial magnetic stimulation, a cutting-edge depression treatment she'd read about in a psychiatric journal. TMS worked by stimulating the areas of the brain most slowed-down due to depression by zapping them with a series of repetitive magnetic pulses via a contraption attached to your scalp.

"You mean it's a machine that will prevent my brain cells from taking a nap?" I said, incredulously. The idea reminded me of someone prodding me with a stick to force myself out of bed every day and then whacking me repeatedly to keep my energy levels up.

Kristina chuckled, not unkindly. "I've never thought of it like that," she said. "But you do have a way with words."

I sighed. "I'm just at this point where I don't think anything could possibly help me. I'm so weak all the time."

Kristina looked at me with an expression that conveyed the opposite of pity—that my words mattered. I hated being pitied, a common feeling when I met with new practitioners: that they'd reduced me to something small and pathetic they'd been hired to deal with. Kristina regarded me as someone with the strength I wished I had.

"I wish you could see yourself as I see you right now," she said. "Here, before me, is a woman who is still so unwilling to give up on herself. You've tried so many things. You're still putting yourself out there to meet new doctors and try new meds. That, to me, is the opposite of weak. That's proof of your fortitude. Of your resilience."

I shrugged off her compliment, but I *was* still curious to try out a remedy I hadn't attempted yet. And as it turned out, one of the country's most renowned TMS therapy clinics, run by a pioneering doctor in the space, was located right in San Francisco. At Kristina's suggestion, I made an appointment.

chapter sixteen

Dr. Waldo Barberi's TMS research had been cited in numerous articles about the treatment, and word was spreading quickly throughout the mental health community about his clinic. During our first meeting, he made it clear that I was very lucky to have snagged an appointment. Like I did for every other professional I'd met in recent months, I dutifully recounted a version of my life story I'd gotten used to hearing myself talk about. Because outpatient therapy, ketamine infusions, and, it appeared, pharmaceutical interventions hadn't successfully alleviated my pain, Dr. Barberi told me I had what was known as "treatment-resistant depression." Lucky for me, his TMS work had shown promising results on other patients whose brains had also resisted other treatments.

Each session was exactly the same. I'd arrive at Dr. Barberi's clinic above the jewelry store in Union Square, with its gray carpeting and matching gray walls, spick-and-span as a dentist's office. A receptionist would hand me a paper survey to fill out, assigning a value of one to five to a bunch of statements depending on how true they'd been in the past week ("I have felt lonely," "I have had thoughts of wanting to end my own life," "I've had a hard time acknowledging my accomplishments"). I'd scrawl a bunch of fours and fives on the sheet and hand it back to her. Then I'd head into another nondescript room deeper in the building, same carpet and walls.

In the second room, a piece of furniture that looked not unlike cartoon depictions of the electric chair faced a giant flat-screen television. I sat in the chair as Ricardo, the technician, put a shower cap on my head and affixed a device that looked like a lamp with a long neck to one side of my scalp (I wasn't kidding about the electric chair). For a full half hour, a series of persistent magnetic pulses would tap-tap onto my head and into my brain. It was mildly uncomfortable, like a pang of minor static electricity or the jab of a needle right before it punctures the skin, over and over again.

In order for the TMS therapy to work, I needed to stay alert and attentive at all times. That's what the TV was for: It was hooked up with Netflix and Hulu and all the best streaming channels. If a good show was what it took for a patient to keep their neurons firing, then they had a top-notch entertainment catalog to choose from.

Dr. Barberi told me that the TMS would only have a fighting chance if I kept up with the sessions regularly. I assumed that meant an appointment or two a week, but he quickly clarified that "regularly" meant "every single day besides Saturday and Sunday." Ideally, I'd get it done on the weekends, too, but his clinic wasn't open then, so I had to settle for business days. As I tried to process this information, figuring out how I could get away with yet another obscure depression treatment without having to explain myself to my boss, Dr. Barberi reassured me that they were open for sessions after working hours. I could easily pop on by during my commute home, he said. I didn't tell him that Union Square was a significant detour from the Mission District. Once I'd committed to TMS, I was determined to see it through.

That's how I wound up sitting in a drab yet freshly painted room above a luxury necklace and bracelet shop every single weekday afternoon for eight straight months, looking like a death row inmate who was lucky enough to watch *Parks and Recreation* reruns during their final moments on earth. I'd always struggled with routine, but something about the everyday hum of the TMS sessions was calming—a steady, predictable activity and a commitment that kept me out of my bed. I never saw Dr. Barberi. I was told he read my daily surveys to keep tabs on my mood and received regular reports from the technician. For the most part, I assumed he was off in a lab doing important research or giving speeches to other mental health professionals.

I soon got used to the feeling of the magnetic pulses against my brain and came to tolerate, even perversely crave, the feeling of the incessant, stinging jabs. During the first few months, I sat there in silence, watching sitcoms on Netflix. I grew to appreciate the stillness of it all, the thirty minutes of each day in which I didn't have to think about my responsibilities, and I wasn't hiding in my bedroom, either. I could just *be*. Eventually, because we were spending so much time in each other's presence that we almost had no choice, Ricardo and I started talking. It started as small talk, little complaints about work or comments about San Francisco's unseasonably blustery summer. But soon our chitchat ballooned into full-blown conversations about almost anything. He loved to hear stories about my travel adventures, and I got him to spill the details from even his cringiest online dates.

I wish I could say those pleasant evenings with Ricardo in a boxy gray room above a jewelry store were enough to pull me out of my depression. But each day, I continued to mark my survey with fours and fives. The truth was, I still felt like shit. My internal monologue hadn't quieted down, and more often than not, I craved the comfort and security of my bed. I still maintained some version of a social life, going on walks with Ari and Devon when I could conjure the energy, working the coat check at the Avalon's legendary annual Halloween party, and masking bad feelings with mezcal and weed and the occasional cocaine bender. But those fleeting highs always made me feel worse in their aftermath.

As my eighth month of TMS therapy drew to a close, Dr. Barberi scheduled an in-person appointment with me. It was now winter, and his office overlooked Union Square's annual ice-skating rink. I stared down at the happy people gliding gracefully in circles, thinking about how I'd always sucked at skating, as Dr. Barberi set a manila folder between us on his desk. Inside the folder were two-thirds of a year's worth of surveys, proving what I already knew: I remained, at my core, a fundamentally depressed person. There was no other label for it.

"Yours is an interesting case," Dr. Barberi said. "You've been so diligent about your TMS treatments. More committed than many of our other patients. And yet, if we chart out your mood scores on a graph, the line remains mostly steady. There's been no shift toward a more positive outcome, like we expected."

I sighed. I already knew all this, of course, but seeing it laid out in front of me made me feel I'd gotten an F on my TMS test. "So, what now?" I asked. "Maybe you can make the pulses stronger? Target a different area of my brain? Extend my appointments to an hour?"

Dr. Barberi only shook his head. "Yours is a form of truly treatment-resistant depression," he said. "One that it doesn't seem TMS therapy is equipped to help with. I wish there was more we could do for you, Carly. I really do. You're a bright young woman with a promising future. I truly hope you discover a regimen that works more effectively."

Just like everything I'd tried before it, my attempt at TMS therapy had been nothing but an attempt. My thoughts turned to the only thing that could possibly comfort me—my warm bed, only a twenty-minute commute away. I zipped my jacket up to my chin and left the TMS clinic for the final time. The skaters swooshed past me as I trudged through the cold night to the BART station.

Why did I end up checking into the psych ward? The reasonable answer was that I felt like I had exhausted all other options—and I was just plain exhausted. I woke up one day and really, really wanted to go back to sleep. Not just for a few hours, or even for the rest of the day. I was too tired to figure out how to make that happen, so I turned myself over to professionals. Sleeping in a hospital, under the care of doctors, seemed like my only choice. At least it would give me a legitimate excuse to call in sick to work.

Since the TMS therapy had failed to have much of an impact on my brain cells, I'd been fielding suicidal thoughts again. They came and went. Sometimes it happened in passing; I'd be waiting for a

BART train and a notion would flicker in my head that it would be so easy to jump onto the tracks. Then I'd board the train and the thought would be gone. But other times, the fantasies persisted; I'd languish in bed desperate to end my life, plotting out every detail of where I would buy just the right kind of pills and lock myself in a hotel room where nobody would find me for at least a couple days.

Playing out the logistics of my suicide in my mind almost always made me feel a tiny bit better; it was like I was finally taking control, even in my imagination, over a condition that otherwise ruled my life. But it was terrifying, nonetheless. And in the moments I was coherent enough to consider my well-paying job, my enviable living situation, and my supportive family and friends, the dissonance and guilt felt almost as overwhelming as the depression itself. My inability to appreciate what I had fed the belief that I didn't deserve to be alive.

Sometimes, when the suicidal thoughts reached a fever pitch, I called my father, the only person I knew who was intimately familiar with this kind of pain. With him, I didn't have to spare any of the ugly details.

"I want so badly to take those thoughts and feelings away from you," he would say, and while his empathy made me feel less alone, it was also a reminder that I was predisposed to my darkness. That my genetics might keep me from ever fumbling my way to light.

Earlier that year, while I was still in the midst of TMS treatments, my dad had flown to California from Connecticut for a visit. I brought him out to hike Lands End along the Pacific Ocean, one of San Francisco's treasures. As my dad watched me heave my body up the seemingly never-ending dirt staircase to the summit, as he saw my blank face stare aimlessly over that world-famous view of the Golden Gate Bridge, he looked at me with a knowing sadness and put his arm around me.

"There *is* another side to all this," he said. "You'll have no choice but to reach it if you just keep moving forward."

Moving forward didn't feel like an option until I took a long pause. I rode to the psychiatric hospital in the back of an Uber, slumped against the window. On the way, I phoned Michael, my boss, and told him I was having a medical crisis and heading to the emergency room. Mercifully, he didn't ask further questions.

In stark contrast to my mental state, my professional performance continued to receive stellar reviews. At work, I could direct just enough of my meager energy into tasks I was well suited for after years toiling away as a round-the-clock news editor. I had a focused set of specific things to do, and I executed them with skills that felt second nature. I could usually shove my depression into a back corner of my mind during my hours at the office. It never went far, though: The commute was still brutal, my walks to and from the BART station a slog, each step feeling like my shoes had ten-pound weights attached to the soles. Sometimes, I took meetings from my bed with the video camera turned off, and I'd taken more sick days than I could count. My output managed to belie the misery of the person producing it.

After I got off the phone with Michael, I texted my mother and told her I was checking myself into the psych ward. She offered to take the day off from work and drive over from Oakland to help me. I was too tired to say no. I waited for her on a bench at the entrance to the hospital, feeling pallid and numb, and gave her a limp hug when she arrived. My mom was a real trooper that day: She stood beside me as I checked myself in, filling out that dreaded 5150 form that turned me over to the hospital's care. She sat with me as I lay down on a cot in the waiting room until a doctor could see me, reading Twitter on her iPad while I curled up in the fetal position.

At one point, in a brief moment of levity, my mom snapped a photo of me waving at her from that cot. The situation *was* pretty outrageous: professional woman takes the day off to nap in a hospital. I'm pretty sure at least five hours passed before I got to talk to a doctor, a harried-looking resident who was even younger than me. They were short-staffed that day, he explained, and there were no beds available yet in the ward. Perhaps I'd be more comfortable waiting in a private room?

"Perhaps," I agreed, and he transferred me to a tiny windowless cell that bore nothing but another sagging cot on wheels.

It was nearing dinnertime by then, and my mom had to leave to feed the dog. "Are you *sure* you'll be okay?" she asked me. "I can just take you back to my place with me; you can rest there for a few days."

I shook my head. I knew, deep down, that I needed more than just rest. I hugged her goodbye and passed out on cot number two. I don't know how long I slept inside that little cell, but by the time a nurse gently nudged me awake, it was the middle of the night.

She handed me a pair of hospital scrubs and waited outside while I changed. I gave her my clothes and my purse, the only possessions I had with me, and she assured me the staff would keep them safe until I checked out. I padded behind her in my papery, hospital-sanctioned slippers, down the hall and into a creaky elevator, to the fifth floor. The elevator doors opened onto what was clearly a psychiatric ward: blinding lights, shiny floors, ghostly hallways, some sort of perpetual beeping noise in the background.

I went through my check-in exercises like a robot. I'm not sure what they asked me, but I'm sure I told them I was not well. The nurse showed me to another cell-like room, this one with a tiny barred window in the corner, and told me my case would be addressed by the daytime staff in the morning. For now, all I needed to do was continue to sleep. Since I had come there to do just that, my first day in the psych ward was, ostensibly, a success. I pulled the stiff white sheet up to my chin and, for a few more hours, turned off reality.

Ari and Devon met me outside exactly three days later—the minimum psychiatric hold the 5150 form permitted. I was so eager to get out of there that I almost felt something that resembled excitement. I hadn't seen daylight or breathed fresh air in seventy-two long hours.

Instead, I'd sat through group therapy sessions with people experiencing very different acute crises from my own, some in states of active paranoia, others hearing auditory hallucinations. I poked my plastic fork around plates of drab microwavable lasagna and canned peaches. I parked myself in a metal folding chair in the gravel "outdoor recreation area" for a few minutes during our daily allotment of sun. I flopped on the couch in the common room while 1980s romantic comedies played on the television. But mostly, I kept to my room, which looked and felt like a prison cell, and I slept on a thin mattress much less comfortable than my own at the Avalon. Yes, I'd achieved the supervised nap I'd craved the morning I checked myself in. But at what cost?

Perhaps the best thing that happened was a chance to talk to yet another highly trained psychiatrist. I shared my complaints about the lithium, and she switched me to Latuda, a more modern mood stabilizer with fewer side effects and a proven ability to treat depression as well as mania. Latuda and Wellbutrin were to become my daily communion, she instructed me, and just like the body of Christ does for the Catholics, hopefully these pills would finally relieve some of my suffering.

Then, because my suicidal thoughts had been replaced by a desperate yearning to go home, she said there wasn't much more they could do for me, and I was discharged.

The sight of Ari and Devon produced something adjacent to real happiness. I ran over to them and we embraced.

"Thank fucking God," I breathed into our three-way hug.

Devon gestured to the hospital building. "Yeah, I don't really get it," she said. "How is this the best place to put sad people?"

We began the long walk home, stopping to take in the view at the top of Tank Hill. "Mental health care is kinda fucked," I said, looking out over the city I loved, thinking back to how suffocating the past three days had been. "I wish more people talked about it."

Ari rubbed my lower back. "You're talking about it," she said. "I admire you so much for that."

In May, more than a year and a half after I left Panama behind, that same hobnobby thought leadership summit I'd helped host at Ico-Inna came to San Francisco. By that point, I didn't think about Ico-Inna all that much. Anytime a memory bubbled up, I felt a pang of regret for my failed relationship and my failed media program, so I'd trained myself to mostly block out those memories. I still hadn't watched the reality show, and Coco Cunningham never reappeared in my inbox or text messages after my abrupt departure. It was almost as if I'd erased the entire experience.

Almost. A couple weeks earlier, I'd received an email from Hendrick, the conference's head honcho, the guy intent on changing the world through his expensive networking events. All Bay Area–based alumni were invited to a "reunion" of sorts at a private Pacific Heights residence (read: giant mansion) for an evening of live music and light bites. In exchange for our attendance, Hendrick asked for a tax-deductible donation to his LLC. As much as I wanted to forget Ico-Inna, receiving the invite had ignited a morbid curiosity that was too big to ignore.

Arm in arm with Pixie, my Burning Man friend, who was a great companion at unfamiliar social events, I ascended the steps to what was indeed a sprawling Pacific Heights estate. Though Pac Heights wasn't that exciting of a neighborhood overall, it boasted some of the biggest and most impressive homes in town, residences that sheltered the likes of the storied Getty family and the bestselling romance novelist Danielle Steel. This particular home had two giant roman columns separating the walkway from the front door. I tapped the brass door knocker, which was carved into the shape of a vine that matched the ivy scaling up the redbrick exterior. Someone I didn't recognize let us in, kissed us on both cheeks, and led us toward a name tag–making station, lest we forget the importance of networking.

The event was mostly mundane and filled with strangers name-dropping to one another, prototypical entrepreneur and venture-capital types who I largely avoided in my social circles even though Theodora and Henry came from that world. A bored-looking violinist played next to a fireplace, and a buffet table offered up snacks I recognized as takeout from a Greek fast-food franchise.

"Seriously? This is all we get?" Pixie said, rolling her eyes and shoving a piece of pita bread in her mouth. I dipped my own pita in a plastic vat of hummus and looked around for the bar.

It was beer and wine only, so Pixie snitched a whole bottle of merlot and we brought it over to an overstuffed velvet couch near the violinist. I noticed Hendrick gesticulating enthusiastically across the room, and I hid my face. I didn't feel like answering his inevitable probing questions about what I'd been up to since leaving the jungle. I just wanted to survey the scene, maybe catch up with a few lower-stakes acquaintances. As Pixie and I took turns swigging from the wine bottle, I felt someone sit down next to me.

"Well if it isn't the famous Carly Schwartz," the person said. I turned around and found myself face-to-face with DeLong, my old Ico-Inna pal. His man bun was gone, replaced with a feathery buzz cut, but it was unmistakably him—one of the first people I'd met upon arriving in Panama and someone who remained one of my favorites until his unfortunate departure.

"Oh my gosh!" I squealed, genuinely thrilled to see him, pulling him toward me for a massive bear hug. "DeLong, wow, what are you doing here? I haven't seen you since the day you guys all up and quit!"

He grinned. "You mean right before the rest of you became reality-TV stars? Seems like I dodged a bullet there." He introduced himself to Pixie, who winked and took another big gulp of merlot.

"What do you mean? Dodged a bullet how?" I asked. As much as I'd tried to avoid the TV series, of course I still wanted to know how it had been received. Luckily, aside from only a handful of text messages I'd fielded the night of the premiere, nobody ever mentioned it to me. I could only assume my appearances had been minimal.

DeLong cackled conspiratorially. "You didn't watch?"

I shook my head.

"Well, probably better off," he said. "You already got to see it all in person, anyway. They must have just let the cameras roll—didn't even have to *try* to make that place look like a pathetic joke."

My mind snapped to the time Max filmed me under the Brooklyn Bridge, clutching my bottle of pills. The unease must have shown on my face because DeLong patted me on the shoulder.

"Don't worry; you're only in the first episode," he said. "They painted you as the sane one who got out while she could. Man, I'm sorry about all the depression stuff, though. I had no idea shit was so hard for you while we were down there."

Relief—mixed with a little schadenfreude, if I'm being honest—relaxed my body. DeLong's review of the show was consistent with Devon's. That, I reasoned, made it as good as a fact.

"So what happened to Ico-Inna?" I asked. "Is it still going strong after all that? I haven't talked to anyone since . . ." I trailed off and motioned to my surroundings, knowing I didn't need to explain myself much more.

DeLong shook his head. "I'm not sure," he replied. "Last I heard through the grapevine, they haven't been able to pull in hardly any students since the show came out. Anytime you google them, all that comes up are TV show recaps. Pretty unflattering ones, at that. Someone told me Coco started a Kickstarter campaign to try to get back all the money he's wasted." He snorted. "Good luck finding backers, Big Guy."

DeLong told me that he currently lived in Detroit and was working for a political-action group focused on legalizing psilocybin, the active ingredient in magic mushrooms. His amateur rap career had also taken off a bit, and he was somewhat of a known entity on the local scene, performing at bars and open mic nights across Michigan. He was in San Francisco just for the weekend, for his cousin's wedding in Redwood City, and he'd gotten Hendrick's email about a reunion and couldn't pass it up.

"I gave that fucker five bucks," he said. "Wanted to make the most of my *tax deductible donation*." I giggled and gave him a high five. I really did adore this kid while I was down in Panama, before he left in a flourish with the other staffers, when I didn't yet know I wasn't that far behind.

"What about everyone else?" I asked DeLong. "You still in touch with the others?"

He shook his head. "Not really, man, I mean I see what's what on Facebook here and there," he said. "Chef Lola was on a road trip a few months back and passed through; we got a beer, it was great. Oh! And I was down in LA last week before I came up here so I caught one of Santi's comedy shows. His new lady-friend was there. She seems cool."

At the mention of Santiago, my heartbeat accelerated. I'd been bracing myself for the moment when I learned anything tangible about his love life. By that point, my memories of our time together were so far removed from my day-to-day realities that they felt more like mythology. But the knowledge that he was happily coupled, living out his comedy dreams—while I suffered just a few hundred miles to the north—all but flattened me.

I grabbed the bottle of wine off the coffee table, where Pixie had left it behind so she could do an interpretive dance to the violin music. I took a huge sip, and then another. And then another, until a small stream of merlot dribbled down my chin and I wiped it off with the back of my shaking hand. I was about to down the rest of the bottle when DeLong swiped it away from me.

"Oh man, I thought you knew," he said sheepishly, setting the wine back on the table. "Santiago told me everything was totally cool with you two, that you'd both moved on. I didn't think you'd be so surprised."

I snatched the bottle back and took another glug. Santiago and I hadn't spoken since that dreadful email arrived in my inbox the day before my new job started. Every once in a while, he made surprise appearances in my dreams, which startled me awake.

"No, no," I said, fumbling to recover, feeling wine-dizzy. "You're right, it's all good. I did hear he was dating someone. I just forgot." Another big swig of merlot. "Hang on, I have to use the bathroom."

I left DeLong on the couch and Pixie swaying around by the fireplace. I wandered around the house in a daze, my heart still thumping, my mind racing between thoughts of Santiago with some mystery woman and images of my sad self hiding under the covers for days at a time.

I wandered up to the top floor of the house, sluggish and syrupy and drunk, spotting a door ajar at the end of the hallway, a sliver of light peeking through the crack. I poked my head inside the room. It looked like an old-fashioned library, lined with fully stocked bookshelves on three walls. The fourth contained a massive picture window with the Financial District on full view.

A bunch of people crouched around a small coffee table. A few women with big blond hair and even bigger breasts, their faces contorted into obvious plastic surgery, and some men with slicked-back hair in dapper-looking suits. They were all speaking rapidly, breathlessly, in another language—Russian, maybe?—as one of the women crouched in front of a pile of white powder with a rolled-up bill shoved in a nostril. At the sight of cocaine, I instinctually lunged toward the scene. One of the men patted the ground next to him and moved over to make room for me.

I spent the rest of the night holed up in that library doing line after line, trying to forget what DeLong had told me downstairs. I only understood about half of what my new friends said; they kept switching between broken English and the original language they'd been speaking. It didn't matter; I was deeply familiar with the phenomenon of flimsy, temporary communities bound together by drugs. When coke was involved, whoever you shared it with was your best friend. Until it ran out, and you became strangers again.

That night, it didn't run out until the sky outside the window faded to indigo and the birds began their early morning call-and-response routine. I dragged my twitchy body and throbbing head back downstairs, a zombie greeting the sunrise, and hailed a cab, trying not to vomit as the car wound its way up and down the hills back to the Mission.

chapter seventeen

I rolled over onto my side and peeked at the clock on my bedside table: 11:48 a.m. My next meeting with my coworkers was at noon. Not a chance I'd be able to scramble into the office in time.

By now, getting out of bed before early afternoon had become the rarest of occurrences. I tried everything: multiple alarms scattered around the room, bribing myself with permission to stay in bed all weekend if I made it up by 10:00 a.m. for three consecutive days. Nothing worked; the idea of leaving the safety of my warm cocoon and joining the rest of society sparked too much dread to overcome each morning.

I propped myself up on two pillows and opened my laptop, signing into our custom video conferencing program. The software gave participants the option to join meetings without turning their cameras on. I stared at the static icon of my smiling face, a photo snapped in one of my favorite mariachi plazas in Mexico City. The rest of my team was either attending in person, sitting up straight around a big table in one of the office's many conference rooms, or from sophisticated-looking home offices that we could all see because their cameras were turned on.

Nobody at work seemed to notice my constant excuses for taking care of my obligations remotely: another one of those pesky migraines, a family emergency in the East Bay. The only punishment I received for my lackluster performance came from my own inner monologue. My self-loathing thoughts played on a constant loop as I lay there in bed, willing myself to get up and wishing I could stay there forever.

As summer unfolded, booze and cocaine became the only compelling reasons to shuffle out of my bedroom. Partying could still pull me, temporarily, from my misery—a fleeting and cheap sense of relief and belonging. Anytime I found myself in a bar or at an event, I sniffed out whatever random acquaintances were willing to call their drug dealers, latching onto their social groups like a tick. The pattern was always the same: party, collapse, party, sleep for days, party, want to die.

The amount of recovery time I needed after every bender was exponentially more than how long I'd been out in the world. I'd spend twenty-four hours in a whirlwind of bodies, music, liquor, powders, and strangers-turned-soulmates, and then I wouldn't leave my room for a week. When the abusive voice in my head finally grew too loud to bear, I'd turn down the volume by peeling myself out of bed and putting more chemicals in my body. But I knew that voice would return, louder than ever, when the party ended. Every time I thought I hit my rock bottom, I learned that there was still space to sink farther down.

I started doing whip-its alone, boxes upon boxes at a time. Most people who have never been in the parking lot outside a Disco Biscuits concert don't even know what whip-its are: small, bullet-shaped cartridges of nitrous oxide that you twist into an old-fashioned whipped-cream canister and inhale for a head rush that lasts no longer than fifteen seconds. They're highly addictive and ostensibly pointless and you can buy them by the hundred-pack at almost any local smoke shop. I didn't know this at the time, but consuming them compulsively can eventually lead to permanent paralysis of the limbs.

I couldn't articulate to anyone who asked—and, to my relief, nobody did—why I gravitated toward such a pointless, damaging pastime, except that it provided yet another escape. Even a meditative one, at that. I'd twist, breathe in, hold, breathe out, get dizzy, and repeat, over and over again, until the box was empty and the little canisters made a jangling sound as I loaded them into my trash can. Concerned that the other Avalon housemates might hear me, I'd gingerly place the cartridges into the garbage one by one to remain discreet.

I didn't tell my therapist, Kristina, who I was now seeing weekly, about any of the drugs. Like my previous omissions to mental health professionals, the more I avoided sharing the truth with her, the less real my behavior felt to me. By that point I knew I should be honest about it with her. But I also knew that if she found out, she would try to make me stop. And I didn't want to stop. I was terrified by the idea of facing life without the option to mask it, without these tiny moments of relief—no matter how much more pain this behavior caused me in the long run.

It felt like a kind of perverse game, avoiding the topic of substance use during my therapy sessions and figuring out other stuff to talk about instead. I would rack my brain for problematic narratives to labor through, delicately neglecting to mention anything to do with drugs or alcohol. When each session ended without so much as an acknowledgment of my benders, I almost believed that the benders hadn't happened in the first place. If a tree falls in a forest that's really far away from your therapist's office, does it ever actually make a sound?

Somewhere along the way, I went to see a nutritionist. Her toned body, glistening skin, chic wardrobe, and seemingly impenetrable peppiness irked me, but she looked like she had things more figured out than I did, so I let her give me some suggestions. She told me my depression was likely caused by vitamin deficiencies and suggested I cut out all gluten, dairy, and sugar. She made me leave her a fecal sample—a revolting act that involved crouching over her office toilet seat, trying to successfully poop into a small jar without getting anything on my hands—and sent me away with a worksheet to document all my caloric intake for the next week.

For a while, I diligently followed the plan: sugar-free coconut-milk yogurt in the morning, chicken apple sausage on a bed of spinach for lunch, arugula salad with oil and vinegar for dinner.

I switched from red wine to vodka and from lattes to black coffee. Devon caught me in the Avalon kitchen one night, loading a tray of roasted sweet potatoes and broccoli into a bowl of quinoa.

"You know, I think all the blow might be counteracting your gluten-free diet," she said matter-of-factly. It wasn't judgmental; Devon never judged me. She was simply stating an observation. Devon hated cocaine and always had, but she never tried to control my behavior or anyone else's.

She had, however, stood by my side as I'd endured what was coming up on two years of major depression. I knew it hadn't been easy for her. Through years of talking to her about my condition, I've learned that the hardest thing about being so close with a depressed person is learning that nothing you do or say will change how they feel. Devon described it as a palpable helplessness, made even more challenging by the fact that even though I hated myself steadfastly, she never stopped appreciating all the things she loved about me.

"I wish you could see yourself the way I see you," she often said, and I would shake my head, sadly, believing nothing about how she perceived me to be true.

The morning after my final bender felt like any other bad hangover. I woke up with a jolt of energy and a crushing headache only a few hours after I'd fallen asleep, my mouth as dry as sandpaper, my eyelashes crusted with two-day-old mascara. I padded over to the kitchen, smeared some Nutella on an apple, and ate it standing up. Downed four ibuprofen pills at the same time and chased them with orange juice straight from the carton. Climbed back into bed, desperate to quiet my anxious mind and slow down my heart rate. Closed my eyes again and passed out until midafternoon, waking up just as anxious, my heart throttling.

The day before, I'd attended a rooftop *Boogie Nights*–themed party with my friend Timothy from work, decked out in leather pants and a see-through lace leotard. The gathering began with mimosas and a light brunch; a bottle of champagne later and I'd convinced Timothy to call his dealer. We spent the rest of the party taking turns going in and out of the host's bathroom, hunched over a plate, as if nobody else knew what we were up to. I'd been miserable the entire week prior, making it into the office only once, and I distinctly remember the relief of that first line of cocaine. *This,* I thought, as that all-too-temporary euphoria glittered through my limbs. *This is what it feels like to be happy.*

Now, my hungover body craved a couple hits of nitrous. Not just craved—*coveted.* Whip-its were the only thing that would quell my anxiety, allow me to focus on my breath, and get me through the rest of the day. I rolled out of bed and pulled my combat boots on over my pajama pants, my face still smeared with makeup. Dragged myself into daylight and down the block to the smoke shop.

The sun smashed against my eyes, making my head start pounding again. At the corner of Valencia and Twenty-First Streets, I surveyed the other people around me. Normal folks, effortlessly going about their Sunday. I could never be like those people. A couple about my age pushing a stroller down the sidewalk. Two teenagers eating ice cream cones. Some girlfriends hauling their shopping bags into one of the many vintage stores. All these people had gotten out of bed that morning, ready for a pleasant weekend. It had been years since I'd gone for a casual stroll on a Sunday afternoon and hadn't either been fucked-up or distracted by persistent reminders of how much I hated myself.

The smoke shop was only a few blocks away, but I was out of breath by the time I arrived. I asked the guy behind the counter for a box of one hundred whip-its, telling myself I'd only do a couple when I got home and save the rest for another time. I wanted them so badly I trembled as he selected a box from the display case and swiped my credit card. I kept shaking as it took far too long for him to authorize the charge and print the receipt. When, at last, he handed me the plastic bag with the box of whip-its inside, I clutched it to my chest and practically ran home.

I dove back into bed and hungrily inhaled my first one, and then a second, and then a third. Before I knew it, the box was completely empty, my bed was littered with little metal nitrous cartridges, and I felt even more anxious than when I'd woken up.

I brushed the nitrous cartridges aside and curled up into the fetal position again. They made a clanking sound as they hit the floor. I passed out feeling pathetic and sorry for myself. When I woke up again, around dinnertime, I had a text from Timothy.

"Wow," he said. "What a mess. I feel like shit. I'm never like this."

To me, this was normal post-bender behavior. I was well-acquainted with the aftermath of hard partying: swirls of shame and exhaustion, wasted subsequent days feeling anxious and mildly sick. This Sunday was like so many others.

"You'll be fine," I wrote back to him. "This happens to me all the time."

His response was quick and offhand; he probably didn't even mean anything by it. But seeing his words was like that feeling when you're in the middle of a horrible nightmare and you suddenly, lucidly, realize you're only dreaming. That it's only a matter of time before you wake up.

"If this happens to you all the time," he said, "then you might have a problem."

My immediate gut reaction to his text message was so quick that it barely registered, so fleeting it could have been just throwaway noise. But for some reason, I managed to grab on to the words as they flicked through my brain.

I need to go to rehab.

And that one simple thought was the most relief I'd felt from my pain in years.

I conveniently had my weekly therapy session with Kristina the following day. Before I lost my nerve, I told her everything. Confessions overflowed like a too-full pot of boiling water: The binge drinking and weed smoking that began in college. My cocaine habits in New York and Panama. My regular dalliances with all sorts of substances in the years that followed. And, most recently, the benders that had reached a crescendo. My horrible day doing whip-its in bed, merely a punctuation mark at the end of a long, run-on sentence of horrible days doing whip-its in bed.

By the time I finished talking, I was limp, deflated, practically out of breath, and deeply, deeply relieved. I waited for Kristina to judge me, to tell me I had to stop. I waited for her to berate me for my self-destructive patterns. But she did nothing of the sort. She simply nodded as if I were recommending my favorite book for her to read and smiled as if we were old friends.

"I'm really, really proud of you, Carly," she said. "What you just did takes a lot of courage."

Pride was the last reaction I'd expected. I exhaled. My therapist's kind disposition, her graciousness at receiving stories of my gross behavior, relieved me even more.

At the same time, I couldn't help but feel like I might be overreacting. I knew all the cocaine was a problem. But it's not like I was doing it every day. And it's not like I ever *really* had an issue with alcohol. I could go days without drinking. Marijuana was certainly more a creativity tool than an addictive drug. Maybe it didn't have to be so black-and-white.

"Do you think I could go to rehab just to get rid of the coke stuff?" I asked her. "I mean, I'm not an addict or anything. I know people who do it a lot more than me. I can go days—even weeks—without drugs or alcohol. It's not like I'm under a bridge, or whatever. Maybe there's a way for me to give up the cocaine, maybe the nitrous binges, but . . . not necessarily everything else."

I couldn't, *couldn't* give up everything else. I wasn't capable of experiencing joy without the help of some sort of substance. I didn't know what real, pure, sober happiness felt like. Or if it was possible for me to *ever* feel it.

Kristina smiled warmly again. "Of course you can go to rehab just to address your issue with cocaine," she said. "Nobody can make you give up any substances you don't want to. It has to come from *you*."

She went on to explain that addiction could take on many forms. It didn't have to constitute chronic, daily use, or even a weekly habit. Addiction, she said, was more about the compulsive behavior I exhibited in the presence of drugs and alcohol. The inability to find an "off" switch, a reliance on intoxicants as an escape from reality. "Addiction comes in all shapes and sizes," she said. "The most important thing for you to know is that there's absolutely nothing to be ashamed of. You've already conquered one of the hardest parts: asking for help."

The conference rooms at work were known for their whimsical, quirky names. Visit any of its offices around the world, and you'd take meetings and calls from places named after sci-fi creatures, mythological Greek goddesses, and cult films. I made the phone call that changed my life while sitting on the floor inside "Paul Thomas Anderson." An ironic coincidence that the place I hid from my coworkers to cold-call a rehab center was named after the director of *Boogie Nights*—also the theme of the party where I took my final bump of cocaine.

That morning, I'd searched online for Bay Area–based treatment facilities that accepted my health insurance. Fancy rehab isn't readily available to people without steady careers or deep-pocketed resources, a dichotomy that struck me as deeply unfair even as I trudged through my own misery. When Water's Edge appeared on my screen, it looked like everything the psych ward wasn't: rolling hills, expansive views, fresh air, healthy food. I wondered why drug addicts received care in settings that looked akin to a spa vacation while the mentally ill languished inside sterile hospitals. Water's Edge seemed like a lovely, rejuvenating environment in which to address my demons.

I was still skeptical, though: After inpatient and outpatient psychiatric programs, nearly a year of TMS therapy, intravenous ketamine infusions, a special diet, and multiple regimens of antidepressants, my depression raged on. There was no reason to think that rehab would make a meaningful difference, either. But the images of Water's Edge were so inviting; its restorative setting beckoned from the screen. The website labeled the program "dual diagnosis," meaning it treated addiction and the concurrent mental health disorders that fueled it. Reading about dual diagnosis was the first time I made any conscious link between depression and getting high. In the accessible parts of my mind, my partying and my mental illness had always existed on two separate planes.

The automatic lights flickered on as I snuck into Paul Thomas Anderson with my cell phone and dialed the Water's Edge intake line. A woman picked up the phone; her voice was kind with an edge of dry humor, the tone of someone who spent her days immersed in a subject matter that wouldn't be survivable without some levity. She asked me the same questions I usually heard from mental health professionals, and this time, I didn't skimp on the raw truth. Instead, I leaned into it, describing my cocaine benders in colorful detail, outlining every moment of the day I needed whip-its so badly I physically shook at the cash register in the smoke shop. I wanted Water's Edge to deem me worthy of treatment. For once, I had nothing to be ashamed of: The worse off I was, the more likely my insurance would cover my stay. Laying it all out for the intake woman felt like sinking into a warm bath.

"Alright, Carly," she said when I was done. "First of all, I want you to know that this all sounds really painful. I'm sorry you're living a life that causes you this much pain."

Sorry? I had never before heard someone say they were sorry I liked to party. I'd always considered my behavior to be a deliberate choice. Something people might judge me for, perhaps, but never something that deserved genuine sympathy. According to the intake counselor, partying was a manifestation of deep pain. Pain that was worthy of treatment.

"I have to run this by your insurers and convince them to cover your stay here at Water's Edge," the counselor continued. "But based on everything you've told me, we've got a really good case. I definitely think you're fucked-up enough to get in here."

She laughed at her own off-color joke, which made me laugh, too. Being a fuckup had never made me feel so accepted before.

chapter eighteen

The Water's Edge campus boasted sweeping views of the San Francisco Bay and all three of the region's major bridges. My mother dropped me off at the nurse's station less than a week after my call with the intake counselor. A technician with a shaved head and tattoo sleeves greeted me like an old pal coming to visit for the weekend. He looked to be about my age and almost immediately told me he was also a recovering addict.

"I know what you're feeling right now," he said. "This is all so unfamiliar. I promise you'll be more comfortable soon."

I surveyed my surroundings: the manicured lawn, the cloudless sky, the striking variety of trees and plants and exotic flower species, the bean-shaped pool, the redbrick buildings with open windows. Definitely not the psych ward.

When I told my loved ones I was heading to rehab, everyone's reaction was relatively similar: supportive, with a glimmer of surprise. I'd managed to keep the worst of my drug use under wraps. People like Devon and Ari knew I'd go on the occasional weekend bender, and my parents had seen me drunk enough times to know that I usually had no "off" switch. But nobody had ever associated me with the "addict" label before.

By that point, I'd been struggling with suicidal depression for more than two years. So mostly, my friends and family were just glad that I hadn't lost the resolve to get better. If rehab was an option I hadn't yet exhausted, then rehab was the place I should go. I told my Avalon housemates about my decision during one of our Monday-night dinners. As I looked around the table at the faces of the people I'd made a home with since returning from Panama, I could feel how much I'd become a part of their shared world. If I could conquer the darkness inside myself, I'd have so much to give back.

I'd read on the Water's Edge website that cell phones were strictly prohibited, so my father sent me an overnight package containing one of his old iPods. He'd loaded it up with all the music we both adored, the jam bands and classic rock of my childhood. My mother took the day off work to drive me across the Golden Gate Bridge and up to the bucolic Marin County hilltop where Water's Edge perched. The night before, she'd helped me pack a duffel bag with my most comfortable baggy T-shirts and pajama pants. It felt good to finally recognize and appreciate little acts of support.

The technician brought me to a room I'd be sharing with someone named Candace, who wasn't there when I arrived. Her clothes were neatly folded next to one of the two twin beds, and the bathroom was full of travel-sized bottles that looked to be the ingredients of a complicated skin-care routine. I hoisted my duffel bag onto the vacant bed and pulled a journal out of one of the side pockets. I'd finally started scribbling some thoughts down after an arduous period of writer's block. Hopefully this whole strange experience could provide fodder for some interesting reflections.

It was just about dinnertime when I finished unpacking, so I made my way up the hill to the dining room, which featured a banquet-style table next to a clear glass wall that overlooked the water and the bridges. A man in a chef's hat was shaving prime rib onto someone's plate, and a line of people wearing similar comfy clothes served themselves delicious-looking asparagus, mashed potatoes, and spinach from a buffet. I loaded up a plate, grabbed a seltzer from a bucket of ice, and sat down at the far end of the table, where two youngish-looking guys in flannel shirts were chatting. One of them sported a face full of scruffy facial hair, and the other's baby-smooth skin made it clear scruffy facial hair would never be an option.

"Hi!" the hairless one greeted me as I joined them. "You must be the new girl."

"I must be," I replied. "I'm Carly."

"I'm Kevin, and this is Roger. We were just discussing the difference between fentanyl patches and painkillers. Do you have an opinion?"

Their bluntness startled me. "Oh, I mean . . ." I began. "Opiates weren't really my thing."

Kevin chuckled. "What *wasn't* my thing?" Roger, the scruffy one, grunted in agreement.

"So, then, what are you here for?"

I hesitated. What *was* I here for? Was I about to be locked up with a bunch of hardcore daily drug users? Wasn't I just a party girl with a tendency to overdo things? A party girl with really, really bad depression? That familiar sense of impostor syndrome, that maybe I'd been exaggerating my problems all along, washed over me.

"I guess you could say I'm here for cocaine," I replied slowly. "I do, you know, a lot of blow when I go out. Which isn't every day," I quickly added. "I'm not, like, you know, a typical addict or anything. I'm mainly just here for a bit of a reset. I need to cut out coke. I don't know if I'd ever, uh . . . give up drinking or anything."

Kevin exchanged a look with Roger and then nodded as if they shared a solemn secret. "Whatever you're here for, Cokehead Carly, you're in the right place," he said, spearing an asparagus with his fork. "Think of this as a summer camp for adults. A self-help summer camp. I've only been here two weeks, and I feel better than I have in my entire life." Roger grunted in agreement again.

"So, then, what are you here for?" I asked them. This seemed like the kind of place where you didn't mince words. Where you could get right to the point, and be brutally honest, even if the person next to you was a total stranger.

Kevin shrugged. "Heroin, mostly," he said breezily. "Lots of heroin by the end there. Only two things made me happy: getting fucked-up and playing guitar. Luckily, I still have my guitar. I even brought it here with me."

"And you just *love* serenading us!" A musical voice said from behind. I looked over as one of the most beautiful women I'd ever seen sat down next to me. Perfectly blow-dried hair, not a stitch of makeup out of place. Even though she was wearing yoga clothes, she looked completely put together, like she would fit right in at an office or on a talk show.

"Hi," she said to me, displaying a mouthful of straight white teeth. "I'm Candace. Are you my new roommate?"

Just like transitioning from the depths of depression to a manic episode, getting better during rehab didn't happen instantaneously. No easy switch to flip that ignited gratitude and self-love. Instead, it was more like that dimmer again, gradually rising upward until the room filled with light.

I settled into the rhythms of Water's Edge relatively easily. It wasn't too hard for me to wake up at seven each morning, buoyed by the knowledge that my day was full of pleasant activities and structured around a sense of purpose. Getting out of bed without an arduous struggle for the first time in two years kindled an unfamiliar spark of energy that kept me alert and present through the morning yoga classes, workshops, and therapy sessions. I took to the group therapy more than I had at my outpatient program; since we all lived together, the rapport felt more natural and comfortable. I found something in common with each of the other residents—all of them struggled with hating themselves, and though the details of how they numbed their pain often differed, our core feelings remained deeply similar.

I enjoyed studying my own life against the backdrop of my peers and learning about the diverse backgrounds and different paths that led us to the same place. I cracked jokes with Tony, the middle-aged meth addict with facial scars and a tendency to interrupt people. I listened to tales of Roger's love life, which was surprisingly colorful considering his standoffish demeanor that first night at dinner. I bought Sour Patch Kids and packs of American Spirits from Kevin, who operated a black market business from his room. I traded work tips with Helena, who was closer to my mother's age and also on medical leave from a corporate job. Their stories helped me piece together my own narrative, to understand myself more intimately.

In addition to group therapy, Kevin wasn't wrong about the similarities to summer camp: We splashed around in the heated pool, went on nature walks, and participated in rowdy drum circles and qigong sessions. Pretty soon, Candace and I became known among our peers for acting the rowdiest of them all.

"Here comes Double Trouble," the qigong teacher, an eccentric Marin County lifer who wore long beaded necklaces, announced every time Candace and I entered one of her classes. We stood in the front of the room, gleefully clapping our hands and throwing our arms in the air.

"You *are* love!" Candace would say, pointing to me.

"I am *love*!" I'd bellow right back.

"*We* are love!" we'd holler in unison, clasping each other's hands.

At the end of each session, the teacher sprayed lavender aromatherapy oil in each of our faces, and the sheer euphoria of that first breath of scented air wasn't unlike how I used to feel snorting a line of cocaine.

During my limited downtime, I wandered the manicured paths listening to the playlists my dad had made me and hung out under the gazebo sharing cigarettes with my new friends. I'd never been much of a smoker, and I'm still not, but the nicotine camaraderie among recovering drug addicts is cliché for a reason.

Candace and I would often sit under the gazebo together before bed, passing an American Spirit back and forth and gazing at the sky. She told me all about how she'd been brought to her knees by alcohol, red wine in particular, which she'd hid under the bathroom sink from her husband. By the end, she was drinking a minimum of two bottles daily. She came to Water's Edge on a court order: A spying neighbor had called the police when she saw Candace run out to the liquor store, leaving her two-year-old kid, Ryan, home alone in his crib.

"Everything I'm doing to get better—it's all for my Ry-Guy," she'd say, a mantra of sorts.

Side by side in our twin beds at night, Candace and I regaled each other with messy stories of drunken shenanigans, like a middle school sleepover for damaged grown-ups. As I recounted tales of my blackout temper tantrums in college and my recent tendency to guzzle mezcal straight out of the bottle, I started to question my alcohol use for the first time. Coming of age in a society that encouraged binge drinking, I'd never before considered that booze might be as problematic for me as the other stuff.

The Water's Edge computer lab is where I became reacquainted with my lifelong love of writing. Part of the rehab program included a series of assignments to reflect on our past behavior: a detailed account of our "rock bottom" moment, our motivations for getting clean, a fantasy account of the life we'd live freed from the burdens of our own minds. I took these prompts very seriously, writing missives on those clunky desktop computers late into the night, getting lost in my craft and feeling passionate about something other than getting fucked-up for the first time in years. When it came time to share aloud with the group, I read my words with the thrill of someone performing at an open mic night.

"I haven't lost everything," I read. "I still have a good job, a respectable bank account, and close relationships. But I need help. I deserve to know what it's like to experience happiness without a bottle in my hand or a baggie in my pocket. I deserve to have a reason to get out of bed that doesn't involve a party. I deserve to walk down the block on a Sunday afternoon and smile not because I'm on my way to buy drugs but because the sun is shining. I deserve to know what it feels like to live."

I looked around at the faces of my new friends, listening attentively. I moved on to the next assignment: a piece about the life I'd design if I could allow myself to be happy. I spoke of writing books, a dream I'd always been too scared to admit aloud, and of using my story to help other people with similar struggles. I described a woman who derived purpose from using mental illness as a means of connection. I detailed a life that capitalized on travel and adventure, dog adoption, live music, abundant community, and secure attachment to romantic partners. None of the fantasies involved starting a traditional family or raising children—that had never been something I aspired toward, and in my lowest moments, I judged myself for it. But there was no judgment from anyone, not even myself, as I read aloud.

The more I talked, the more the woman in my dream scenario started to feel real. I knew she was in there somewhere. If I kept doing this work, maybe someday, I'd set her free.

My time at Water's Edge, of course, wasn't a vacation—far from it. Each day, I traveled deep into the crevices of my psyche to explore my relationship with drugs and the way they interacted with my depression. As much as I was learning how to pass time enjoyably without getting wasted, I remained acutely aware that reality had ostensibly been suspended, that rehab was merely a liminal break and most of the outside world didn't include so many leisurely pleasures or indulgent therapy sessions.

I waffled on my shaky intentions around future substance use, writing long diatribes in my journal about how I could never imagine going to a party, or on a date, or to a wedding, or out to a fancy dinner, without having a few drinks along the way. I couldn't comprehend how I'd spark any kind of visionary thinking without smoking weed. In idle moments, I craved cocaine and whip-its, but in the safety of my fenced-in campus, I was able to talk about it openly until those cravings passed.

One of the people I spoke to the most was my assigned therapist, Dr. Yasmine Gomez. Dr. Gomez was a few years younger than me but already an accomplished psychiatrist—and a recovering addict herself. Her long black hair was dyed pink at the tips, and she wore it in a messy bun atop her head. Ceramic skulls stretched her gauged earlobes. An army of floral tattoos marched up and down both forearms to her elbows. I loved her from the moment I met her.

No topic was off-limits in Dr. Gomez's office: my low self-esteem, my perpetual sluggishness, my addictive tendencies toward boyfriends, my addictive tendencies toward sleeping, my addictive tendencies toward so many other things. Her office, replete with framed 1980s rock and roll posters and an impressive collection of Japanese wall clocks, was the most comfortable place I'd ever explored my flaws and afflictions.

Early on in our sessions, she had me write a "breakup letter" to my bed, which I read aloud from the comfort of her overstuffed cheetah-print sofa. "Goodbye to sinking into your false security, your faux release," I wrote. "Goodbye to long nights that turn into long days that turn into long nights again. Goodbye to my aching back after too many horizontal hours." At that point, I'd already been rising early every morning and avoiding naps for most of the day, but the act of reading that letter evoked a sense of finality. It would be a balancing act once I left Water's Edge, Dr. Gomez explained, because sleep remained an essential part of a healthy life. The trick would be to no longer use sleep as an escape.

Dr. Gomez and I explored my relationship with success at length. I told her all about how I'd spent most of my twenties chasing a career that looked impressive on paper, aligning my self-worth with my résumé or whatever latest promotion I got, even if reaching those milestones never ended up having a lasting impact on my confidence. We discussed the misalignment with Santiago as I watched him relentlessly chase his own goals, the cognitive dissonance of wanting to succeed as fiercely and conventionally as he did while preferring to spend my free time restfully ("lazily," as I referred to it, and "leisurely," as Dr. Gomez corrected me). I spoke of the guilt I felt around my easy tech gig, that I'd abandoned my roots as a real journalist in favor of corporate comfort.

"Forget, for a moment, how it looks to the rest of the world," Dr. Gomez instructed me during one of our sessions. "What would you do if money were no object, and if it didn't matter what anyone else thought of you?"

"I don't know," I admitted, because salary and status had always been two of my primary professional motivators.

I thought about it for a minute. "I've always wanted to start a magazine," I finally said, reaching back for one of my childhood dreams. "Not online clickbait, but a nice, monthly print magazine, where my writers could really take time and be creative with their storytelling."

"A magazine," Dr. Gomez repeated. "How cool. What else? This is a safe space, an alternate universe where all your dreams will come true."

"Writing," I continued, thinking about how happy I'd been the other night, reading my pieces aloud to the group, and as a kid, scribbling whole worlds onto loose-leaf notebook paper with a freshly sharpened pencil. "I've always wanted to write a book. And I've always known it, too, I just hate admitting it. I'm terrified I would suck. That I would fail."

"Sucking and failing are irrelevant right now," Dr. Gomez replied. "We're just dreaming. It doesn't cost a thing. What else?"

"Helping people like me," I answered immediately. This exercise was starting to get easier, an extension of the fantasy life I'd laid out for my peers the other night. It was like a treasure chest of goals and desires was buried right under the surface, and I'd never allowed myself to unearth it because I'd never believed I deserved happiness.

"I want to help other people who suffer the way I do," I continued. "Use my own voice to show them they're not alone. I want to fight for people who want to end their lives. Nobody deserves to know that pain."

Dr. Gomez nodded. "A beautiful, valiant goal," she said. "Anything else? What does *true* success mean to you, when you dig deep within yourself and come face-to-face with your own personal truths?"

I thought for a moment. The answer was so obvious, I couldn't believe I'd never acknowledged it before. True success had nothing to do with my name on the masthead of a news website, or an edgy media program in the jungle that drew acclaim from impressive people, or the short blip of notoriety that came along with a minor appearance on a reality show. Success was staying out of bed. Success was quieting the perpetual noise in my head that constantly reminded me why I wasn't good enough. Success was learning how to experience happiness without drugs and alcohol. True success, in its purest form, was loving myself. To wake up every day genuinely loving myself would make all those other things come true.

I told Dr. Gomez as much. She smiled proudly, as if I had just discovered one of the great mysteries of the universe. Indeed, it felt like I *had* discovered one of the great mysteries of the universe.

"So tell me this," she continued. "Do you like your job?"

I nodded. "The work is totally fine and interesting," I said. "It just doesn't mean a whole lot. It's not connected to any of my dreams."

"And you've said to me many times before that it's quite easy for you to complete your tasks. Complete them well, even."

I nodded again. "That's how I get away with spending so much time in bed."

"Well, what about this." Dr. Gomez leaned forward as if she were going to share a piece of juicy gossip. "What if there's nothing wrong with having a pleasant job that pays you good money and gives you the gift of free time to do other things? What if your job is merely a foundation to support your other dreams? If true success, to you, is learning how to love yourself, then you should be extremely proud of the time you're investing here at Water's Edge, moving closer to that goal. And your job is the reason you're here, right? If I'm not mistaken, your company offers excellent health insurance."

I listened to her, rapt, hanging on to every word.

"If your job is allowing you to make this big investment in self-love, think of all the other things it might let you do, too, once you're able to keep yourself out of that bed," she continued. "Think of how well on the way you are to actualizing your own definitions of success—without even needing to change anything about your career. Maybe, just maybe, you're right where you need to be."

I let Dr. Gomez's flipped perspective of the life I'd built sink in. With a few simple questions, and a handful of elegant sentences, she'd cracked my longstanding perception of success, of what was worth striving for and appreciating. Like any true shift in values and viewpoints, I didn't leave her office that day completely transformed—my beliefs continued to develop and gradually solidify after she first introduced the ideas. But that conversation marked a shift, a stray from a route I'd been walking for almost my entire life, so familiar I could traverse it blindfolded.

I'd heard all the tired expressions about how loving yourself and loving what you did meant you never had to work a day in your life. Until that session with Dr. Gomez, those had always felt like hollow words, meaningless aphorisms people tossed around to sound wise and preachy. But talking it through and landing, organically, on the idea that I could derive success from within myself—by loving and appreciating everything I already had access to, by pursuing activities that produced joy regardless of how they looked to others—marked the first time this notion hit me emotionally. Maybe I *did* have lazy tendencies. Maybe I had ambitious ones, too. Maybe I was a million different things, all of which added up to make me a whole person.

Pretty soon after that session with Dr. Gomez, I started making gratitude lists, another tactic frequently employed by recovering addicts. I didn't write them daily, or even on any sort of set schedule, but whenever I felt inspired to scrawl down the many things I had to feel grateful for, the more I actually started to believe it. That perhaps, as Dr. Gomez had suggested, I was right where I needed to be.

I tried my first twelve-step meeting mainly as a chance to get off campus and shake up my surroundings. And as the most devout recovery warriors instruct you to do, I kept going back. Each evening, a big van painted with the Water's Edge logo transported interested parties from the rehab to a local meeting, usually in some sort of church basement or community center. We nicknamed the van the "druggy buggy" and fielded looks of recognition from other attendees when we piled out. Many of the folks, as it happened, had once been in our shoes.

Candace and I would dress up for the meetings as if we were primping for a big party. She curled my hair and lent me her eyeliner and lip gloss, and I put on the only nice outfit I'd brought with me, night after night. It felt no different from getting ready for a Saturday night with my friends, though instead of bar stools, we'd sit on metal folding chairs, and instead of beers, we'd drink weak coffee and nibble Oreos.

The conversations at these meetings were much more interesting than idle party chitchat, though. Former addicts and alcoholics got *real,* and fast. They didn't skimp on the grimiest, dirtiest details of their stories: living on the streets, suicide attempts, reckless sexual escapades. One man who frequently got up to share had a steel rod for his left leg after jumping off a building in a drunken stupor.

I was fascinated by what everyone had to say. Even though I didn't exactly jive with the dogmatic overtures, the "higher power" stuff, I saw a part of myself in every single person who spoke up, be it the widow of a former celebrity or a truck driver in his seventies or a college kid who stumbled upon her second chance early in life.

After many of the meetings, people gathered outside in the parking lot, smoking cigarettes and hanging out, for the better part of an hour. They were as bustling as San Francisco's most bar-studded blocks, and ten times more enjoyable. In fact, I had more fun in those parking lots than I ever had at one of my neighborhood watering holes. There was no such thing as small talk. Everyone was welcoming and open, with no hidden agenda, unafraid of your darkest parts and just as comfortable sharing theirs. The things we'd normally be ashamed of became the ways we connected.

A few weeks into my time at Water's Edge, Candace and I got all dolled up and rode the druggy buggy to my favorite Thursday-night meeting, held in a rickety white church in the quiet beach community of Tiburon. It attracted tons of young people and often spilled over into standing room only. We arrived early enough to snag seats in the front row, and we balanced plates of cookies and paper cups of black coffee on our laps. The facilitator introduced the night's speaker, a young woman from nearby San Rafael. She wore her jet-black hair in a blunt bob, a sharp fringe of bangs cutting across her pale forehead. Her cat-eye eyeliner and bright-red lipstick looked effortlessly chic as she sidled up to the microphone to tell her story.

"My name is Dahlia, and I'm an alcoholic," she said. "I'm going to start by saying two things. One, my story isn't really about alcohol—it's about other drugs. In fact, I never actually considered myself an alcoholic. The only reason I use that label now is because alcohol always led me to other things. And two, my shit was more about mental illness than anything else. Depression. So I'm gonna talk about drugs and depression tonight. I hope that doesn't trigger anyone." Her red lips curled into a shy smile.

As Dahlia told her life story, I felt like she was addressing me directly. She could have been talking *about* me. A relatively conventional suburban childhood, followed by an adult lifetime of depression. Persistent weed smoking in college, a cocaine habit as a young adult. Inpatient and outpatient stints in the psych ward.

"Nothing made me feel better," she said. "Depression ruled my life. I tried everything to get over it." She paused, and in that moment, I swear she looked right into my eyes. "I tried everything, that is, except getting sober. And getting sober was the only thing that worked."

There it was. It sounded so clear, coming from her. Why hadn't I *truly* considered this option, wholly and absolutely, no pot, no booze, none of it? In the past two years alone, I'd tried all sorts of professional mental health services and cutting-edge therapies, along with a pupu platter of pills. Nothing had worked. Because all along, I hadn't been willing to give up partying. I was too afraid to really sever ties—all ties, not just the cocaine excuse that brought me into rehab—with the one thing that gave me any form of relief. As Dahlia spoke, I thought about how much all that phony relief had cost me.

What if I thought of sobriety as a new sort of substance in itself? For the past fifteen years, I hadn't spent even a full day completely sober. Like trying a new drug for the first time, prolonged sobriety would be a whole new experience for my mind. Maybe one that led to real, lasting relief.

After the meeting ended, I went up to Dahlia as if she were an old friend and gave her a big hug. She smelled like peppermint soap and she hugged me back with the familiarity of a kindred spirit. I knew I'd never see her again, but I also knew her words would stay with me. That night, back at the Water's Edge computer lab, I searched for San Francisco's twelve-step meetings and printed out a list.

I dipped my oar into the water and pushed my kayak away from the dock. I could see Candace and Kevin ahead of me, threatening to capsize each other and howling with laughter. Beyond them, the San Rafael Bridge cut the skyline in half: bulbous hilltops on the bottom, speckled clouds above. The sun heated my arms as I glided toward my new friends.

It was "Sober Fun Day," a reward for Water's Edge residents who completed all their required programming for a full week. That morning, a group of us had ridden down the hill in the druggy buggy to a boat-rental shop along the bay. After ninety minutes in the water, our rehab counselor would take us to a coffee shop—a real coffee shop, where we had permission to order anything we wanted on the menu!—and we'd make it back to the facility in time for qigong. That night, a jazz trio planned to come on-site to teach us about music therapy. I was genuinely excited for the day's events, and the excitement felt unfamiliar and pure.

In a few days, I'd be discharged. My transition counselor, Shelley, and I had outlined a detailed plan to ensure I'd be set up for success. After Water's Edge, I'd enroll in a ninety-day outpatient program just up the Embarcadero from my office, where I'd attend sessions three times a week after work. Shelley also helped me come up with a list of ways to pass idle time that didn't involve sleeping or partying, and she helped me make plans to redecorate my bedroom: repositioning the furniture, buying candles and throw pillows, installing a couple standing lamps to change up the lighting.

"You can't return home to the same little den that kept you spiraling and hidden," Shelley explained. She was also in recovery. She knew what was up.

I paddled my way over to Kevin and Candace, who were splashing each other and trying to bump the noses of their boats together. Kevin grabbed the side of my kayak and jiggled it.

"Dare you not to fall in!" he taunted as I playfully shoved him away.

I couldn't help but join in their laughter, dipping my fingers into the bay as my kayak jostled back and forth. I was in hysterics by the time my body tumbled over the edge and I plunged into the frigid water. I squealed and caught my breath and flapped my hands, spraying droplets everywhere, as the cold overtook me. I felt alive, present, and free. I felt happy.

I didn't yet know that this was just the beginning. That my depression would remain a memory that grew more and more distant in the coming years. In that moment, splashing around in the bay, my wet clothes sticking to my shivering skin, all I knew was that for the first time in my adult life, I was experiencing happiness that hadn't been induced by some sort of drug. Real happiness, with no caveat. Just plain happiness.

I pulled myself back into the boat and paddled on.

epilogue:

ONE YEAR LATER

It's a particularly cold and windy night in the desert, even for Burning Man. I wrap my giant fur coat around my body as I ascend Gregoire's art car, a massive, roving construction of a snail, strung top to bottom with lime-green LED lights, its steel antennae leading the way.

I look around for Leo, but he's already pedaled out to the depths of the desert. His bike is nothing more than one of the many bright dots in the distance.

"Hurry!" I command Henry, who's steering the snail toward the glowing activity. "Maybe we can still catch that hot guy from my camp."

He ruffles my sticky, dusty hair. "You are so boy crazy sometimes, you know that?"

I giggle and ruffle his hair back, which is caked with so much debris that it stays stiff and wild even as I remove my hand.

I met Leo earlier that day, at one of Burning Man's many twelve-step meetings that take place throughout the week. I never knew it before, but the event has a big underground network of sober attendees. This year, with eleven months of sobriety under my belt, I decided to forgo my usual crew and join one of the recovery camps.

When Leo introduced himself to me after the meeting, I was instantly attracted. He's tall, tan, and chiseled, with thick, nerdy glasses shielding brown eyes that remind me of Santiago's. In a spate of confidence, I invited him out for a ride on the snail with my Avalon pals and felt giddy when he agreed to join.

But he brought his own bike out with him for the night, and he pedaled away as soon as the snail's wheels started rolling. Now, I'm distracted by his absence and determined to find him.

Since returning from Water's Edge almost a year ago, I've remained clean. It doesn't even feel like a hard choice. When my mom drove me back to San Francisco after my discharge, she said my demeanor seemed different: I stood a little taller, acted a little lighter, hugged my new friends goodbye as if I were a kid leaving summer camp.

As the weeks continued to unfold, the correlation seemed clear. I continued not to drink or do drugs, and I continued to feel good. The more I felt good, the more I wanted things to stay that way. I came to enjoy the routine of my outpatient program and the local twelve-step meetings I began attending after it was over. The more I invested in my sobriety as a way of life, the more motivated I was to stay sober.

One evening, the counselors at the outpatient center gave us an assignment to write a letter to a loved one. I chose my father, my genetic source of depression. I reflected on the affliction he passed down to me, thinking about the profound empathy for pain and darkness I'd amassed as a result. In my letter, I thanked him for bestowing upon me those superpowers. For showing me a type of hardship that can serve as a means to connect with others.

"We might not realize it," I wrote to him, "but our depression is the greatest gift we've ever been given, if we treat it that way."

Visiting my father on the East Coast that Thanksgiving, I slipped him the letter under the dinner table. He read it on the couch after our meal with tears in his eyes, and he still carries it with him in his backpack to this day.

I only relapsed once, a few weeks after leaving Water's Edge, during an idle evening at the Avalon. Cleaning up my room, one of my first assignments from my transition counselor Shelley, I stumbled upon an old stash of weed. I took a pre-rolled joint out of the bag and hit it a few times. Its effects overtook my body almost instantly, and I began to feel anxious and paranoid for the first time since enrolling in rehab. My mind racing, I wandered into the kitchen for a snack, acutely aware of my every move, unable to converse with any of my housemates. I absolutely hated it.

The next day, I gave the rest of my supply to Theodora and Henry. I've remained clean since then. Sure, I've been tempted to partake in old indulgences from time to time, craving a glass of red wine with dinner or feeling a pang of envy when friends stay up all night partying. But those desires always pass, and they never stick around long enough to impact my behavior. I make the choice to go to bed sober every night because I know the next morning, I'll always get out of bed again.

The longer I've stayed sober, the more I've learned to love myself. I don't know if it's because my medication is finally working in earnest or if it's because I can appreciate my good qualities with a clear head or if my newfound healthy habits have allowed me to develop an equally healthy perspective on who I am. I *do* know that these feelings have led to an equilibrium and confidence that continues to blossom in unexpected ways: spending one-on-one time with friends without worrying I'll run out of interesting things to say, facilitating a series of storytelling workshops at my company's international offices, taking on new leadership roles at the Avalon, and spending time with people I actually care about instead of fleeting party pals. I've even figured out how to hang out and enjoy myself alone, a prospect that used to terrify me if I wasn't safely tucked away in bed.

Over the past year, a handful of my housemates moved out—Ari and Devon included—and as new people came in, I settled into my home more deeply. The house's culture and traditions remain strong, a sharp contrast to my time in the jungle. It's not perfect: I still can't relate to the lavish and orchestrated gatherings, some of the "intentional" and "consciousness" lines of discourse make my eyes roll, and I question the tech industry's overall impact on San Francisco. In the years to come, those hesitations will lead to other shifts: I'll switch careers, give up Burning Man, and become more directly involved with the longtime residents of the Mission District and the issues that matter to them.

But for now, my time immersed within such a steady community, idiosyncratic as it may be, has led me to appreciate the importance of belonging. The longer I stay sober, the stronger those ties and the more grounded I feel.

It's been a year of firsts, each one less nerve-racking than the last: first sober date, first sober wedding, first sober party, first sober holiday season, and now, first sober Burning Man. Tommy is on the decks, DJing a rowdy techno set he debuted at a nightclub in the neighborhood earlier this summer, and Drue and Eliza are swing dancing inside the snail's belly.

Ari, who now lives in her own house in Portland, has reunited with us in the desert for the week, as have Devon and her new husband, Nico, who married each other in a beautiful outdoor ceremony earlier this summer. I was maid of honor, and during my speech, looking into my best friend's eyes and telling some of our favorite stories, I noticed how different it felt to experience such an important moment without a layer of substances between us.

Now, Ari and Devon stand on either side of me, our arms wrapped around each other as our hair whips in the wind and the snail weaves its way through the desert's dusty, neon revelry.

The vehicle pulls to a stop near a massive wooden structure built to look like a castle. One of its towers is on fire. Soon, the entire structure will burn to the ground. Dancers surround the perimeter, some beating drums, others wiggling Hula-Hoops around their hips. I scan the crowd for Leo. I really want to find him.

A few weeks before Burning Man, I saw on Facebook that Santiago had gotten engaged. By that point, we hadn't spoken in several years, and my shame and regret over my failed Panama experiment had morphed into appreciation for a full, heart-wrenching, undeniably entertaining story. The kind I might even write about in a book one day. But I still felt a little pang in my chest upon seeing Santiago's engagement. Unlike him, I haven't felt that kind of love again. Maybe I never will; maybe ours was the kind of rare, gobsmacking connection I'd be lucky enough to experience only once in my life. Or maybe the best is yet to come.

"I can't find the hot guy from my camp *anywhere*," I complain to Ari and Devon, still searching the throngs of people for Leo. "I really want to hang out with him."

"Who cares?" Ari replies. "You're with us. Isn't that good enough?"

I look over at Tommy, concentrating hard on his DJ setup, and Drue and Eliza, helping each other dismount the snail. I see Gregoire in his ridiculous fractal-patterned leggings, swaying around by the fire dancers. I glance at Henry taking a sip from his flask, and he winks back at me.

Ari's right. I'm with my people. I'm loved and supported—by them, and by myself. As I watch my friends with mutual admiration, that does feel good enough for now. In fact, it feels more than good enough. It feels exactly right.

I shake off the feelings of today's fleeting crush and grab Ari's and Devon's hands. We jump off the art car, into the dust, and out toward the night.

acknowledgments

Elizabeth Kaplan, Elizabeth Kaplan, Elizabeth Kaplan. When I first met you at a Le Pain Quotidien on the Upper West Side and told you what a hot, unhinged mess I was, I never could have possibly guessed that would be the beginning of a decade-long journey to make my dream come true. You are so much more than an agent. You are a spirit guide, a fairy godmother, the bearer of the best and worst news, a mentor, a dear friend. One of the most important figures in my adult life, someone I consult before almost any major decision, whose advice and straight talk I cherish, my favorite long-lunch companion. Anytime I've pictured writing acknowledgments to a book, an embarrassingly frequent fantasy, you are so completely obviously the person who comes first.

Thank you to Brooke Warner, Shannon Green, and the inimitable team at She Writes Press. Brooke, from the moment I met you I could tell you were a kindred soul. I'm in awe of the work you've done to champion women storytellers and the pioneering path you've carved in the publishing industry as a whole. It's an honor to publish a book with a team I not only respect but also deeply admire. Shannon, thank you for bringing this book to the finish line and for supporting me through the whole process. A huge thanks to Julie Metz and Rebecca Lown for creating a provocative, bold cover that so closely aligns with my (non-professional) design vision.

Thank you to Marissa DeCuir, Angelle Barbazon, and the crackerjack team at Books Forward for working tirelessly to help this

this story find an audience through thoughtful, creative, deeply personal channels. Thank you to the talented team at John Marshall Media for bringing this book to life for audio listeners, including the director, Nikola Hamilton, who sat patiently with me in the booth for four days; Kevin Stillwell and James Zachary for working your magic, and Michael Trageser for making sure I didn't lose my voice.

Thank you to my brilliant writing teachers, Hope Edelman, Andrea Wilson, and Leslie Schwartz, who helped me unpack and sift through the chaos of what I wanted to say and hone my craft so I could do it well. And to Hope for reading the first version of my messy manuscript with enthusiasm and without judgment, helping me uplevel it to its next phase, and giving me a master class on memoir writing over the course of only a few meetings. You're a legend! I'm floored when I think about how much you guided me.

Thank you to my earliest readers—though I'm mortified you slogged through such raw, unfinished thoughts, I'm also touched that you took the time and delighted that you were even mildly entertained. Every thought you gave made this book better. And thank you to my fellow writers who share their work with me, help me navigate the choppy waters of media and publishing, and motivate me to keep going via their own talents: Kate, Zach, Adam C., Eliot, Robin, Topher, and Niels. We must be insane to be called to such a thankless, solitary pursuit—and yet it's the most rewarding one in the world, made more rewarding when you know you're not in it alone.

Thank you to the incredible mentors, teachers, and colleagues who stuck by me while I balanced the final phases of this book with other professional endeavors: Libby, Roberto, Josh, Jodi, Vanessa, Vince, and all the other clients I'm fortunate to learn from through telling your stories. Thank you also to the folks at the real-life company who supported me through my journey of getting well and beyond, especially Emily, Abbi, Matt, and Harrison. I'm astounded there's a workplace out there where people truly have your back to that degree.

Thank you to the best therapist on planet earth, Catherine, who often knows me better than I know myself. You've seen me through so many phases, cheered me on the entire time, played a pivotal role in my sobriety journey, and even read the book. For these reasons and more, I will (almost) always follow your advice. Thank you to all my kindred spirits in the recovery world, especially Lily, Katie, and Lee Lee. Your zest for life keeps me coming back. And thank you to the entire staff and community of the real-life Water's Edge for holding me as I got well.

Thank you to all the artists and writers and creators who continue to inspire me and push me to be better, to the authors of the books I devoured while writing my own, and to a certain jam band I had on in the background the entire time. ;) Thank you to the Puzzle Sluts, who ignite a totally different form of creativity and form the reason for my happiest two hours every week. And thank you to my *Trix* magazine cofounder Jess, who helped me rediscover my own creativity during a time I forgot it existed. We built something together that I will forever be proud of, and your confidence in me feeds my confidence in myself.

Thank you to my tribe of exceptional friends I haven't mentioned yet. My buddies since birth: David and Kate C. My high school gals: Megbag, Jenny, Maria, and Clare. My college pals: the incredible women who quite literally saved my life, Shelly and Ashley, and the dear friends who stuck with me during some of my most challenging years and beyond, Jenn, Collin, Dave, Serena, and Amy. The people I came of age with in early adulthood and beyond: Kate W., Mike, Edo, Jake, Modesta, Zach, Kyrie, Molly, Adam, Annie, Bryce, Claudia, Holly, Liz, and Cak. All the special souls from the real-life Avalon and its surrounding world: Shanza, Maryna, Lucia, Alfred, Cezar, Johnny, Diana, Mehdi, Nada, Nick K., Ellie, Dillon, Maggie, Perry, George, Joe, Ysiad, Alex L., Colin, Justine, Christian, Lydia, Mike, and everyone else who touched me during my time in that magical mystery house where I got sober, overcame some serious stuff, and wrote most of this book. And those of you who defy the aforementioned categorizations but I adore just the same: Eliot, Siobhan, Taniko, Alice, Melissa, Inas, Kimberly, Nick Mc.C, and Meg. One of you once told me that we invest in our communities to make the hard stuff easier and the easy stuff extraordinary, and you were right.

Thank you to the children in my life, some of my most important teachers, who motivate me to give a shit about this world we're leaving behind: my perfect nephews Atlas and Forest, my four-year-old best friend Nina Rae, and Iggy, Audrey, Fin, Thea, Peter, Cammie, and Tripp. You're all way too young to read this book, but maybe I'll tell you about it when you're older.

Thank you to my family. It's pretty miraculous to be forty years old and still have three iconic, living grandmothers—thank you to Gerda, Heather, and Mimi, who taught me how to write and always corrected my grammar along the way. When I said I'd dedicate my next book to you, you replied, "Okay, I guess." Thank you to my aunts and cousins for reminding me strong women are a part of our heritage: Biz, Toodie, Nancy, Erin, Emma, and Amy. Thank you to my aunts, uncles, and cousins (by birth and otherwise) for your unconditional love and support: Lenny and Donatella, David, Ben and Maryam, Norm, Rob, Grant, Chris, Sean, Max, Jack, Larry, Tony and Irene, Donald and Mary, Steve and Josette, and my godmother, Auntie Judy.

Thank you to my stepmother Ronni, with whom I've connected in a way I never thought possible. I cherish our deep conversations and the unlikely, special combination of mother figure and dear friend—so much of what we talk about helped inform my perspective for both this book and my life. And thank you to the extended family members you've brought into our lives: Jeremy, Tyler, Tara, Carly, Nina, Leo, Palmer, and Asher. A big, blended tribe is the best kind.

Thank you to my father, Chuck, the funniest person I've ever met (and the bravest one for reading the unedited version of this book before I cut out all the sordid stuff). My idea of perfection is laughing until I can't breathe and seeing live music with you, both of which kept me chugging ahead during the many phases of this book. Thank you to my mother, Alison, the strongest person I've ever met (and the sanest one for avoiding the unedited version of this book before I cut out all the sordid stuff). Your badassery is a huge part of what made me believe I could do this (thumbs-up emoji). Thank you to my brother, Alex, my lifelong best friend, and my sister-in-law, Ally, a best friend for life. I'm in awe of the world you've built together and hugely lucky to be a part of it. I'd follow you two anywhere, and I probably will.

Thank you to my "platonic domestic partner" Topher, my intellectual soulmate, the only person I want to torture with my singing first thing in the morning. I appreciate you reading my manuscript and editing my text messages—you'll always be my number one number two. Thank you to Nacho, who had no idea I wrote a book and will never know what a book is. But you curled up next to me all the way to the end, and when I finished, you barked at me so I'd take you out. I love you more than I knew it was possible to love something.

And thank you to Cory and Kelsey for telling me to do this, making me keep going, and reading every word. My greatest fortune is to bear witness to your lives and have you do the same for me. Thank you for being my forever people.

about the author

Carly Schwartz is the former editor in chief of the *San Francisco Examiner* and founding editor of *HuffPost*'s SF bureau. *Editor & Publisher* magazine named her one of ten "women to watch," and her writing has appeared in the *San Francisco Standard*, *Elle* magazine, MSNBC, and more. As an advocate for suicide prevention and addiction recovery, Carly has been a spokesperson for the Jed Foundation and Google's Recovery Month. She lives in San Francisco's Mission District.

Author photo © Niels Joubert

Praise for *Just Diagnosed*

"The days and weeks after hearing the words 'You have cancer' can be among the most overwhelming moments in a person's life. Drawing from her lived experience, Jennifer shares thoughtful, practical guidance and resources for patients and families as they take their first steps on the cancer journey—because survivorship begins at the moment of diagnosis."

—**Jun J. Mao, MD, MSCE**, Chief of Integrative Medicine and Wellness Service and Laurance S. Rockefeller Chair in Integrative Medicine at Memorial Sloan Kettering Cancer Center

"You are not a statistic; this guide ensures you won't feel like one. *Just Diagnosed* transforms fear into actionable steps, blending personal insight with practical tools—from diaphragmatic breathing techniques to navigating clinical trials and medical bills."

—**Ting Bao, MD, MS, FSIO**, codirector of the Dana-Farber Cancer Institute's Leonard P. Zakim Center for Integrative Therapies and Healthy Living and associate professor at Harvard Medical School

"Cancer survivorship is most often measured retrospectively. *Just Diagnosed* reorients the cancer journey by affirming that survivorship begins at diagnosis. By acknowledging the existential shock of a new cancer diagnosis, this book guides patients to build their care team, surround themselves with support, and pursue evidence-based treatment while remaining open to complementary approaches."

—**Robert A. Figlin, MD, FACP**, Steven Spielberg Family Chair in Hematology Oncology, professor of medicine and biomedical sciences, and interim director of Cedars-Sinai Cancer and the Samuel Oschin Comprehensive Cancer Institute